The Picara

The Picara:
From Hera
to Fantasy Heroine

Anne K. Kaler

Bowling Green State University Popular Press
Bowling Green, Ohio 43403

Copyright © 1991 by Bowling Green State University Popular Press

Library of Congress Catalogue Card No.: 90-086056

ISBN: 0-87972-515-X clothbound
0-87972-516-8 paperback

Cover design by Gary Dumm

Dedication

To my mother—
    in many ways,
        the greatest picara of them all
. . .
And to my father,
    who loved her for it.

Contents

Acknowledgments

Unlike a picara, an author does not have autonomy. I am indebted
...to my many fine teachers, colleagues, and librarians who helped me through
the years, especially the Sisters of Mercy at Gwynedd Mercy College.
...to Philip Stevick who gave me the initial idea to investigate Roxana.
...to Pat Browne of the Popular Press who made it a reality.
...to Sister Berenice Marie, Pat Smith, and Carmella Benjamin who ordered
every book they thought I might need.
...to Sister Mary Delaney who gave me moral support.
...to Carol A. Breslin, whose scholarship and friendship inspired me.
...to Patti Traub who taught me more about mythology than most books.
...to Cynthia L. Louden, who always gave me time and space.
...and, finally to Pic'lo, my mother, Mary G. Kaler, who listened for hours
and who taught me what autonomy really means.

Picara

I might as well have been a picara,
 for I wander
  down the paths
   of my own thoughts

in search of sustenance—
 regurgitate it all,
  transformed, I think,
   in the honey of my words—

but knowing still
 that I prostitute those thoughts
  for those voracious maws
   of my students.

Only, sometimes,
 when I least expect,
  a fragment such as this
   floats free.

From it
 and others like it
  I piece together
   the child I never had.

Picara-like
 only to abandon it
  only to survive, of course,
   only to survive.

Anne K. Kaler

Chapter One
Introduction
Tapestry, Picara, and Autonomy

The origin of the craft of weaving is lost in the mists of antiquity...by exploiting the special features of the technique of tapestry weaving...readers can be made aware of the special qualities of tapestry weaving...to give them a greater appreciation of the superb technical skill seen in the masterpieces from the past. (Rhodes, *Small Woven Tapestries*, 9)

Imagine, if you will, that we have entered the workshop of a medieval tapestry artisan. Natural sunlight from high windows traps motes of bright lint and the oily smells of wool and linen tickle the nose.

The weaver sits behind the high tapestry loom. The vertical warp of coarse undyed wool passes through two sets of needles which raise and lower alternating threads. The warp stretches from a huge spool on the ceiling down past the weaver's face and hands and under a bar by his feet, to be wound on another spool, which receives the finished tapestry. Inch by inch, the weaver passes the finer woof or weft yarn through the opening or "shed" formed by the raising and lowering of the warp threads; after each pass, he combs the woof yarn tightly to form the weave of the fabric, adding as part of the weave the colored yarns which define the figures. Inch by inch, the weaver fleshes out the black and white outline of the artist's cartoon, suspended behind the hanging warp. Inch by inch, he compares the figures on the mirror hanging in front of the tapestry with the artist's design. In and out, colored yarns wrapped on small bobbins dart to the front of the warp to catch a few threads before retiring back to the weaver's hand—three, four, five warp threads ensnared before the next color is introduced. When one color is finished, its cut ends are dovetailed back into the tiny section of weaving so the small slits texture the finished front with vertical shadows. The smaller slits will remain open while the larger ones will be stitched together in the finishing stage. The figures are built up by adding color next to color. The shadow of a gray underlines the gleam of an eye; a flicker of crimson adjacent to a pale pink defines a lip; the shimmer of white silk accents a cheek. A face begins to emerge—the face of the picara—the figure of the picara.

The image is not farfetched. In literature, the figure of the picara is an elusive and neglected one, despite her colorful design. Often mistaken for the feminine counterpart of the picaro or for the feminine extension of the picaresque, the picara has her own identity separate from and preceding that of the picaro. Yet critics to date have ignored or misread her presence in the tapestry. They

1

condemn her as a wanton; they revile her as a sinner; they dislike her as a woman. Why are their criticisms so harsh? Perhaps it is that the distinguishing feature of her tapestried figure is the white silk of her autonomy.

Despite her persistent appearances in the literary tapestry, the picara is never considered a hero. Only as an archetypal pattern of autonomy does the picara pursue the hero-quest common to human nature. Specifically, the picara seeks her identity through the masculine outward quest of the hero: her call to action is her abandonment as a child or wife; her mentor is her confidante; her magical weapons are her wit and sexuality; her trip to the underworld is her criminal career; her adventures are her wanderings; her obstacles use her warrior abilities; her return to this world appears in the retelling of her memoirs. Yet she lacks some particulars of the hero's journey for she never finds peace or reconciliation as heroes do.

In the same manner, the picara neglects the complementary inward feminine quest toward spirituality—the creativity symbolized by motherhood. This quest is seldom accomplished by the picara; she ignores the awakening to motherhood, letting her tricks serve as her creative outlet; she is too busy surviving to contemplate her sins; her repentance is always suspiciously self-serving; she never reconciles with her society or her nature; she is trapped in a survival mode, struggling for an autonomy neither her nature nor society will grant her. If she follows the masculine quest more readily, it is because her nature is one of action rather than of contemplation. Still, she does rely strongly on the intuitive side of her personality to accomplish her contradictory goals of security and autonomy.

Consistently she falls short of heroism. She is too subjective to be a hero and too objective to be a heroine, who is at best a complacent secondary character, lending the hero moral support while waiting to be rescued. Nor is the picara an anti-hero whose satire provides a foil for his society's flaws. Nor is the picara a female hero, an emasculated male who "masters the world by understanding it, not by dominating, controlling or owing the world" (Pearson and Pope 5) as the male hero does. Nor is the picara a romance heroine who must capture a man strong enough to provide a marriage in which her creativity, in the form of children, can flourish. Nor is she a sacrificial mother who surrenders individuality for the continuation of the species or for the common good. Nor is the picara an Amazon whose glory rests in patriotic self-sacrifice or battle. Nor is she a villainess, except when she must be. Nor is she a witch, except when she must be. Nor is she a bitch goddess, except when she can be nothing else. Nor is the picara a nymphomaniac, except when it profits her. While she is immured within the tale or the novel or the genre, the picara transcends them all precisely because she is not a hero or a heroine or a female hero. She is the archetypal pattern of autonomy.

As the "hero," the picara goes back beyond the word to its root of the word in Hera, the chief mother of the Olympian gods, sister and wife to Zeus, and a powerful goddess in her own right. When her followers did deeds for her sake, they adopted a name signifying their accomplishments; thus Herakles did deeds for the glory of Hera. Critics might find the adoption of Hera's name for such a woman a cleaner, simpler way to distinguish her from a female hero or a heroine; a woman who does great deeds might be called a "hera" rather than a "hero." But, the picara even precedes and predates Hera because she is the literary emanation of the Great Goddess quaternity of Hera (mother/wife), Aphrodite (prostitute), Athena or Diana (virgin), and Sophia or Hecate (wise woman/hag). While this configuration of the Great Goddess has long been woven into the tapestry of myth and literature, we see the picara best in the four stages of her literary development: as the counterpart of the historical picaro; as the Puritan picara of Defoe; as the Victorian and modern novel picara; and finally as the fantasy picara. Since any discussion of the term "picaro" includes and suggests the picara, we first need a brief history of the picaro, of his socio-economic and literary origins, and of picaresque literature itself before we can attempt to distinguish the picara from her fellow characters in the tapestry.

The Picaro

The etymology of the word "picaro" is as complex as the social development of the picaro himself and just as deceptive. Harry Sieber in his work *The Picaresque* traces the word's origin to the euphemism for a kitchen or stable boy or basket-carrier, a *picaro de cozina*, as far back as 1525, where is was used in its adjectival form nearly thirty years before the appearance of the character of the picaro in *Lazarillo de Tormes*. By 1548 the term *picaro de corte*, the low or unscrupulous courtier, was contrasted with the *cortesano*, or worthy courtier in Eugenio de Salazar's *Carta del Bachiller de Arcadia* (Sieber 5-6). Interestingly, the word "cortesano" is also the root of the word "courtesan," another euphemism for the picara as prostitute. Sieber also cites Joan Corominas who sees the word "picaro" as a form of the verb *picar* meaning to prick or puncture or bite. Chandler and Schwartz claim it comes from "*picante*, a biting meal, or perhaps *picado*, contaminated meat, or even *pico*, sharp tongue" (179) while other critics suggest its origin in the word "*picado*" or pitted from smallpox.

Spanish political incursions into the Netherlands may have affected both the word and its connotations as a corruption of the French word *picard* for a native of the often disputed section of Picardy near Spanish-occupied Flanders. When Spanish soldiers were garrisoned in the Flemish towns, a linguistic tie was forged in the Spanish term for the pike-men, *pica secas* or *piqueros secos*. When those same soldiers were forced to find their own way home after Spain's unsuccessful military campaigns, they resorted to the picaresque traits of survival by begging and stealing on the way. An epic poem by Alfonso de Pimentel detailing his adventures in the 1567 Flanders expedition identifies "picaros with the beggars he encountered...real as well as false beggars...It is possible that some of the deserters carried their previous military title of *piquero* with them into 'civilian' life" (Sieber 6-7). In sixteenth-century Louvain, for example, the garrisoning of Spanish soldiers in the beguinage, reinforced and further confused the origin of the word. The beguinal communities of independent women which developed in most cities in Northern Europe, partly as a result of the relative scarcity of marriageable men and partly of the penitential movements, had the origin of "beguine" or "begijn" in Flemish shrouded in mystery. Some claim the word came from the name of their putative founder, Bishop Lambert the Stutterer (the "Begue") or from St. Begga, a sixth-century nun who founded churches; still others said it derived from the "baga" or hood similar to the scapular and hood of monastic orders. Archbishop Jacques de Vitry, the defender of the beguines, attributed the word "beguine" to the color of their homespun dress, "beige" or "bege," hence the word "beguines."

Their male counterparts were called the "beghards" or "bigardos," words which may have provided roots for concept of the picaro. The male weavers who linked themselves into penitential lay orders (as opposed to religious orders) tended to wander in search of work because towns would not grant them citizenship. When the guild system excluded weavers like the beghards from selling their goods within the city by imposing hallmarks on all cloth produced, they limited the amount and the type of cloth the beghards could produce to inferior products (linen, not English wool; homespun, not dyed stuffs). Although the beghards were never as numerous in the textile trade as the beguines, by the sixteenth century both terms had fallen into disrepute, although in opposite ways; the beguine who was almost cloistered in her beguinage where she owned real property was tarred with the same brush as her mendicant male counterpart of the wandering weaver, the *beghard*, who owned nothing. Another factor lay in the Church's persistent opposition to the organized beggars' guilds and of mendicant orders, an opposition which extended to these quasi-religious under the name of the sect of the *"Pyghard"*; since both beguine and beghard alike were periodically charged with heresy, the similarity of "beghard" to "bigardo" may have suggested a "strong and persistent connection between beggars and *picaros*" (Sieber 7). So intense was ecclesiastical disapproval that papal bulls attempted to disperse the beguines and beghards and writers like Dante and others satirized them as frauds.

In literature, the origin of the picaro is no easier to determine. Essentially the archetypal pattern of the trickster, the picaro is aligned with the criminal world in Frank Chandler's *Romances of Roguery* as a "rogue" or "scoundrel"; Robert Alter prefers "picaroon"; Parker prefers "juvenile delinquent" or "unattached outsider" or even "gate-crasher"; Michael Alpert likes "swindler." The French translate the picaro as a "larron" (thief) or "belistre" (rascal) while the picara is a *narquoise* or *vivandiere*. The Germans call the trickster the *Schalksnarr*; the English prefer "adventurer" or "buffoon" while in his criminal element, the English picaro is a "vagrant" or "cheating beggar." Richard Head's 1665 *The English Rogue* adopts the Spanish "ladron" and French "larron" or thief for his character of Meriton Latroon, a "Witty Extravagant" and James Mabbe's 1622 translation of *The Rogue* identifies his picaro Guzman de Alfarache as a "rogue."

Whatever his etymological origin, the critics agree that the picaro began as young male servant or errand boy. Although a "picaro" might be a person in menial occupation especially a basket-carrier or kitchen helper, he was not considered a rogue until after the middle of the sixteenth century; at that point, the critic Joan Corominas "correctly reminds us that implicit within this semantic shift is a change in emphasis from the *picaro*'s social situation to his immoral and delinquent behavior" (Sieber 6). This characteristic is almost always consistent; Chandler and Schwartz categorize the picaros as "porters, errand boys, or the like...crafty, sly, tattered, hungry, unscrupulous petty thieves" (179). A. A. Parker's *Literature and the Delinquent* stresses another phase of the picaro as "an offender against the moral and civil laws; not a vicious criminal such as a gangster or a murderer, but someone who is dishonorable and anti-social in a much less violent way" (4). He always challenges authority, upsets the social order, and poses as the Lord of Misrule. Modern critics transform him into an anti-hero, a fragmented and alienated man in a hostile society, an artist of the deception and trickery whose innocence causes him to reorder the world and to satirize it. Yet, as the literary picaro steadily accrues characteristics of delinquency, autobiography, journey, and satire,

the picaro's 'tainted' ancestry defines him as an outsider...The picaresque novel finally becomes what it pretended to be all along: the autobiography of a 'nobody' and his adventures in a 'repressive' society. The discovery of the picaresque as a mode of fiction is a failing enterprise in itself [because] the picaro's self-creation in words is at odds with his attempt to be more than 'mere' language. The very nature of his 'speaking presence' is obliterated through the 'writing' of his life. (Sieber 74)

Critics now tend to discount the 1554 *Lazarillo des Tormes* as the first of the picaresque novels, calling it a precursor rather than an originator. Parker claims that the 1559-1604 Guzman de Alfarache by Mateo Aleman is the first picaresque prototype because it introduced the realism necessary for a novel structure and sparked a new interest in Lazarillo. Such modern critics further insist on separation of the picaro from picaresque literature, claiming that the emergence of the trickster archetype can be distinguished from the literature in which it is embedded; those who stress his literary origins preserve the genre as the distinguishing mark of the picaro while those who center on the social conditions as forcing the satiric picaro into bloom discount his literary ancestors. A more liberal view is taken by Sieber who claims that the "term 'picaresque' can still be of some use as a literary-critical category...pointing out the genre's internal uneasy blend of humor and seriousness" (3-4). A "cluster of 'picaresque conventions' " can lead to a " 'picaresque myth' " (3-4) which can be applied to all literature. What he calls the "picaresque myth" provides a happy blend of terminology to extend legitimately the picaresque traditions into later literary genres, specifically those of the historical novel and the modern feminist fantasy novels.

Monteser's claim that the term *"picarismo"* existed before the word or archetype of "picaro" allows us to apply the larger term of *picarismo* to all picaresque literature. While this claim allows us to expand the narrow limits of the picaresque literary genre without rupturing it, it also encourages us to refine *picarismo* into *picarisma*, the epitome of the picara's autonomous archetypal pattern of individualism. Indeed, the argument of this work lies in the explication of those traits of the general literary origins and characteristics of the picaro and picara which will form the second and third chapters. Subsequent chapters will develop the specific picaresque traits of hunger, avarice, and criminality, of sexuality and children, of marriage and prostitution, of wandering and warrioring, of disguise and deception, and of isolation and inferiority, as they apply to the picara.

The Social and Economic Origins of the Picaro and Picara

6   The Picara

As we undertake the tapestried trail of the picara, we cannot neglect the major woof or weft threads of her picaresque socio-economic background. Because those strong binding cross yarns are equally neutral in shade to those of the warp, they support the overlaid colors but do not conflict with them. It is those neutral shades of economy and social origins that must first be seen because implicit in them are the complementary or oppositional pairs of the picaresque traits which will form the succeeding chapters.

Like the mystic and the murderer, the picaro and the picara exemplify the continual tension between the community and the alienated person. The hierarchical whole of the feudal system imposed a structured order on society which assigned each individual to a position and expected him to stay there. However, as the historian J. Huizinga suggests, when excessive pride became the symbolic sin of the dying feudal system, the man who was common or ordinary was lost within the vestigial courtesies of an earlier chivalric code. "Long after nobility and feudalism had ceased to be really essential factors in the state and in society, they continued to impress the mind as dominant forms of life...undervaluing altogether the social significance of the lower classes" (Huizinga 46-7).

In such an order, even the alienated man was a part of the natural hierarchy: his deviance proved the need for the same structure; his roguishness was an example of what would happen without some controlling order; he could be used as a scapegoat in times of communal repentance, as a shibboleth to the aberrant, as an example to the young, as a pariah to maintain right conduct. When the unifying force which accepted the anti-social person as an integral part of his community disappeared, the picaro was born. But, where the hierarchical feudal order once provided shelter for the wanderer, the Renaissance contempt of the common man excluded him from all activities, save those of the lowest order. Machiavelli's *Discourses* and *The Prince* established the unusual man of *virtu* as the desirable leader to be emulated, while Castiglione's *The Courtier* established elaborate rules of conduct in love. This exaggerated concern for trivial custom increased as the Renaissance man strove to retain feudal pomp when his feudal power base had failed and the town structure emerged.

If the excessive pride of feudal chivalry had cast off the wanderer, so also did the contradictory actions of the dissolving church structure shake him from his spiritual moorings and set him adrift. Preaching reconciliation, the Church consistently excommunicated those already cast out by society—actors, defiant princes, gypsies, minorities. Preaching peace, the Church sponsored the Crusades, whose lengthy voyages, restless adventurers, and returning soldiers brought new cultures and new ideas to the embastioned west. Preaching stability as the fourth monastic vow, the Church encouraged pilgrimages of devotional piety and financial gain until the familiar figure of the pilgrim colors the pages of medieval history with his religious fervor and his insatiable curiosity. Preaching reconciliation, the Church's distrust of the mendicant orders, such as the Franciscans and Dominicans, solidified into the "special hatred for the begging friars [which became] an indication of the most important change of ideas...People were beginning to regard poverty as a social evil instead of an apostolic virtue" (Huizinga 161-2). Preaching charity, the Church's acceptance of the pilgrim beggar saints emphasized the necessity of charitable works. At the same time the stringency of the Poor Laws often forced the alienated man to continue his journeying thereby isolating the wanderer further until he became an object dangerous to the community. The "expelled prince, roaming from court to court, without means" (Huizinga 10) presented as great a threat as the impoverished second sons of the nobility, who could not inherit under the laws of primogeniture, presented.

Where property had once meant financial security, the modern age replaced land with capital as the touchstone of wealth. Where land owners felt some responsibility to the people who tilled the land, the lure of tangible and immediate return for capital led to a disregard for the workers. Suggesting that the demographics of towns and guild structures might provide a clue to begin a "search for the origin of the picaresque in literature, perhaps for the germ of the novel" (6), Peter Lazlett postulates that the wanderer may have developed from the medieval craft system where the apprentice-turned-journeyman was caught between the dissolution of the medieval craft system and the surge of capitalism. When the division and specialization of labor lowered his value as an individual worker, the later wanderer lacked both the sufficient education to be a productive member of specialized society and the incentive to learn a skill. While the emphasis shifted, the wanderer was relegated to an arcane representative of a lost epoch since he could neither toil nor spin. As a rootless person, unsupported by family name or wealth, he was forced to search for his livelihood wherever he could. Because of his valueless position in society, the wanderer gravitated toward lower levels of employment, usually servitude, as more fitting to his lack of a trade. Since the position of a servant is often a temporary one, requiring little skill, the alienated man found no disharmony in his lower social level, preferring to keep his menial job rather than to commit himself to a programmed apprenticeship. Ironically, the outcast chose that form of employment where insecurity is embodied in the whim of the master. The basic inferiority he felt may have supplied a need or humiliation to counteract his pride. Not being able to judge his own worth, the wanderer assumed a false pride in his own accomplishments and his tricks. By blindly adopting the values of his society as criteria for himself, the outcast discovered that he failed to meet those criteria: in retaliation, he took a lower position in society to atone for his deficiency.

The search of the alienated man for security is also hampered by his isolation, the severity of which is determined by his anti-social offenses as a criminal. The distinction between anti-social and criminal lies in the values of the society itself rather than in those of the wanderer. One measure of the degree of criminality is in Emile Durkheim's definition of an act as being criminal "when it offends strong and defined states of the collective conscience" (80). The "conscience" of the Middle Age and of the Industrial Age refused to let the wanderer have a place in society and then condemned him for seeking his livelihood outside the law. However, the levels of criminality in which the wanderer dabbles are relatively minor: "criminality is often merely an alternative reflection of the general values of a social system in which great emphasis is placed on the success goal...and relatively slight emphasis is placed on the proper means and devices for achieving this goal" (Sutherland, in Kirkman xi-xii). The picaro's offenses seem to be aimed at striking back at society; in a materialistic society, theft is serious; in a sexually rigid society, prostitution is serious. Since he is a non-professional criminal and sometimes an inexperienced one, he does well to stay on the move since his usual crime is petty theft and slow-footed thieves are easily caught.

Life for the wanderer is precarious, chancy, and volatile. If the early picaro's life seems less hard, it is also less complicated: his needs are immediate and concrete—he is hungry, cold, wet, humiliated, naked. The later picaro of the more sophisticated societies experiences more sophisticated needs: he is hungry because he can not earn money for food; he is cold because he can not afford clothes. While his needs are one step distanced from those of his earlier counterpart, he can not satisfy them any more easily.

The shift from the medieval world where Fortune was a whimsical woman to the industrial world where the Machiavellian man of *virtu* dominated served to isolated the picaro further. Mired in an economic system which valued fragmentation over the integrity of the human personality, the wanderer rejected his new environment; as the trickster/jester, the symbol of honest and satiric rebellion within feudalism, he was reduced to a non-entity, stripped of vocal powers in an industrial age. Since he could not or would not orient himself to the newly forming society, his only course was to become a scourge to the society which rejected him.

No social revolution or single historical event can account for the persistent phenomenon of the wanderer. In religious matters, the increased stress on personal interpretation and individualism shifted the responsibility of salvation from the church to the individual man; within politics, the decline of the monarchy spread responsibility of government among individual men; within economics, the decline of feudalism's self-sufficiency shifted responsibility to the individual entrepreneur. What distinguishes the wanderer from his early ancestors is his tenacious, satiric, clamorous, humorous, and impudent demand to be heard. It was the ears of the picaresque novelist, finely attuned to social satire, that heard and answered these demands.

The Picara

The picaresque novelist, however, was not the first one to write about the picara. Christine J. Whitbourn in her essay on "Moral Ambiguity in the Spanish Picaresque Tradition" claims that literary picara preceded the picaro in the bawd characters of Trotaconventos and Celestina in the 1330-43 *Libro de buen amor* and the 1499 *La Celestina*. What distinguishes the picara from the stereotype of the bawd in these pieces is her avarice and her autonomy.

"From the twelfth century downwards people began to find the principle of evil rather in cupidity than in pride...what haunts the imagination is still the tangible yellow gold" (Huizinga 18-9). If the first capital sin, pride, caused the fall of the feudal system and, by implication, caused the rise of the picaro, then the second capital sin of avarice or cupidity, the major sins of the industrialized society, forced the picara into her emergence. The other five capital sins flash their staining colors onto our tapestry after pride and avarice—gluttony, sloth, lust, envy, and anger—with the picara specializing in all of them from time to time as she recounts her life's story.

What especially separates the picara from the picaro and the picaresque literature is her autonomy which serves as a highlighting white in our tapestry. One strand of white is traced in her survival instinct to know, to experience, to adventure, and to venture where only the picaro had gone before. Starting with the mythical tale of the fall of Lucifer and continuing down through Faustus' pride, the picara's quest for self-knowledge is always one of pride. So powerful is this pride that it appears in Lilith, the proto-wife of Adam, whose assumption that she was his equal so disturbed him that he rejected her for the more submissive Eve who, in her turn, also sought knowledge. The desire for such complete knowledge implies a desire for power or autonomy, which in a religious aspect represents a disordered or disobedient willfulness. When the picara risks damnation to obtain knowledge which will complete her, she becomes an eccentric, anti-social person; while her pride is the natural form that the sin of knowledge takes, its corollary sin of avarice becomes the picara's worst offense and greed becomes her victim's weakness on which she preys.

Knowledge does not always imply formal education. When the schooling given to young women is slight and feeble, when domestic chores and the managing of a household means the acceptance of responsibility, when the feeding of others is a full-time job, the picara scorns learning. Like the grasshopper, the picara would rather play than prepare for winter like the ant; likewise, she scorns any community involvement implied by the dedicated ant, opting for the freedom of the grasshopper's solitary flitting. After all, the possession of knowledge might mean the acceptance of responsibility and the hampering of her autonomy. However, while the picara refuses to learn an honest trade, she pursues an informal education in her skills as a thief, con-artist, and prostitute. Often her skills in deception and disguise carry a taint of magic. For example, a fantasy picara might have some skills that might seem magical to one unskilled but those powers are usually developments of natural abilities rather than gifts from the supernatural. As sciences demand empirical proofs, the charge against the picara of working magic and miracles fades in the world of the realistic novel. Witchcraft appears only in her sexual prowess; the human failings she preys upon are not supernaturally induced; the assignations the bawd arranges are not diabolical rituals; the love potions the soubrette uses are made of natural ingredients. Only with the rebirth of fantasy did the older mythological links to magic resurface.

Wit is another matter. Like the picaro-trickster, the picara lives by her wit and her knowledge is focused on that natural ability to survive. The folk tales of Reynard the Fox and Brer Rabbit retain the reader's interest only in the recounting of his tale and his tricks. When playwrights calculate the effect of a good confession on an audience, the retelling of the tale has dramatic impact which stress the confessional motif. When the picara retells her story, it is not as a confession for repentance, but as a braggadocio performance, because she is stymied by her survival mode, unable to progress beyond it to the self-sacrifice needed of a hero or a saint. Partly this is due to the restrictions of the tale genre in which her story is lodged; partly it is due to her short-sighted view of the world; part is due to her cultural milieu from feudalism.

If modern man is fragmented, then modern picaro or picara feels at home in a disordered world. If the picaro did not fit into the industrial society which demanded that each one contribute materially to the community, then he will not fit into a technological society any better. When the picaro emerges in literature, he takes on characteristics of the hero of a novel to be different or antithetical to the establishment. Just as the heroes of novels are traditionally victims or minorities—the child, the woman, the black, the disfigured, the outcast—the picaro works as a catalyst in the society, forcing it to see itself from another angle. This satiric role is not found explicitly in the fantasy picara, however, since the created world which she inhabits has little to do with the real world. It is fine for a Lazarillo or a Celestina to mock the social and sexual practices of their day, but the picaresque heroine of fantasy must accede to her society's wishes. For example, the heroine may indeed be an outcast by her birth or her powers or her abilities; instead of conforming to society, she often changes society to insure or to suit her own acceptance into society. In doing so, she assures her own survival but on an individual basis. While the survival theme may justify a mother's sacrifice, seldom does it provide a motive for the picara, perhaps because the picara's tales were originally written by men.

In fantasy, the modern picara comes into her own. No longer is she at the mercy of a society; rather, the fantasy picara changes the society to suit her own needs. As women writers rediscover the archetypal pattern of the picara, their picaras gain autonomy which becomes the shaping, highlighting color in the picara's tapestried figure. Prolific writers such as Marion Zimmer Bradley steadfastly claim that an "egalitarian heroine is *necessary but not sufficient* to a modern story...heroines in S&S must *start out* as strong, liberated, and enlightened...they should not have to prove their right to existence/equality" (*Sword* III, 8). Sharon Green, author of over a dozen books, writes about "women who become entangled in unusual situations...even a seemingly helpless person—male *or* female—can very often do *something* to make the mess they've landed in less messy, but they have to *try*. Sitting around crying and/or complaining is worse than useless" (*Authors*, 120, 139). Another prolific writer, Jo Clayton, claims that in her dual role as an artist and as a writer she is concerned "with the human being who manages to gain a measure of self-respect and self-reliance in spite of manifold difficulties—especially women" (*Authors*, 81-4, 92). As one of her characters claims, "all my life I've had to fight to keep a piece of myself for me" (*Bait* 76). Jessica Amanda Salmonson argues that, while "women in the heroic fantasy of the recent past have been either helpless, evil, absent, drawn funny, or at most inferior companions," newer attempts in creating female heroes may return fantasy to its "nobler heritage of ancient mythology, intelligent extrapolation, and good storytelling" (*Amazons!* 14). Ignoring the divisions of science fiction and high heroic fantasy, fantasy as a encompassing genre provides the most recent emanation for the picara. It is from the folds of fantasy that her figure emerges from the tapestry.

As critics of the picara, we must explicate the warp, the weft, and the spectrum of bright yarns which make up her colorful figure. To analyze her, we must trace each separate shade to its origin to see how the shade plays with the light of different time periods. To do this, we can assign "color" or color values to each characteristic which contributes to her formation: her shadowy criminal origins can be assigned a blue-grey, her lust a vibrant red, her wanderlust a moon-like silver. These powerful hues can be mounted on the neutral background of the bleached wool of the social and economic conditions crossed by the creamy texture of the literary characteristics, just as the neutral background of literature and culture allow the more colorful archetypal patterns to emerge time after time. Thus, the explication of the picara may unravel her origins, her present dimensions, and perhaps suggest her future configurations.

Chapter Two
Literary Origins of the Picaro and the Picara

The word tapestry is derived from the Latin *tapete*, which means a carpet, tapestry, hanging or coverlet...the hand-woven material that was produced on either a high or low-warp loom by weaving with soft woollen thread weft threads over hard warp threads and pressing the weft threads down so that they entirely covered the warp. (Rhodes 9)

The crossing of the weft and warp causes interstices which give strength to the fabric and provide a neutral background into which the design of the tapestry can be woven. In literature, those points of conflict and of similar strengths must be established before the picara's figure can be fully outlined. If a weft thread is the same weight and thickness as the warp thread, the fabric will be evenly textured but, if the weft is finer, the fabric will be uneven in texture. The texture of the picaro and the picara will appear to vary in literature as the colored yarns pick out their specific designs over the years and over the cultures. Like all archetypal patterns, the picaro and picara are elusive combinations of "types" which exist in human nature and which are solidified from time to time in literature, like insects imprisoned in amber or figures frozen in tapestry. Such solidifications are easier to analyze in a literary form where they can be viewed from all sides; when, where, why, who, and how the picaro and picara became trapped in the tapestry are the concerns of this chapter.

The Picaro
The picaro is an easily recognizable sixteenth-century Spanish literary type who lent his name to the picaresque genre which already encompassed the archetypal pattern of the trickster. However, while the picaro is a male literary figure who can be located in time, the archetypal pattern of the picara underlies the entire tapestry, first appearing in her role as the Great Goddess and continuing as an archetypal pattern distinct from the picaro and the picaresque. At some point in time, the picara meets and melds with the picaro, using his wandering roguish skills to strengthen her own mythological origins to form the picara of modern fantasy. It is at that first interstice of warp and weft that we must begin our investigation of the picaro.

As the drafts of historical winds move our tapestry slightly, the light of criticism reveals the picaro's emergence from one of the vertical folds into full light; in reality, he has always been in the tapestry as a trickster archetype whose nature is in itself shadowy and sly. Historians trace the origin of the picaresque novel to the disintegration of the chivalric code. Critics accuse him of being the last stage of chivalry, a leftover knight who pranced across the tapestry in the dying light of feudalism. A literary critic like Charlotte Morgan in her *The*

Rise of the Novel of Manners views the transition of the courtly romances into the cynical rogues as a necessary antecedent to the picaro (1). Frederick Warren views the rise of the picaro as a series of literary reactions to the chivalric romances like *Amadis de Gaul* and *Don Quixote* (288-9). Frank Chandler agrees that the emergence of a picaro is a "literary recoil" (7) against the ineffectiveness of the effete chivalric ideal of honor in Spain. A.A. Parker sees the picaresque novel as an "exposition of the theme of freedom [which] does not arise as anti-romance in the sense of an implicit parody of idealistic fiction [but as] a deliberate alternative, a 'truthful' literature in response to the explicit demands of the Counter Reformation" (19, 22). Warren further sees the picaro as coinciding with Spanish interest in fortune-hunting wayfarers and the resulting poverty of those who stayed at home; Frederick Monteser maintains that because "social disruption" produces good literary figures, the Spanish seedbed of "hopelessly, eternally and, worst of all, resignedly poor thieves and idlers" (1-3) produced the picaro. Chandler further sees the "direct current of the literature of roguery [which] flowed from Spain through France to England" (35) while Stuart Miller cites the exchange of traditions as necessary to the international picaresque genre which "must exist in examples that cross linguistic boundaries and occur over a long period of time" (4). Harry Sieber provides a terse but provocative delineation of the social conditions which engendered the picaro; Frederick Monteser does likewise. While Robert Alter concurs "that the picaro is by origin a deliberately de-idealized version of the knight errant" (77), Warren agrees that the first picaro in "the appearance of *Lazarillo de Tormes* was a direct challenge to the eulogists of banished knight-errantry" (288-9).

The grandfather of all picaros is the character of Lazarillo de Tormes. The original incident—that of the blind beggar and his boy (lazaro)—is so ancient a tale that it appeared as early as the thirteenth century in a French farce entitled *Lazarillo de Tormes* and continues down to a variation in the 1607 *The Woman Hater* by Francis Beaumont (Baugh 572). The progress of the wily Lazarillo from his dramatic form into his novel form is lost in literary history; even the authorship of the sixteenth century novel *Lazarillo de Tormes* in uncertain, although most critics attribute it to Huertado (or Diego) de Mendozo and some claim that it was written as early as 1530s.

Coming from the Greek "Eleazar" meaning "God helps," the name Lazarillo or little Lazarus in Spanish can be traced back to 1528 tale of the Andaluzian picara Lozana, a tale which precedes Lazarillo by a quarter of a century. The name Lazarus first refers to two men in Scriptures: the first is the brother of Mary and Martha, the friend that Christ raised from the dead; the second Lazarus appears in Christ's parable of the poor beggar at the gates of the rich Dives. Both men named Lazarus exhibit some state of decay: because of his four days in the tomb, Christ's friend's winding cloths resemble the scales of leprous skin while Lazarus of Dives is a beggar with open wounds which the dogs lick. Thus, pious tradition gives the title of "lazar" to any poor or undernourished person likely to have a scrufulous skin disease which resembles the lesions and scars of leprosy. Indeed "lazar" was so common a name for any beggar that the Military Order of St. Lazarus founded during the early crusades in Jerusalem nursed the lepers and the *lazarone* or poor men of the streets; the hospitals were thus called *lazariums* or *lazaretto* because they cared for the lepers and indigents.

Chandler and Schwartz indicate that the name gave "a new word to the Spanish language, as Lazarillo now signifies a youth or dog who guides a blind man" (182).

The concept of Lazarus' human suffering and its final defeat of death long intrigued artists from catacomb artisans to Van Gogh's rendition of Rembrandt's Lazarus. Iconography insists on merging Lazarus the leper at the rich man's gates and Lazarus of Bethany into one imaginary St. Lazarus, the sufferer who is a human equivalent of the suffering Christ. While medieval Spanish iconography stressed the passion of Christ with its imagery of realistic and blood-stained crucifixes, the need to name and sanctify human suffering was so pervasive that many European cathedrals and infirmaries claimed St. Lazarus as their patron. Later, statues of actual suffering beggar saints such as St. Roch and St. Peregrine filled the niches and walls of the churches as reminders of the need for charity to alleviate human suffering. Since these saints were pilgrims and wanderers, their legends became one basis for the picaro's tales in literature and in iconography. For example, the 1681 Verdussen edition of *Guzman de Alfarache*, printed in Antwerp, has an illustration of Guzman being treated for his painted-on sores on his legs. As he is seated with thankful eyes and hands raised to the Cardinal, his head bandaged, his left leg is extended while a doctor unwraps the ersatz bandage from his leg. A brazier with a cauterizing poker sits to the left, fresh bandages and scissors lie nearby with broken bits of bread; while bread is symbolic of the hunger motif of the picaro, it is also used to treat the supposed suppurations of infection on the picaro's leg (Parker 37). Guzman is imitating the "seventh class of Italian beggar listed by Giacinto Nobili in 1627, that of the '*Accaponi*,' or Ulcerated, who made ulcers on their legs with powder, oats, and hare's blood" (Parker 153). The iconographic representation of such a scene is a common one in European museums and cathedrals; the Stedlijke Museum in Leuven shows a similar scene with an unnamed beggar having his leg wound dressed by St. Elizabeth of Hungary while Flemish beguines look on. So pervasive still is this image of the wounded beggar that statues of St. Lazarus appear in religious goods shops; one such statue appears in the opening shots of recent television situation comedy, "Frank's Place" because it is set in New Orleans, Louisiana, whose humid climate begets disease and cures it at Carville, the leprosarium; another appear in an MTV video.

Lazarillo de Tormes is the episodic story of the son of a thieving miller who flees into the army where he dies. Poverty forces the boy's mother to become the mistress of the local black stablehand-thief, to bear him a child, and to become a servant-prostitute in a inn where Lazarillo becomes the "fine little boy who ran errands for the guests" (Alpert 7). When she is not able to feed Lazarillo, she apprentices him to a blind beggar. Through a series of masters, Lazarillo learns to survive: the priest teaches him about hypocrisy, the hidalgo about false pride and hunger, the others about human depravity, until he ends up in the relatively secure position as the cuckolded husband of the archpriest's mistress. The story is an open-ended, episodic, satiric, pseudo-autobiographical journey of a self-deceiving trickster who values survival over honor. Played against the background of the Spanish scene with its impoverished economy, heightened religiosity, and exaggerated code of honor, Lazarillo takes his place as the first in the line of tapestried pilgrim beggar saints.

As the picaro accrues those characteristics, we can begin to pick out the glimmer of the picara's underlying warp threads under his nature. Lazarillo's story establishes outlines common to all later picaros and picaras. For example, his introduction to the world occurs when the blind beggar first instructs the boy in the ways of the trickster by bashing his head against the bridge, warning him,

... 'You'll have to learn that a blind man's boy has got to be sharper than a needle!'

And he cackled with glee. At that moment I felt as if I had woken up and my eyes were opened. I said to myself: 'What he says is true; I must keep awake because I'm on my own and I've got to look after myself.'

We began travelling and in just a few days he taught me thieves' slang, and when he saw I was quite sharp, he looked very pleased. He kept on saying: 'I won't make you a rich man, but I can show you how to make a living.'

That was true because, after God, he gave me life, and though he was blind he revealed things to me and made me see what life was about. (27-8)

It is doubly significant that Lazarillo's first master is both blind and a beggar. The medieval concept that begging is an honorable profession which allows the rich to exercise charity to less fortunate coincided with the popular fascination of criminal literature and criminal language. For example, only ten years after the picara/bawd appeared in *La Celestina*, the *Liber Vagatorum* or Book of Beggars of 1510 was versified in 1517 and turned into prose by Martin Luther in 1528. The English *Fraternitye of Vacabondes* and *A Caveat for Common Cursitors* appeared only twelve years after the picaro's tale of *Lazarillo* in 1566.

As the religious motivation for charity waned, the beggar was bereft of any sympathy because no one felt responsible for him; society had grown intolerant of the pilgrim saint and wandering sinner when he became the financial responsibilities of the towns where a man was valued for his ability to produce work. In essence, Lazarillo de Tormes represents the death of the feudal system and the inhospitality of the industrial systems to non-productive workers. Satirically, his story of moral blindness reflects the classical origins of the blind prophets—Teresias and Oedipus, who comment on their societies because they cannot see, and Homer, who traditionally "saw" better for being blind. The continuing popularity of the Spanish blind beggars' ballads is reflected in the insistence on physical blindness of Lazarillo's first master's blindness which is, in itself, both real and symbolic.

As a novel, Lazarillo is characterized by the increased realism inherent in the novel form; his portrait may be incomplete but it is sharp in outline. This formal realism, as Ian Watt defines it, is the mark which distinguishes the picaro from his sub-literary delinquent ancestors. Citing narrative techniques, Watt establishes the novelistic traditions on a wider basis than just the narrow picaresque ones. For example, he argues that realism is not the reverse image of romance but that "the novel's realism does not reside in the kind of life it presents, but in the way it presents it" (11). By mentioning names as a stereotyping device and by citing the novelists' eventual break with it, Watt establishes verisimilitude and truth-seeming as the definitive elements of the new novel form. Autobiography is also a way to effect realism and Lazarillo's author uses it as such: thus, Lazarillo can introduce himself chummily with a casual "Well, in the first place, Your Excellency should know that they call me Lazarillo" (7) and can conclude with the pompous assurance that "as to what happens to me from now on, I shall keep Your Excellency informed" (152).

Of the certain major color motifs woven into the tapestry, the first is the dull grey of the hunger/survival theme that Lazarillo exemplifies. In sixteenth-century Spain, starvation was a close comrade whose clamor dinned out any strains of honor in the *danse macabre* and whose cries for survival overrode individual consciences. Thus, Lazarillo forever seeks food—immediate food and food for that day alone; as a Catholic, he may mention his daily bread as he says his "Pater Noster" but the picaro has not even the assurance of such a blessing. The transformation of this grey hunger theme into the picara's sickly white avarice will be discussed at length in a future chapter.

If the first color that Lazarillo lays down is the grey of hunger, the second is the inconstant moon-silver of the wandering servant who changes masters as the moon changes phases. As a servant is an aristocratic society which often could not afford to feed itself much less its servants, Lazarillo scrabbles for food for his proud hidalgo master; his servitude connects him with the parasite of Greco-Roman comedy and the Harlequin figure of the *commedia dell'arte*. He becomes part of the dispossessed civilization, following the breakdown of the feudal system, unable to earn a living in an industrial world. Specifically, Chandler delineates those non-productive elements that formed the picaro as the beggars, the church (which needed the beggars as object of charity), the gangs of illegitimate children abandoned by their destitute parents, and the gypsies who migrated to the warmth of the Spanish climate, to Andalusia, the origin of the first picara Lozana (*Literature* 29-33). As a beggar, Lazarillo is the prototypical "suffering servant" who aligns himself in iconography with the mendicant religious orders, wandering pilgrim saints, and the medieval beggars' guilds.

Although most critics acknowledge that Lazarillo was the first picaro, the generic form and traits of the picaresque had been floating about in the literary air. Although the picaro appears in trickster folk heroes like Til Eulenspiegel, Reynard the Fox, the jester Skoggin, and even in Thomas Nashe's 1594 *The Unfortunate Traveller*, these attempts were only "separate accounts of wit employed at the expense of others...strung as anecdotal beads along the thread of a single name" (Chandler 8) of picaresque literature. They lacked cohesive unity which the infusion of the Spanish social conditions onto the literary form could bring. If we were pressed to name the major gift that Lazarillo contributes to his genre, it would be the glue-white of cohesiveness because Lazarillo's story is more than a series of episodes linked by concentration on one figure; it is a completed action (albeit with an open-ended conclusion) which deserves the name of novel. Parker argues that, although *Lazarillo* "is generally considered the prototype of the novel, it is better called the precursor" (6). The publication record of *Lazarillo* shows so poorly that its one reprinting and one expurgated version caused a 1587 editor to refer to it as " 'forgotten and worm-eaten with age' " (Sieber 11).

Far from being "forgotten and worm-eaten," Lazarillo's portrait on our tapestry is still outlined in the crudely bright shades of his growth and his inability to develop. Because of his cohesiveness, his episodic stories multiply into an odd sort of growth; however, his adventures never mature into a development. And, while he is often called a delinquent, a rogue, and a scoundrel, he is the same person at the end of the book as he is at the beginning—good-humored, adaptable, scheming, and hungry.

In denying that Lazarillo is the first picaro, Parker claims that title for Guzman de Alfarache as the "first fully developed picaresque novel and the first full-length realistic novel in European literature" (22), because only after the 1599 production of Guzman did the genre of the picaresque find popularity. Parker based his assumption on the fact that the Madrid publisher Luis Sanchez reprinted an expurgated edition of *Lazarillo* some nine weeks after printing *The First Part of the Life of Guzman de Alfarache* by Mateo Aleman in 1599, with the second part of Guzman following in 1604. It was not until the 1599 publication of Guzman that Lazarillo was established as a picaro and as a model for picaros. Even Sieber also attributes to Guzman the identification of Lazarillo as a picaro, reasoning that, while *Lazarillo* is a collection of episodes, lacking central character unity of a narrative, *Guzman* is a conscious effort to construct a moral tale because it unites the adventures of a picaro with moral digressions.

Like Lazarillo, Guzman is an impoverished youth from a less than moral family who soon finds his way as an accomplished rogue bent on deceiving his fellow man. In Madrid, he acquires his picaresque nature, imitating Lazarillo in his hunger theme; his story continues with the young man forced to join the ubiquitous beggars, becoming a "basket carrier" or, more specifically, one who uses a basket to beg food for himself like the mendicant orders so that the term "basket-carrier," when applied to the picaro, indicates beggary, not honest work. His comparison to Lazarillo continues as he complains that being a tavern boy was worse than being a blindman's boy, both occupations Lazarillo attempts.

Sieber points out Guzman's interest in outward appearance and his love of clothing as a disguise which aid his scams. Fleeing to Toledo and posing unsuccessfully as a wealthy noble, he wanders along established pilgrimage routes as a pilgrim beggar, finding adventure along the way until he reaches Italy where a cardinal befriends him. Rather like Jean Valjean in *Les Miserables*, Guzman betrays the cardinal's trust and steals from him. At one point, he marries but his wife, like Lazarillo's, is a prostitute who supports him. After posing as a saint and attempting the clerical life for financial security, he returns to Madrid and Seville where he is imprisoned in the galleys for stealing from his employer. His final passages reassert his intention to reform his life by the writing down his progress in criminal life (and in criminal diction) so that others can avoid his errors. However, when the second part of Guzman was written by Juan Marti in 1602 to capitalize on Aleman's popularity, it failed to meet the picaresque standards.

On a wider canvas than that to which Lazarillo has access, Guzman constructs a bright plaid of criminal experiences and an awareness of an organized structure of criminal underworld of beggars and thieves. Lazarillo is at best a minor criminal but Guzman's experiences are tinged with an autobiographical hue. As a government official, Aleman interviewed galley slaves to uncover possible mistreatment and, as a result, became involved in correspondence with the chief social reformers of his day. Chandler and Schwartz cite the "curious coincidence in his [Aleman's] life was that he was in debtor's prison in Seville at the same time that Cervantes was there for similar reasons, although the two men were not friends" (183). Written at the same time as Guzman, Cervantes' *Don Quixote* has the rogue Gines de Pasamonte refer to *Lazarillo* as a direct model for his autobiography and to *Guzman* as an oblique source when Gines refers to his life as a galley slave. The modern musical version of Quixote, *Man of La Mancha* sets Cervantes' work within a prison, with Cervantes interacting with the prisoners, some of whom are galley slaves.

There is a difference in the two outlooks, however. Sieber claims that Cervantes' insistence that the picaresque should not "stand as an autonomous art form" (26) is ignored in Aleman's melding of Guzman to the earlier sketchy picaro Lazarillo, to the wandering impoverished beggars, and to the imprisoned galley slaves of Spain. Guzman thus emerges as a picaro whose tale does not encompass a feminine picaro or a picara. In contrast, Cervantes recreates a picara in his character of Dulcinea, the tavern-maid/prostitute, who is as much the picara as Quixote is the knight-errant. He creates others in his short stories, (collected into the *Novelas ejemplares*) and in his dramatic interludes, which connect him with the picara's stage tradition.

While Guzman unleashed a horde of imitators in the following century, not all of them are equally important to the development of the picaro, although each one has his supporting critic who claims that work as seminal to the picaro and to all picaresque literature. Most of these subsequent Spanish picaros are pale descendants of Lazarillo or Guzman. For example, when Francisco de Quevedo wrote *La vida del Buscon, llamado don Pablos* in 1608 and published it in 1626, he added the character of the swindler to the picaro. Born into a criminal family, Pablo wanders his satirizing way through society until he, like Lazarillo, marries a prostitute and retires from the scene. In 1604, Gregario Gonzalez's *El quiton Honofre* follows the satiric bent of the previous picaros, centering on Honofre as a false beggar or pilgrim who, after a life of adventure and low tricks, pretends to be a penitent to enter a religious order to escape civil punishment as a thief. The other picaresque novels that emerged in the hundred years between 1550 to 1650, the *Siglo de Oro* of Spanish picaresque literature, are repetitions of picaresque conventions.

Although the picaro was undeniably a Spanish invention, his story quickly jumped national boundaries with each country adding its own flavor of cultural modifications to the original mixture. Understandably, the first imitators of the Spanish picaresque were the French whose translation of *Lazarillo* six years after its publication led to increased interest in books of thieves' jargon, gypsies' language, and beggars' guilds like the *Histoire Generale des Larrons* [beggars or thieves]. These translations as well as the French comic narratives, bridged the gap until the picaro was fully transported into French life in the works of Paul Scarron and Charles Sorel's 1622 *La Vrye Histoire Comique de Francion*. A Gallic re-interpretation of the anti-hero, Francion is "no longer a servant but rather the scion of nobility, a gallant adventurer, and a most enthusiastic exponent of eroticism" (Monteser 27). Sieber claims that the French so emasculated the picaro that the picaros are "presented as full-grown, experienced satirists and comedians whose 'innocence' is soon lost after they enter the novels" (47). As such, because the French picaro is never of low lineage, his adventures serve to expose the corruption in his society, stressing the hypocrisy which found its ultimate in *Tartuffe*. Despite this, Alain-Rene Lesage created one French picaro in his novel of *Gil Blas de Santillane* in 1715 who, is more concerned with criticism of society than in deceiving it. He is of poor but honest parents, resents the world because he does not receive the education he thinks he should, becomes an apprentice to a doctor, and ends up as a devoted father and husband. The picaresque qualities lie mostly in his wandering between masters who, in their turn, tell him of their adventures. *Gil Blas* is more a comic novel because it neglects the very real conditions such as starvation and deprivation that caused the Spanish picaresque novel to emerge.

But, if Lazarillo is created against a sparse background, there is another picaro whose realism is "exaggerated, burlesque, and obscene for the purpose of throwing his fantasies and his moral and religious concerns into relief" (Grimmelshausen 34). Like many of his English ancestors, the German picaro has his origins in Germanic folklore of the jest books like the fifteenth century Til Eulenspiegel character and in the protonovel design of the *Erziehunsroman* in Wolfram von Eschenbach's *Parzival*. This latter type, more commonly called a *bildungsroman*, traces the development of a young man from his innocence to his acceptance into society, such as in Dickens' *Great Expectations* and Samuel Butler's *The Way of all Flesh*; the feminine form of this type of novel is the "educative" novel like Fanny Burney's *Evalina* or Charlotte Bronte's *Jane Eyre*.

An early form of such initiation novel can be seen in the figure of Simplicius in *Simplicius Simplicissimus*, the 1668-9 set of ten novels by Hans Jacob Grimmelshausen, which provides a depth of characterization absent in the early picaro. As George Schultz-Behrend points out in his translation of *Simplicimus*, "Simplicius develops from a naive child into a sophomoric fool; then deteriorates into a show-off, a rake, and a gigolo...and a saintly hermit" (xii). Grimmelshausen employed the German translation of *Guzman* which incorporated the unpublished third part by Machado de Silva where Guzman becomes a member of the Third Order Franciscans and retires to a hermitage beside a hospital, the idyllic resting place for wandering beggar, saint, or sinner.

Set against the background of the Thirty Years War (1622-52), Grimmelshausen's ten books on Simplicius use various interlocking characters to stress his attitude toward the military. Born of a nobleman who is revealed at the end of the book as his hermit-mentor, Simplicius is made a wanderer when soldiers destroy his home. Serving under many military masters, he becomes an accomplished sharpster and thief, pilgrim and prostitute, buffoon and soldier, ending his life as a hermit. In many senses, it is the war which best characterizes the picaresque because Grimmelshausen translates the picaresque wanderings into military pursuits. As Sieber points out, "Grimmelshausen captures the basic 'instability' of the rogue's open-ended life by preventing his characters from escaping war...War, then, is their ultimate master" (44). The other picaresque characters in Grimmelshausen's novels are so affected by the war that one of them, Courage, becomes a soldier, plunderer, sutler, and camp follower, taking and marrying several military men until she settles for the trickster character of the musketeer Skipinthefield. Courage's entire life is seen in relationship with the war which, as Parker says, recreated the disorder of delinquency of the human will which "is presented in human society rather than in the individual...as war which is the delinquency of men against their own nature as social beings" (135). Even in so small an item as where Simplicius finally rests gives his author a reason for social commentary against war. Because his neighbors in his homeland fear that his hermitage will draw unwanted attention to the mineral spring near his home, Simplicius is forced to choose another spring: "He cannot return 'home' because he is no longer 'simple'...On another level, Grimmelshausen seems to be saying that thirty years of war have left precious little to which the participants are able to return" (Sieber 43).

Other genres taint Grimmelshausen's picaro: the baroque novel which demanded the exaggerated dependence upon coincidence and obscure family relationships; the repentance theme of spiritual autobiography; the *bildungsroman* of the education and disillusionment of the young Simplicius. Such straying from the Spanish picaro is typical as the novel form developed and as the conditions which engendered the picaro dissipated. While Simplicius' similarities to Lazarillo are those generic to the picaresque—autobiographical narration, roguery, theft—Simplicius' differences from Lazarillo are found in the increased depth to which he knows himself and to which he returns in his calling as a hermit. It is this progression which involves so many items which attract critics; Miller, for example, sees Simplicius as "vivid, changing, alive before our eyes. Even the possible contradictions among his comments may give us the sense of the character constantly changing in accord with a narrative and a narrated world that is not fixed or ordered" (115).

The English participation in the picaresque genre is rather like that of the French, starting with an interest in the control of law and order through the *Liber vagatorum* or thieves' cant books. So avid was the interest that the picaresque tricks were elaborately catalogues in several pamphlets such as Robert Greene's 1591-2 "Conny-Catching Pamphlets" and 1592 *Black Bookes Messenger* with their revelations of charlatan schemes. A further interest in detailed hierarchy of criminal types appeared in John Awdeley's 1560-1 *The Fraternitye of Vacabondes* where the orders of the criminal world imitate the medieval craft guilds. In the same way, Thomas Harman's 1567 *Caueat or Warening, For commen Cvusestors vvlgarely called Vagabondes* specifies the different types of criminal women. The popularity of such tales caused David Rowland to translate *Lazarillo* in 1568, a text which, although it was not published until 1576, was often reprinted. However, only the full-bodied autobiography of a criminal satiated the English taste for detailed adventure as they trimmed the picaro to fit an English mold. Although Andrew Borde produced his tale of a single hero, *Geystes of Skoggan*, as early as 1565, one of the earliest rogue biographies is Thomas Nashe's 1594 *The Unfortunate Traveller* which Chandler calls the "earliest English fiction of pretension in the picaresque genre" (193), because of the emergence of Jack Wilton as the hero. Critics differ on its importance to the picaresque genre since it bred no imitators, although it is often considered one of the proto-novels.

Where Lazarillo failed to inspire many English imitations, Guzman spawned imitations like Richard Head's 1665 tale of Meriton Latroon, *The English Rogue*, based on his own life experiences as a drunkard, gambler, and literary hack. Michael Shinagel in the introduction to his edition of Meriton's life claims that he is not a picaro is the sense of Lazarillo because his "rogue autobiography...represents a vulgarized version of the pure picaresque, the moral distinctions between good and evil becoming blurred, if not blackened, by an oppressive atmosphere of unmitigated villainy and eroticism" (vii). English literature has produced a long and valid list of descendants in characters as diverse as Ralph Ellison's *Invisible Man*, Saul Bellow's *The Adventures of Augie March*, and even Mark Twain's *The Adventures of Huckleberry Finn*. The trickster, the con-artist, the riverboat gambler, the rogue scoundrel are all legitimate sons of the picaro whose figures are incorporated into our tapestry with bold strokes and bright colors. But underneath we perceive the outline of the archetypal pattern of the trickster. We notice his motley dress, his elusive glance, his perky insouciance; we are attracted to the suffering underlying his false smile. Now we must look to his feminine counterpart, the literary picara, to discover how the intricate colors of her personality match and blend in our tapestry.

The Picara

Imagine that, after all the primary colors that the picaro left us are blended into crude figures, the artist introduces a true blinding white which is laid on top of all the other shades to highlight prominent points.

Autonomy is such a white—a brighter, larger, obtrusive, awkward, unpredictable, crystalline, visible, shattering white. For it is around and about and in and through her autonomy that the picara takes her distinctive literary form, separate from the subdued shades of earlier literary forms. If her autonomy clarifies her picaresque traits, autonomy also magnifies the shapes and colors of the earlier picaresque forms. Asserting that her autonomy is her distinctive characteristic, this part of the chapter will seek to prove that her existence not only precedes the emergence of the literary picaro in time, but also that her picaresque traits diverge sharply enough from that of the picaro to force us to look beyond him for their cause. For, where Lazarillo, Simplicius, and Guzman are more affected by their society than affecting it, the picara adapts the brilliance of her autonomy to survive in her society. She controls her own destiny. The picaros might serve masters but the picara is never a mistress—that is, she is never a mistress unless it will profit her.

The assertion of her autonomy over her sexuality brings the picara to the notice of Western literature: the Greek *hetaira*, the desert harlot, and the Renaissance courtesan, all possessed autonomy over men by bestowing their sexual favors. While the Song of Songs might praise women's breasts as apples and the images of Eve's tempting apple and of Israel as the unfaithful bride of the covenant might pervade the Scriptures, Christianity found sexual autonomy, such as the Lilith myth demanded, too dangerous a tool for women. While Christ's teachings upgraded the status of women by giving them the protection of marriage, some church fathers rejected feminine sexuality in their misogynist list of evil women. While the Church lauded Mary of Nazareth for her obedient submission to the will of God, it ignored her autonomy over her own destiny in choosing to be the bearer of Christ; she could have said "no" but her *Fiat* became the hallmark of acceptance of her feminine role and the model for all women. In contrast, Eve's apple is a borrowing from the cult of Aphrodite and her sin of "disobedience" was thought to be a sexual one akin to that of Lilith— a sin of rampant feminine sexuality gone wild. In iconography, Mary's crushing the head of the serpent with the apple of Eve's temptation still in his mouth exemplified the defeat of the spiritual over the material powers.

If the white of the picara's autonomy highlights the vivid green of her prostitution, the yellow of her courtesanship, and the dark green of her bawdry, her entrance point into literature is marked by her emergence, not by her sexual role as a prostitute, but by her role as the bawd. What characterizes her first is her avaricious greed. When the sin of usury prohibited Christians from the charging of interest because money should not beget money—Mammon should not beget Mammon—the bawd's major sin was her avarice, not her prostitution. While her traffic in fornication was serious enough, her more serious sin was that she profited from prostitution. Ironically, she is an early entrepreneur investing her capital—her time, experience, and efforts—in her prostitutes and living from the rewards of their labors: as Lynne Lawner in her *Lives of the Courtesans* notes, "the courtesan is one of the first examples of modern woman achieving a relatively autonomous economic position" (4). The later mercantile society chastised her for encouraging men's wastefulness and the lack of good stewardship; like coins debased with inferior metals, the man who frequented prostitutes wasted his efforts since no children resulted. So repugnant was this unproductive form of sexuality that the bawd was assigned to be the gatekeeper to hell, further tying her with the devil of Mammon. It took the satirical humor of Spanish literature to characterize the bawd as a woman worthy of notice.

In Spanish literature, as early as the fourteenth century, the bawd is the "sempi-eternal figure of Spanish literature" (Cohen 15). Prefigured as the go-between and the duenna in the *Roman de la Rose*, the bawd figure first entered into the tapestry of the young lovers in the Archpriest of Hita Juan Ruiz's 1330-43 tale of *El libro de buen amor* or the *Book of Good Love*. Often compared with the realism of *The Canterbury Tales* of his contemporary Chaucer, Ruiz's tale resembles the Wyf of Bath's Tale with the wandering knight who must marry the old hag when she gives him the correct answer as to what women want most—sovereignty. The hero of the *Book of Good Love* calls on Venus and the bawd to aid his amatory conquests. Using a twelfth century dramatic remnant of Terence and Plautus' comedies as a basis, Ruiz popularized the bawd under the title of "Trotaconventos" whose name describes her function, a woman who "trots" between convents or religious events to secure assignations for her clients. While Trotaconventos obtains for the narrator the object of his desire, Dona Endrina, the young widow is disgraced while the picaro narrator lives to bed a series of ugly shepherdesses (or cowherds), Moorish girls, and chaste nuns before Trotaconventos dies and he ends the book. That a bawd would have religious implications is not unexpected in a country like Spain where religious events were also social events and where church services provided a natural trysting place for women secluded by family and custom.

Such a mixture of religious and secular themes places Ruiz's book among goliardic or juglaresque literatures for his love songs jostle elbows with his hymns to Mary, his comic touches abut his serious moralizations, his autobiographical style compliments his misery at his imprisonment. He categorizes and castigates love in all its forms, rendering the nature of the book closer to *carpe diem* verses of goliardic literature in its celebration of wine, women and song. The narrator is a wandering cleric who writes for the wandering artists, actors, journalists of his time, for "blind men, for begging scholars, for Jews and Moors and wise women and serenading lovers" (Brenan 83). While all of these characters types are found in picaresque literature in some form and all contribute to the picara, so many literary genres are used by the author that the work becomes a satire on literary forms and pretensions of his day. The theatre, for example, is a natural environment for the picara and the drama a natural way to express herself. The church's use of *auto sacramentales* or religious drama heightened the use of dialogue as a worthy medium of literary exchange, as appears in the *debat* form of psychomachia of later literatures and in the later *La Celestina*. Ruiz's book contains drama in the *debat* between Dona Quaresma (Lent) and Don Carnal (Feast or Carnival), with Don Amor welcomed as a conqueror over Dona Quaresma. Still, the author creates the character of the memorable bawd with a gentle and humorous understanding of her necessary position in his society.

A century later, the 1438 work of another churchman presented the darker green-black view of the bawd. Nicknamed the *Corbacho* the work of the Arciprete de Talavera Alfonso Martinez de Toledo solidified the medieval litany of evil women by embroidering on the bawd of Boccaccio's *Corbaccio* until the bawd became a fit ancestress to Celestina. Unlike Ruiz, Martinez de Toledo introduced a lower form of dialogue to characterize his bawd, a form which continues into *La Celestina*. So intent is Martinez de Toledo's work that Chandler and Schwartz claim that the author made "misogyny a studied art" (165) in his indictment of types of evil women.

In the 1528 picaresque work of another churchman Francisco Delicado, *Retrato de la lozana andaluza*, the Andaluzian girl Lozana travels to Rome where she becomes an eavesdropper on courtesan life in her occupation as beautician. Lozana's autonomy appears in her recording that the Renaissance courtesans were exalted as *cortesanae honestae* or honorable whores in their roles as the personification of earthly beauty of Eros in contrast with the spiritual beauty. As Lawner in her work details, Rome was the "city of celibates" and of Renaissance artists where the "theoretical Neoplatonism idealizing the female figure as 'heaven on earth'—literally the stepping stone to, or shadowy copy of, divine beauty— converged with a practical epicureanism to allow a quite concrete image of the desirable woman to emerge" (4). Entrepreneurs to a woman, the courtesans used portraiture as an advertising medium to increase belief in their role as necessary deities in the Roman society much as their later descendents used pictures to lure clients. As women who lived in secluded houses and attracted only the highest quality of clients, the courtesans' solemnity in their portraits shows the seriousness of their vocation.

Many of the picaresque traits are imitated in stories of these courtesans— they adopt fanciful names, change lovers, seek money; in Lozana's case, she travels from her home to Rome and from lover to lover, combining two major traits of the picara. While not quite knowing what to call her—Chandler and Schwartz settle for the term of "anti-heroine" (181)—they admit that she is the first of the picaras. What is of interest is the fact that the term "Lazarillo" for a beggar is mentioned in connection with her, proving that the name was in existence as a type long before Lazarillo became the literary picaro.

The most famous Spanish bawd, however, appears in the 1499 closet drama of Fernando de Rojas' *La Celestina* which achieved such popularity that more than sixty editions and even more imitations were produced in the century following its publication. While Rojas probably wrote the piece in 1499, the first act differs from the rest of the play in so many particulars that critics feel that it preceded the play by as much as a quarter of a century. In a letter accompanying the 1501 edition, Rojas claims to have reworked an old "auto" or interlude he found while on vacation from its one-act concentration on Celestina the bawd into the romantic story of Calisto and Melibea.

The Spanish *auto sacramentales* (short skits used as moral teaching devices akin to the Corpus Christi miracle and mystery plays of the English stage) employed the one-act structure of the morality play, personified vices and virtues, and were usually performed within a procession. For example, the "ship of fools" which convention appeared in Gil Vincente's 1519 *Barca de la gloria*, an "auto" based on the medieval *danse macabre*, was a familiar theme to a society who held the bawd as the gatekeeper of hell and who had sin and death as the children of the devil. Akin to the story of Dame Siriz in the "Interludum de Clerico et Puella," *Celestina* was adapted by confreres of St. Thomas More as an interlude between the courses of banquets where it served the same purpose as a morality lesson to warn society of the evils of procuresses. Because the drama and the tale both come from similar sources of oral tradition, to find the same story in two genres is not any more unusual than to find the story of Tevye in a short story or in a musical comedy or a movie.

Critics agree that Celestina is actually a novel; Chandler and Schwartz refuse to place it in drama and insert it under the novel because it "was obviously never intended to be acted" (72-3). Yet the dramatic structure increases the play's connection with the picaresque novel. "What is gained by the use of uninterrupted dialogue is a condensation [with] no description of places or situations, which arbitrarily change. Everything is conveyed by conversation, stifled asides, and soliloquy," J.M. Cohen claims in his introduction to his 1964 Penguin translation entitled *The Spanish Bawd* (9). Such paucity of details, such concentration on episodic action, such interchange of dialogue rather than description is characteristic of the picaresque tale and becomes the mainstay of picaresque novels.

Celestina is a bawd who, like Lazarillo, lives near a Spanish river with her two prostitutes Elicia and Areusa and two servants Sempronio and Parmeno. As a peddler of notions and potions she has access to the women at church services and in their homes. When Parmeno suggests that his master Calisto used Celestina's services to obtain the secluded Melibea, Celestina's professional skills become a *tour de force*, justifying her existence as a bawd. When she is successful, her servants kill her in an argument about the reward she has received for arranging the assignation between Calisto and Melibea. These star-crossed lovers are unfortunate; during one of their meetings, Calisto is killed in a fall from the ladder and Melibea throws herself from a tower in mourning.

Cohen asserts that Celestina's origins can be traced back to the lighthearted madam and bawd of Plautus and Terence because the names are Latin rather than Spanish in their origins (9). Monteser claims that in Plautus' parasites are early picaros and that in *Truculentus* the courtesan Phronesium is "clearly a sister-at-heart of Celestina, and therein is to be found a direct connection between Rome and the *Siglo de Oro*" (35). So popular was Rojas' combination of the bawd figure with the sentimental and romantic story of Calisto and Melibea that it was first translated into English as early as 1526. James Mabbe's famous translation entitled *The Spanish Bawd* in 1631 brought Celestina into prominence, prefiguring Shakespeare's combining the love story of Romeo and Juliet with Juliet's nurse as the bawd. Chandler and Schwartz claim that Shakespeare used an Italian edition to form his Juliet's nurse (172); as a descendant of Celestina, the nurse's practical, i.e. non-romantic comments, on the interchangeability of lovers shows her basic survival trait. Count Paris is as attractive as Romeo and he is available, she reasons the nurse's husband exists for no other reason than to provide lewd remarks to Juliet. This bawdic callousness in the face of love flaunts the convention of romance and is typically picaresque; love does not pay the rent nor buy the bread. By defying the traditional concept that marriages were arranged for the society's good and not for the individual's pleasure, Romeo and Juliet plunge into modern romanticism. Similarly, Celestina exemplifies the old morals while Calisto and Melibea employ the new romanticism of the individual. The entire play/novel can be read as a moral lesson on how unbridled passions of the individuals can lead to their deaths and to the rupture of society's communal growth.

While Celestina's tale remains a truncated picaresque morality play, in the hands of Rojas, however, the major love story develops leisurely in dialogue before it expands into a social commentary on the hostility of Spanish culture to its Jewish "conversos." Because recent critics believed Rojas may have been such a "converso," Cohen argues that the union between the lovers cannot take place because they are of different castes, religions, and social status, citing "the lack of Christian language in the speeches of Melibea and her father" (13), the superior attitude of Calisto, and Rojas' initial hesitation in acknowledging authorship as the signs of a "certain nervousness" (13) about censorship. Indeed, the anonymity of much Spanish literature, even *Lazarillo des Tormes*, Cohen claims, may stem from the fear of censorship that forced Rojas to include his name in an acrostic in the 1502 edition. For example, the same is not true of Celestina's story which remains an undeveloped and functionally picaresque tale of the bawd who dies for greed whereas the time and leisure of play's dialogue allows the lover's characters and backgrounds to develop; of special note is the fact that the story of Celestina dominates the first edition with the love story being expanded in later editions.

The picara is often accused of being a witch because she practices herbal or folk medicine under her cover as a seamstress. Celestina's witchcraft is associated with the prostitute/picara's occupation of cloth and sewing when she pictures herself as a peddler who deals in needles and thread. Parmeno the servant claims that she "had six trades in all. She was a seamstress, a perfumer, a master hand at making up cosmetics and patching maidenheads, a procuress, and a bit of a witch. Her first trade was a cover for the rest" (37). For over a hundred lines, Rojas details Celestina's lists of medicinal compounds and love potions with which she would "paint letters on their palms in saffron or vermilion, or give them wax hearts stuck full of broken needles [or] draw figures on the ground and recite spells" (39). Furthermore at the end of the third act, Celestina's list of ingredients would put Macbeth's witches to shame as she conjures up the dark forces of classical hell of "melancholy Pluto [to] wind this thread around you, and do not let it go till the time comes for Melibea to buy it. Then remain so tangled in it that the longer she gazes at it...she will forget her modesty, reveal herself to me, and reward me for my labours" (68). Ironically, Parmeno delivers a diabolic litany of her titles, the proudest of which is "old bawd" (36). As a witch and a procuress, she is a social outcast, her house "on the edge of town...stands a bit back from the road, near the tanneries and beside the river. It is a tumbledown place, in poor repair and badly furnished." (37).

While Celestina harkens back to the personified Vice of Avarice in playing the archetypically greedy old woman, she is uniquely autonomous even in Spanish picaresque literature where she is worth of recognition in a society that is obsessed with servants and servitude. Whereas the later European derivatives of the picaros are usually free men and women, the Spanish picaro is a servant while the picara is not. Whatever her status, Celestina is a manipulator of people and industrious in her own cause, an independent entrepreneur who must adopt a servile guise but one who has "lived an honourable life, as everybody knows. I'm a person of note" (63). Like her avaricious sister-picaras, she demands and gets one hundred crowns to secure Melibea for Calisto by seducing Parmeno from his innocence into greed, counteracting his "I don't want ill gotten gains" with her own statement, "I'm for gains by fair means or foul" (48).

While Celestina adds the green of procuress and seamstress to the picaresque colors, the character of *La Picara Justina* adds the moon-silver of the wandering rogue to the nature of the Spanish picara. Where Trotaconventos trotted between lovers and Celestina went between the houses of the lovers, Justina moves from city to city, not in pursuit of love or lovers but for adventure and fun. Justina, Parker claims, "adds nothing new to the exploration of delinquency, but it does add a new element to the literary material of delinquency by the creation of a female rogue" (50-1). She is the first of the picara rogue/tricksters without being a bawd or prostitute herself.

Controversy still exists about Justina's authorship with most critics accepting Francisco de Ubeda as the author, although Frank Chandler claims that a Dominican friar Andres Perez of Leon wrote the work during his student years and used Ubeda as a frontman. Written in 1603, the story was classified with other picaresque tales, quickly passed into other European languages, and finally was condensed under its English subtitle of *The Country Jilt* with tales of Celestina and other minor picaros and published in 1707 by John Stevens.

As a literary work, Justina is perhaps more conscious of its literary style, although most critics see it as a *roman a clef* of Ubeda's court scene; it has three prologues and four books, an introductory preface, and little literary merit for its interest lies in its relationship to the other picaras and picaros. The subtitles of the books indicate the author's use of cultural and social customs in the different types of picaros and picaras: Justina is a *picara montanesa* whose concern with a high place in society implies the denial of Jewish or Moorish blood, a *picara romera* or pilgrim rogue, a *picara plietista* or deceiving rogue, and a *picara novia* or engaged rogue (Sieber 27-8). She compares herself to Celestina, Lazarillo, and other lesser picaros in the description she sends to Guzman prior to their marriage. For example, in the fourth book, Justina marries a soldier named Lozana, the same name as the first Spanish picara; in the promised but never delivered sequel, Justina was to marry Aleman's Guzman de Alfarache. In fact, Frank Chandler notes that the frontispiece of the first publications of *Justina* shows Celestina and Guzman accompanying Justina toward the Port of Death with Lazarillo in a neighboring boat (428).

Well aware of her position in such august company of the picaros and picaras, Justina is closer to the trickster-picaro than to the bawd Celestina. Justina is an anti-heroine to the romantic heroines as much as Lazarillo is an anti-hero to the knights errant. Like Lazarillo, she is much more of a trickster who seeks her identity and her inheritance by her cunning ways. What the world will not give her, she takes through chicanery. She has made the step from the hunger theme to the avarice theme because she needs money or goods rather than food itself to survive; in a sense, she feeds off the thrill of the adventure itself. As Frank Chandler points out, "the picara thus secured inevitably greater freedom of movement than the picaro, and through her was to come the evolution of the rogue novel to a higher stage, where the theme was not so much the classes in society as individual adventures and aspects of life" (239).

After establishing her picaresque genealogy, "for a rogue should prove roguery a heritage" (Chandler 235), and the death of her innkeeper parents, Justina wanders to the Spanish cities, joining with occasional con men to pull off tricks, returning home to Mansilla at the end of each book, marrying finally, and leaving her readers at that point. Because she is not a courtesan, Justina does not follow the picaresque exchange of masters; because she is not a beggar, she is never a picaresque parasite; because she is seldom a servant, she is not subservient. "Justina herself had but one mistress, the *Morisca*, and thereafter, down to Moll Flanders, the women of the romances of roguery were treated rather according to their lovers and their personal exploits than according to their changes of service" (Chandler 239). The picara had begun to wrest autonomy from a reluctant society.

Spain contributed other picaras, all of whom are variations on the same themes—courtesan, trickster, romantic heroine, adventuress—all of whom push the picara into the criminal/trickster image. The titles alone give a hint to their contents. In 1631, Castillo Solorzano wrote *Las harpias en Madrid y coche de las estafas*, a collection of four novellas about four fatherless girls who use a coach from a deceased admirer to defraud hapless suitors and to acquire wealth. The four retire to Granada, promising new adventures. His romances include *Teresa del Manzanares* [Teresa, the Child of Frauds] in which Teresa follows the sharpster tricks of Justina in defrauding and satirizing society. She joins the theatrical troupe, marries four times, and settles down, promising to "a new volume to treat of the avarice of his [her husband's] and her family" (Chandler 314). Solorzano's other novels are about the picaro Trapaza (whose name means deceit) and his daughter Rufina whose story in *La graduna de Sevilla* in 1642 gave rise to many translations and imitations; Scarron used it in his 1651 *Roman Comique*; John Davies printed *La Picara or the Triumph of Female Subtilty* in 1665 which was later titled *The Life of Donna Rosina*; in 1717, *The Spanish Pole-Cat: or the Adventure of Senora Rufina* appeared.

Influenced by the lists of evil women prevalent in the writings of church fathers, the picara acquired the darker shades of the villainess so that every evil woman becomes a picara. For example, Salas Barbadillo's 1612 novel *La hija de Celestina*, known also as *La Ingeniosa Elena*, departs from the picaresque genre into that of the murder mystery in which the heroine is executed for her crimes. Confusing the sordid reputation of Helen of Troy with the contemporary picaras, critics agree that Elena has strayed into the realm of villainesses: to Chandler and Schwartz, she is "the typical evil, vice-ridden woman...the most depraved of all the picaras" (186) and the tale of such a picara has deteriorated so that it is "no longer communicating with the birth of the rogue, and dispensing entirely with the service of masters, its observation of low life was only such as would contribute to the working of the plot, the intrigue standing out as supremely important" (Chandler 291).

Written within seventy years of each other, the early picaras' stories contribute additional colors to the basic formula: Lozana is a wanderer; Celestina is a full-time bawd, Justina is a trickster. While French and Italian authors never developed the picara beyond her Spanish origins, the German Grimmelshausen constructed his picara Courage as a countervoice to his picaro Simplicius. Hans Speier claims that it is unlikely that Grimmelshausen consciously used *Celestina* or *Justina* as sources of his picara while Monteser claims that "*Trutz Simplex* was probably based" on the French version of Justina, *La Narquoise Justine* (31). Indeed, while she does imitate the other picaras, Courage is very much her own individual; her contribution to the tapestry is the sparkling blue of the adventuress and the purple of the warrior.

Her name is intimately tied with her vice. When she is the daughter of an unidentifed Bohemian nobleman, she is called Libuschka; when she is the military serving boy, she is Janco; when she is revealed as a woman, her captain names her Courage because, in her fight to resist discovery of her true sex, she refers to her opponent's grabbing her "between the legs because he wanted to get hold of the tool [male genitals] that I did not have" (99). Just as the name Lazarillo delineates his character, the various translations of Courage's name and subtitles color the reader's view of her. For example, Speier's translation refers to her as the "adventuress," a word used by G.B. Shaw for his female heroines. Yet an "adventuress" is somehow less than an "adventurer" who is defined by Webster's as "one who engages in new and perilous enterprises" and "a soldier of fortune" while an "adventuress," on the other hand, is a lesser being, a "female adventurer; a woman who seeks position or livelihood by equivocal means." The older translation of George Schulz-Behrend's calls her the "Runagate" Courage, a word which confuses the Latin word "to deny" or "renegade" with the Middle English words "to run" and "agate" or "on the way." Monteser calls her by the first German words of the manuscript—"Trutz Simplex"—"to spite Simplex" because he feels that it best describes Grimmelshausen's intent to weave Courage into his ten-novel series as a female rogue and antithetical contrast to Simplicimus. Most critics call her a picara.

Courage's life story, interwoven as it is with that of the picaros Simplicimus and Skipinthefield, ultimately revolves around the Thirty Years War. Because of the constant war, she adds a dimension not used by the Spanish picaras like Celestina and Justina; where their survival efforts center on wresting food from their reluctant societies, Courage's survival is even more basic because she is constantly uprooted by the chaos of war; it is not surprising to find her as a warrior of sorts. However, Speier notes that, while Courage is "as much an amazon as a harlot," she also "has many of the quantities of the heroines in the idealistic novels of the baroque era...a manlike, vigorous creature, a virago...the ideal of the Renaissance, fashioned after illustrious ancient models" (32-3). He cites the several contemporary German baroque novels which helped form Courage but maintains that she has several picaresque elements which set her apart.

One of those elements is the variable final status of the picaras: Celestina is murdered; Justina survives to marry happily; Courage survives but at a lesser status as she is reduced from being the daughter of a nobleman to the "Madam General" or queen of the wandering gypsies. Within her military career, she is increasingly less fortunate as she is reduced from an actual combatant and plunderer, to her trade as a sutler, to a lesser position as dealer in minor tobacco and brandy, finally to a psuedo-military leader of a raid for stolen food from peasants. Fortune is often flexibility for the picara and what autonomy Courage has is linked with her military career as it parallels the Germany's war-ravaged destiny. Her picaresque nature allows her to move as easily within military ranks as she can in civilian life. While she cannot control the actions of war, she can control her participation in it as a combatant, plunderer, sutler, camp follower, or soldier of fortune; her fortune may decrease but Fortune still protects her.

In her marriages, her career is equally downward as she starts with marriage to a cavalry captain, descends to a infantry captain, to a lieutenant, to a sutler, to a musketeer (Skipinthefield), and ends up with a gypsy husband. Despite her checkered career, she outwits Fortune by her survival in the face of the horrors of war. At the end of the novel, she claims that she and the gypsies are "of no use to God or man and do not want to serve either of them, but to the detriment of both the country folk and the great, whom we relieve of many a head of game, [we] live on nothing but lies, fraud, and theft." (223). The operative word here is "live" because she does survive into her seventies. Even then, as the wife of the gypsy lieutenant, blackened by "goose drippings and various salves for lice on my skin and from the use of unguents to dye my hair," Courage is "so struck by the change I had undergone that I had to laugh at myself out loud" (216-6). Change, growth, Fortune, chance, choas—all color the tapestry with their hues but the grim black-red of war dominates Courage's story.

The streaked black and red of the chaos of war are the natural foil for an autonomous picara; war and social change establish the disordered universe of the early picaras which later novel picaras use merely as backgrounds while many fantasy picaras adopt it as integral to their character as warriors. Parker claims that war is the ultimate delinquency derived from pride or the inability to submit the individual will to the common good (135), a vestige of the primal capital sin of pride. Courage prides herself in gaining revenge on Simplicius by abandoning a child for him to raise and on various lovers for their ill-treatment of her. Her pride leads to her concern with vanity about her loss of beauty which in turn might lead to a loss of money and an attack of avarice, the second deadly sin. She accuses herself of other faults—anger, indolence, melancholy, wantonness, lust—to construct her own version of the seven deadly sins that are so much a part of the makeup of Celestina and other Spanish picaras.

Courage uses the military aspect of war as a secondary source of her two vices: avarice and sexuality. She is aware of these as faults as she mentions in her first chapter: speaking of herself, she claims that "her sauciness and wantonness have subsided, her stricken conscience is anxiously awake, and the listless old age she has reached makes her feel ashamed of keeping on with her excessive follies...What I am lacking is repentance, and what I ought to be lacking are avarice and envy" (89-91). Always her chief characteristic is her avarice which drives her to her revenge on Simplicius; her ultimate trick, she claims, is that she has left her maid's child to be brought up at Simplicius' charge. Thus, her avarice is both motivation of her need for survival and a demonstration of her skill of survival. Even when she tries to settle down as a farmer, she is able to gain financially on the soldiers billeted at her house, so that she found that her "prosperity and income exceeded the expenses incurred through the war" (202). Her rapaciousness in accumulating plunder leads first to her dabbling in trade and then to her acquiring goods through tricks and scams; again, there is a downward movement as she participates in legal theft on the battlefield to illegal thievery with gypsies.

Just as the military setting satisfies the restlessness of the picara, so also does it provide a natural environment for her lustfulness. The change of military husbands and lovers serves as the picara's version of the picaro's change of masters, a form of autonomous control. With the help of her nurse, Courage first tries to avoid losing her virginity by disguising herself as a boy; when that disguise is about to be uncovered, she gives herself to the cavalry captain who promises to protect her. Even then she is autonomous because she controls the situation: "I liked the touch of his lascivious hands much better than his fine promises, but I resisted gallantly, not in order to get away from his or to escape his desire, but in order to arouse and excite him to even more fervent efforts" (101). Her assessment of her sexual powers achieves autonomy for her; once she understands that she has a marketable body, she uses it to obtain her survival by marrying and prostituting herself to her financial advantage. Thus, war has satisfied her need for chaos of Fortune, for pride in her military accomplishments, for her avarice in accumulating money, for her lust in sexual endeavors, for her need to travel, and for her general restlessness. Onto the picaro's colored skeins of wandering, hunger, and trickery, the picara laid her colorful skills in bawdry, avarice, and war. The next color to be applied came with the transportation of the picara into English.

The primary colors of these Continental picaros and picaras were muted down into softer shades of the English female rogue, derived partly from life and partly from the prose fiction forms of autobiography (criminal, spiritual), jest biography, joke books, fabliaux, drama. Although the English fictional picara is slashed in the bold outline of the criminal biography, her introduction of humor, literary realism, and social criticism capture the more complex tones and values to define the English picara.

Just as the *epylla* cluster around a central hero to become an epic, so do the stories within a generation center on the most prominent person of that century. In such a mythopoeic process, the subjects of the jest biographies or *Schwankbiographen* could not have created all the tricks and riddles assigned to them any more than Abraham Lincoln could have experienced all the anecdotes attributed to him. In England, the citrus yellow of jest biography—the treasury of jokes, riddles, and anecdotes—tinged the popular mind in various literary forms. Because such books needed justification for their existence, many overlapped characters with Lazarillo and Celestina, Justina and Guzman, frequenting later editions of each other's works. This spin-off effect or "visiting star guest" format is most familiar in television but its purpose is the same as that of the jest book: to provide "a whetstone to mirth" as the prologue of the 1635 edition of *Long Meg of Westminster* does when it compares the heroine's escapades with those of Robin Hood and Bevis of Southampton (Mish 83).

Despite the fact that her biography was entered in the Stationers' Register in 1590 and her story has continued down as an example of the jest biography, debate as to whether Long Meg was an actual living person is still going on. The actual persons mentioned in her biography place her in the early sixteenth century in the time of Henry VIII through Queen Mary's reign in 1557. According to the epitaph by a later writer Gayton, Long Meg of Westminster was buried in the Abbey: "I, Long Meg, once the wonder of the spinsters/ was laid, as was my right, i' the best of Minsters" (Burford 47).

Long Meg's name stems from her extreme height of more than seven feet and from the "length of her proportion [where] every limb was so fit to her tallness that she seemed the picture and shape of some tall man cast in a woman's mold" (Mish 84). When she leaves her Lancashire home to London to "serve and to learn city fashions," she is accompanied by several young women. Encouraged to find work as a tavern-maid at the Eagle tavern in Westminster, she is tested by two historical jesters—Will Summers and Doctor Skelton; when she defeats a third man in combat, a Spaniard, Sir James of Castile, she is hired as a "bouncer" for the tavern. That Sir James is a Spanish knight heightens awareness of the picara's origins in the Spanish picaresque, jest books, and anti-romantic spoofs. When this latter *miles gloriosus* again engages her in combat in her male attire, the braggart knight pleads with the disguised Long Meg for his life, declaring that the duel was only "for a woman's matter; spill not my blood" (Mish 91). When Meg agrees to spare his life if he serves as a page at dinner, she reveals herself as a woman and enjoys being "master of the feast, Sir James playing the proper page, and Meg sitting in her majesty" (Mish 92).

While Long Meg's two occupations of soldiering and tavern-keeping seem to lift her above the tradeless picaro, the trades actually precipitate and emphasize the later picara's autonomous abilities. Her original military career is precipitated by her taking the place of her servant. Nowhere is she called a camp follower but rather a "laundress [who caused] her women soldiers to throw down stones and scalding water" (104) on the French soldiers. When Meg is challenged by a braggart Frenchman, she defeats him in single combat and sends his head to his commander. For her military efforts, she is granted lifetime pension by the King of eightpence a day, not an uncommon practice for many of the actual women who soldiered in various wars. (The seventeenth century Christian Davies fought with the British army and was awarded a shilling a day pension (Thompson 69).) In peacetime, Meg also resorts to physical means to defend her business from a persistent constable who tries to count "what guests she had"; she promised to "beswinge you as ever constable was beswinged since Islington stood" (107). She keeps order in her tavern by enforcing a list of rules of conduct yet within her own marriage she gives apparent autonomy to her husband by refusing to fight with him when she is challenged.

The taint of prostitution was so intimately linked with picaresque soldiering and tavern-keeping that Long Meg is accounted as a prostitute everywhere but in her telling of her own tale. The closest the original text comes to prostitution is a reference to her house at Islington where "oftentimes there resorted gentlewomen thither and divers brave courtiers and other men of meaner degree, [so that] her house was spoken of" (107). Even here her soldiering affects her tavern-keeping. While her biography itself does not detail any prostitution, the house she kept at Islington with "lodging and victuals for gentlemen and yeomen...surpassed all other victuallers in excess of company" was kept "quiet" (108) and peaceful through a series of posted rules which, while generous to the impoverished, were enforced by Meg's strong arm. The only reference to other women is in one of these house rules where, if a "ruffler [who caused] an alehouse brawl...would not manfully...fight a bout or two with Long Meg, the maids of the house should dry beat him and so thrust him out of doors" (Mish 108). Whether the maids were prostitutes is not clear, although the assumption in picaresque literature is that any tavern or inn provided maidservants as temporary prostitutes.

Contemporary reports attribute prostitution to her tavern. For example, a tract "The Golden Grove" by William Vaughan assumes that she is a bawd: "It is saide that Long Megg of Westminster kept alwaies twentie Courtezans in her howse, who by their pictures she solde to alle commers" (Burford 47). Mentioning the practice of advertising the prostitutes by their pictures ties Meg with the same practice used by the Renaissance courtesans, the Dutch and Flemish brothels, and by Holland Leaguer's, the most famous brothel of its time. Perhaps her military career may have gotten tangled up with Holland Leaguer's reputation for defending itself against attack by the law. Somewhere after 1562 and before 1578, Long Meg was the alleged owner of the Manor in that area around the Bankside, infamous from its mention in the twelfth century rules laid down for licensed brothels. According to the anonymous 1632 pamphlet, the estate called Holland's Leaguer was known for "the memorie of that famous Amazon, Longa Margarita who had there for manie yeeres kept a famous Infamous House of Open Hospitalitie" (Burford 46).

The autonomy of the English prostitute rests with the strange Elizabethan institution of Holland's Leaguer and again it involves actual people rather than literary ones. Holland's Leaguer was originally the estate known as the Liberty of Old Paris Gardens on the south bank of the river Thames, so called because it provided a natural defensive front with its moat and porticullis. Playwright Shackerley Marmion's tract describes it as "a Fort citadell or Mansion Howse so fortified and envyroned about with al maner [of] fortifications that ere any foe could approach it he must march more than a muskette shotte on a narow banke...betwixt two dangerous ditches...then a worlde of bulwarks rivers ditches trenches and outworkes" (Burford 53). Holland's Leaguer lay very near the three major theatres of the day—the Swan, the Globe, and the Hope-Bear-pit—outside the environs of London proper and subject to its own laws because it was an "ancient Liberty with rights of asylum...and with very ill-defined means of law enforcement even by the king's officers" (Burford 55). It was called "leaguer" because of the difficulty anyone would have in beleaguering or capturing it. Easily reached by city clients who could walk over London Bridge or ferry across the river, the brothel was equally approachable by the court.

Its uniqueness does not lie with its defensibility alone but in the famous procuress and prostitutes who were sheltered by its walls. E.J. Burford in his *Queen of the Bawds* claims that the majority of information comes from a 1632 tract, possibly by the playwright Shackerley Marmion whose later play uses the house of prostitution, Holland's Leaguer, as it title and the theme. The pamphlet creates an early history from sparse facts to concentrate on the life and adventures of a young London housewife in the 1590s. During the Elizabethan and Jacobean era, the most famous prostitute of her time was Elizabeth Holland or Dona or Madame Brittanica Holland. Lured to London by the glitter of court life, the girl entered into genteel "service" in the household of an city alderman where his pictures of famous classical "curitizans" or courtesans encouraged her that to "synne wysely was to synne safely" (16). Such influences affected her choice of occupations.

Like Aphra Behn's mysterious disappearing husband, Elizabeth Holland's husband apparently contributed only his name before retiring from the arena while his wife started a lucrative brothel in London near the playhouses. While Elizabeth's merchant-husband may actually have been a member of the Holland family who ruled the Elizabethan underworld, there is considerable doubt about which Holland, Elizabeth or otherwise, owned the brothel and, indeed, so many references to Hollands being fined for prostitution during those years may point to the existence of an entire family who governed the vice. While her husband's position as a merchant may have first served to introduce her into the international set in bustling London, her liaison with an Italian courtier Alberto Gentile encouraged Elizabeth to provide a brothel for multi-national foreigners, streaming into prosperous London.

What is of importance is that Elizabeth Holland changed her name to Madame Britannica Hollandia in keeping with the regulations, stemming back to Roman times, that registered prostitutes must adopt a professional name to avoid confusion with street walkers or casual prostitutes. Also, it would hardly be political wisdom for "London's most popular well-known high-class Brothel Queen" (40) to bear the name of the Queen. This change of name allowed Elizabeth to follow the old custom that brothel "madams were either Flemish (including Dutch) or French [and] that whores should bear fancy foreign names, in line with the tradition that continental harlots knew their business better than local British ones" (Burford 40). One contemporary critic complains of the Bankside stews that "English women disdayned to be Baudes; Froes (women) of Flaunders were women for that purpose" (40). One of Elizabeth's prostitutes was known as Longa Margarita whose name, beside being connected to Long Meg, may have been a variant of the Flemish saint Margaret who died defending her employers' or relatives' tavern from being robbed; many Flemish taverns are named after her.

The connection of the Netherlands, France, and Italy with prostitution is a frequent one in English literature. Burford cites an instance where the apprentices' annual Shrove Tuesday shutting down of the Shoreditch brothels forced a brewer-owner, a Mrs. Leake or Leeke of Flemish heritage, to protest to the courts. According to Burford, Holland's Leaguer in Paris Gardens was the "congregating place for all the Dutch Whores at the end of the 16th century, and was popularly known as Hollands Laager" (119), in imitation of the "famous 'Schoen Majken' (The lovely Little Maiden) in Brussels, renowned at this time for its excellence in every respect" (73); Holland Leaguer's popularity depended on the business-like atmosphere in which it was conducted, its good food, luxurious surroundings, modern plumbing, medical inspections, clean linens, and high class prostitutes. Thus, the Continental brothels made popular by the Elizabethan poets and sonneteers sported English whores imitating the Dutch or Flemish "froes" imitating Italian Renaissance *cortesanos* imitating Roman courtesans imitating Greeks *hetairai*.

The civil authorities always threatened brothels and Elizabeth, employing her girls in Duke Street, near the docks but within the town walls and jurisdiction, came under the London court's harsh punishments. In 1597 she was imprisoned in the infamous debtor's prison of Newgate charged with running a brothel. While Elizabeth's literary sisters—Moll, Amber—find themselves in the notorious prison as harlots or thieves awaiting the punitive sentence to Bridewell—the prison for rehabilitation or punishment for women—or transportation to the colonies, Elizabeth had enough money to buy a comfortable existence in the Newgate. She paid her fine for running a brothel but escaped the physical punishment and humiliation of a public whipping at a cart's tail by fleeing to sanctuary outside London's jurisdiction. Stung by the law's inroads into her affairs, she swore to fight off any forces which might seek to disrupt her again. Consequently, she leased the estate outside of London and entered history as the Dona Hollandia Britannica, madam of Holland's Leaguer.

Elizabeth's ability to be autonomous is her most outstanding quality in a business where she competed with skilled whoremasters like Henslowe and Edward Alleyn. Frank Chandler, sees her as the "English Celestina, who had taken up her abode on the south shore of the Thames in an establishment impregnable except to her well-wishers and furnishing for the moment the scandal of the town" (147). As the bawd of a thriving brothel, Elizabeth became the major subject of a pamphlet by Nicholas Breton and the minor subject of a play by Marmion, where she is rendered as a "fierce imperious creature full of defiant spirit" (Burford 89). She is able to defend her house against the law from within; ordered by Privy Council to surrender, she defied the law and abandoned the house without answering any summons with no trace of her being punished or fined. Thus, Holland's Leaguer lived up to its name by withstanding the law's beleaguering to give its mistress time to escape unharmed. Shortly afterwards a balladeer Lawrence Price who wrote in "*News from Holland's Leaguer*" that "Hollands Leaguer is lately broken up/This for Certain is spoken" suggests that disappointed young men keep a lookout for the new brothel "at *Bewdley* where they [prostitutes] keep their musters" (Burford 116).

Burford asserts that King James must have known and probably visited her establishment. This tradition of the courtesan's connection with the king pervades the literature of the picara as the ultimate goal to be achieved, even though the picara's fortunes invariably decline after her liaison with the king. Courage has affairs with the military "king" of her high-ranking captain; Roxana's liaison with the king is a highpoint of her life and her French prince is another. Amber's one-night stand with Charles II frustrates her when she is not called back and Becky's affair with Lord Steyne is the highest she goes in the nobility. Even Scarlett marries Rhett who sets out to be the "king" of Atlanta society so that his daughter can be the "princess." (This concept carries over into the film version where the "King" of movieland, Clark Gable created the role of Rhett Butler.) Liaison with the king does not usually continue into the fantasy picaras, although the created worlds which they inhabit often boast a monarchy of sorts; the fantasy picaras do not sleep their way to fame; either they earn fame themselves or they have affairs with men whom they consider "kingly" by their picara standards.

If the vivid green of Elizabethan courtesans did not clash with the earthier greens of the bawdic imitations of Celestina, the green of English picara broadened to incorporate the subtle camouflage greens of the trickster/confidence women like Justina. For example, Mary Frith was better known as Moll Cutpurse, a term arising from her thieves' jargon as a gangster's woman, a "moll" or a "doll," and from her specific occupation as a pickpocket. Best known through her alleged diary of 1662, Moll was probably a hermaphrodite, according to her biographer C.J.S. Thompson; she was brought up as a girl but soon adopted attire akin to that of the hobby horse—a doublet on the top and a skirt on the bottom. As an actual person, Mary appears in court records for wearing men's clothes for which she had to do public penance in St. Paul's. So disguised she joined a group of thieves or "land pyrates" (21) who preyed on tourists near Covent Garden and the theatrical neighborhoods. She fenced stolen items for a network of thieves and, using her reputation as a fortune-teller and finder of lost items, returned the stolen goods for a reward: " 'The world consists of the cheats and the cheated,' " Mary claimed and there was no doubt which side she favored.

Just as Elizabeth Holland was immortalized in drama, so also did actual English female rogues like Mary Frith appear in plays as subjects and possibly as actresses. According to William Macqueen-Pope, "there had been rumours of a woman appearing before at the Fortune Theatre in 1610, in a play by Middleton and Dekker called *The Roaring Girle-or Moll Cutpurse.* Presumably the character was drawn from life for the author in an epilogue promised that Moll herself should appear if the public wanted her to do so" (27). She was also mentioned in Field's 1618 play *Amends for Ladies* and, over a hundred years later, Defoe knew her so well that he referred to her in *Applebee's Journal* of March 23, 1723 and, very possibly, used some of her experiences as a base for Moll Flanders.

Criminal autobiography further formed the English picara. In the life of Mary Moders Carleton, who appears in James Kirkman's 1673 criminal biography, *The Counterfeit Lady Unveil'd*, was so popular that twenty-four books emerged on her between 1663 and 1673, according to Spiro Peterson's introduction to Kirkman. Mary Moders Carleton was a swindler and impersonator who for twenty years bilked unsuspecting dupes. Charged with bigamy, she fled to Germany where she so infatuated an old man that she was able to abscond with his money. Arriving in England again, she posed as an impoverished German princess, swindled several men and was charged with bigamy for her third marriage. In one escapade reminiscent of Defoe and Amber, she and her maid posed as young men to escape with their loot; in another, she pulled the "jealous husband" scam, blackmailing a young lawyer to preserve his reputation. When she was apprehended, she was sent to Newgate, transported to Jamaica, returned to London, arrested again and hanged in January 1673. Her life story reads like a summary of the picara's archetype; her use of male clothes as a disguise to escape prosecution is typical picaresque action; her willingness to deceive by altering her name is also. The German Princess, as she titled herself, possessed the picaresque elements of roguery, vanity, thievery, disguise and deception; so widespread was her influence that Defoe has Roxana title herself the German Princess (271). In fact, critic Ernest Bernbaum, the early editor of the *Mary Carleton Narratives*, sees a foreshadowing of Defoe when he states that "Kirkman maintains the manner commonly associated with Defoe…serious moral tone, minute depiction of occurrences, the coherence of plot, the tracing of the motives of the character and the elaborate creation of verisimilitude" (90).

Not all the picaras existed before 1700, however. Another set of more subtle shades influenced by increased realism, the sharper light of criticism, and the color-hungry readers created the picaras of Behn and Defoe, the immediate ancestresses of the novel picaras and the distant ancestresses of the fantasy picaras.

The beginnings of the novel show glimmers of the picara as a subject worth writing about. Nicholas Breton's *The Miseries of Manuilla* lacks the force of character associated with the picara because for, while Manuilla suffers the troubles of a defenseless young woman in a wicked world, she escapes the fate of the disillusioned picara by dying while she is still innocent. Aphra Behn's heroines, on the other hand, present a variety of types from innocent to villainess. Unusually strong in mind and in action, Behn's heroines are determined to pursue their survival. Philadelphia in *A True History* suffers a Clarissa-like brothel imprisonment by her brother, survives, and emerges as a rich and honored widow, capable of choosing her next husband. Arabella in *The Wandering Beauty* escapes from an unwanted marriage by a journey of flight and disguise, finally choosing the husband she wants. The villainesses exhibit the same ferocious feminism. Ardelia in *The Nun: or The Perjured Beauty* is lustful, malicious, and vengeful; Sylvia in *Love Letters* is little better than a nymphomaniac; the heroine of *The Fair Vow-Breaker* is so evil that she murders one man and accidentally kills her husband. The subjects which Behn selects range from an Oedipal incest motif in *The Force of Imagination* to vanity as a reason for murder in *The Fair Jilt*.

Defoe's female heroines are logical steps in the development of the picara from her mythical origins through her counterpart with the picaro. Using the older forms, Defoe is a pivotal writer whose works both reflect his traditions and forecast the future of the novel. Just as Richardson developed *Pamela's* epistolary style from his books of letters and Fielding developed his comic epic of *Tom Jones* from earlier satires, so did Defoe rework criminal autobiographies as major themes in his novels. With the wealth of picaresque literature at his disposal, Defoe was in the enviable position of creating the first picara who blends the awkward primary colors of the picaresque forms with the subtler shades of the novel heroines, while still remaining very much her own autonomous person.

An innovator seldom perfects the form and Defoe's attempts are not generally considered novels. While each of Defoe's novels is different and each one is *sui generis*, Defoe makes the prefaces of *Robinson Crusoe, Colonel Jacque, Moll Flanders*, and *Roxana* complement each other in their insistence on the autobiographical confessional intent as the sole motive for their writings. *Crusoe* uses a variant of the spiritual pseudo-autobiography: thus, "the story is told with modesty, with seriousness, and with a religious application of events to the uses to which wise men always apply them, viz. to the instruction of others by this example" (n.p.) In *Moll*, Defoe comments that "as the best use is to be made of even the worst story the moral 'tis hoped will keep the reader serious, even where the story might incline him to be otherwise" (3). With *Roxana*, however, Defoe departs from his cautious statement of purpose; although he maintains the facade that the novel is meant for instruction, its fullest impact centers on its entertainment value. Nor apparently did Defoe feel that *Roxana* needed much apology for its existence since, "the advantages of the present Work are so great, and the Virtuous Reader has room for such much Improvement, that we make no Question, the Story however meanly told, will find a Passage to his best Hours; and be read both with Profit and Delight" (2-3).

Although *Moll Flanders* has been accorded the title of Defoe's most picaresque work, his *Roxana* is the stronger example of our argument because she is a full-bodied, full-blooded picara. Critics stress only some of the picaresque traits within *Moll*: Alter calls her an "anti-heroine" (73): Monteser sees Moll as "in the direct tradition of the picara" while Roxana is only one of the "samples of the picaresque romance" (48). As Starr points out in his preface, Moll is closer to a criminal autobiography; he cites several actual persons whose lives may have been the sources for Moll but denies that she is wholly taken from any one person. By limiting her to criminal autobiography, Defoe is able to expand on this familiar theme of what Starr calls the "callousness of society towards the unprotected and the unproductive—orphans, debtors, criminals, single women without trades, and other marginal types" (xiv). Within the larger scope of the picaresque being discussed in this book, Moll comes up a poor second to Roxana as a picara who overrides her genre. This is not to deny that Moll is a picara. She is a fine one but one whose picaresqueness is limited to her ability as a thief, as a wanderer, as a prostitute because, after her picaresque birth and background, Moll's story swerves into conventional marriage and economic problems, with only the second half involving her picaresque journey. Roxana, on the other hand, is immersed in the picaresque from her first memory as an immigrant from France; while the stability of her early upbringing aligns her more with the Continental picara, she is early forced into prostitution and deception for her survival before her autonomy asserts itself. Roxana is a picara; Moll is picaresque.

In developing an updated picara, Defoe did not need to create a character beyond Roxana because he had reached the zenith; this only possibility lay in creating an imaginary heroine and that was too far from the historical and literary realities to suit him. In *Roxana*, Defoe flexes his novelistic muscles into the showmanship of an older genre rather than the creation of a new genre. Having once finished *Roxana*, he had exhausted the genre and Defoe was too practical a man to pursue a dying genre. No matter what critics decide *ex post facto*, Defoe's experience with Roxana did lead him back to expository prose and away from a fictional suitable for a novel. Ironically, as Defoe's last fiction, *Roxana* is his most critically neglected work because his other novels distract from it. Within the history of literature, *Roxana* has been seen from the wrong perspective. The novel is not an example of an early novel—an archetype of the eighteenth century fiction or a prototype of the sentimental heroine's tale of misfortune. *Roxana* is Defoe's version of picaresque novel about a picara and, as such, it exhibits his unique adaptation of all the picaresque traditions.

Yet, *Roxana* has long perplexed critics who felt comfortable with Moll's picaro origins but not with Roxana's picara origins. (One critic even commented that he suspected that Roxana enjoyed being a courtesan. Chandler considers Roxana to be "almost without emotion. She certainly wins no sympathy...with characters so perverse in motive, with personages who are simply puppets, it is only natural that the morality of 'Roxana,' should be external and distorted" (196-7). Maximillan Novak calls her "Defoe's least attractive character" (50); Harrison Steeves sees her as "vain, avaricious, hypocritical, and a ruinous influence" (33). Is it her flagrant sexuality that offends them; is it her feminine approach to the masculine world that disturbs them? Or is it that critics avoid Roxana because they cannot recognize the archetype of autonomy? For our argument, Roxana presents a sharp outline of what the picara has been, should be, and will be.

Departing from the creamy homespun wool and the primitive herbal or vegetable dyes of the early picaresque genres, the colors of the picara in these early novels began to imitate the industrial practices where yarn was spun on mechanical wheels, looms were owned by factory owners, and colors expanded in numbers to over two thousand shades for the tapestry. The subtlety of the picara's figure deepened as new shades of picaresque color were developed in a group of novels classified, for the sake of our argument, as the later "novel" picaras, to separate them from the picaras of Defoe.

Primary among them is Thackeray's *Vanity Fair*, that novel without a hero, which presents another version of the picara, one who has learned how to mingle in society while milking it. Here, the actual actions of the picaresque are masked in the satire of polite society, journeying through the Fair. Just as Becky's hunger theme has been transmuted into her greed for goods and security, Thackeray's Puppet Master device distances the author from his work and gives him a set of impartial archetypal patterns which the picaro, telling his own story, never achieves. Becky is not an autobiographer and the lack of this viewpoint must be assumed by Thackeray as he does when he defends his heroines for their actions. What he admires are Becky's survival techniques and, consequently, he stresses her autonomy. However, Amelia is equally a picara: as the emanation of the Widow of Windsor archetype, doting on her child and her memories, she fights mightily for her autonomy in a mass of sentiment and Thackeray is as critical of her as he is of Becky. But, while Amelia is an economic outsider, Becky is still the emotional outsider who cannot find a place in her society; nor does she care to as long as she has the means to survive. Just as the somber black of Amelia's widows' weeds is a fugitive dye, so also the sharper reds of Becky's villainy that tint her sandy hair pale into insignificant and unobtrusive pink when she achieves some measure of respectability.

In contrast, another redheaded modern picara Scarlett O'Hara in Margaret Mitchell's *Gone with the Wind* marches onto our tapestry, trailing the red clay of Tara in her wake. Critics claim that it is a satire on Mitchell's own culture as well as a reordering of the antebellum South. As a historical romance, it might be expected to end happily as its subsequent bodice-ripping novels do. But, of course, it does not. What Scarlett does is to rise above her literary romance heritage to become an archetype of the strong southern woman who insists on her own way; she is the first picara to become accessible in novel and film, the first to capture the popular imagination, the prime figure in our modern tapestry.

Another novel picara is Amber in Kathleen Winsor's *Forever Amber*, written some ten years after *Gone with the Wind* and in direct imitation of it and of early picaresque forms and novels. Closely derivative of Moll Flanders, Roxana, and Scarlett, Winsor's use of historical details and scandalous liaisons made the book an instant bestseller with its recreation of Restoration England. By alternating chapters of the fictional life of Charles II, the novel differs from later historical novels by featuring a picaresque heroine in opposition to the well-balanced fictional biographies of historical figures such as those written by Jean Plaidy and Antonia Fraser and Norah Lofts. Amber has few morally redeeming values and the book was roundly condemned for its immorality by contemporary critics. So potent was the novel that Winsor carried autobiography to the ultimate by writing another book *Star Money* about her experiences as an author of a best-seller whose character became confused with her author in the eyes of the public. It too was made into successful film.

The last category of the picara is that of the fantasy picara who apparently developed from science fiction heroine. I say apparently because a quick look at the heroines of science fiction disproves this: in science fiction, the heroine is a pale appendage of the hero, the object of desire, usually sexual, the reward for the quest. She has no identity of her own because she seldom acts on her own; she lacks autonomy as she waits to be rescued. Not so the fantasy picara who is an autonomous hero who is a woman rather than a heroine. While she appears to have "ridden the coattails" of science fiction until she gained strength and identity to launch her own sub-genre in fantasy, we have only to look at her origins in the picara to see that such is not the case.

The fantasy picara is both the newest and the oldest picara. Built on the warp threads of the Great Goddess archetype, the picara is never far from any genre; in fantasy, she uses the background colors of the science fiction genre as foils to show off her skills but she is a clearly woven figure of her own. She is more than the feminine version of the hero because her quest is so vitally different; as a woman, she was different goals and different obstacles to overcome; her monsters are society's disapprovals, her mountains are galactic spaces, her hunger is for self-knowledge. The picara simply highlights the existing warp threads underlying her modern design because her autonomy demands full participation in any action involving her life. Furthermore, where science fiction is more hospitable to the nature and needs of science, fantasy includes the overwhelming need of the picara to tell her story.

The increase in women authors of fantasy and in the genre itself has made necessary some investigation as to why the fantasy heroine is a popular species. This leads immediately to the conclusion that the fantasy heroine often partakes of the nature of the picara, intentionally or unintentionally, consciously or unconsciously. The fantasy picara is an imperfect one because she is tinged with a humanism not found in early picaras. While she is motivated by the same needs—survival, hunger, traveling, adventure—as her sister/picaras, she is always subject to compassion. This somewhat limits her, as a fully functioning picara. Because the fantasy picara inhabits a created world and not a real one, she is seldom in science fiction which limits technology to that which is in existence. The fantasy picara can extend into the realm of fantasy in her use of pseudo-scientific psychic powers or magical powers which enable her to cope in a created or unreal world. That she carries over the same worries as a woman in the real world and how she handles them make her a picara. To maintain interest, the authors of fantasy, usually women, must create a sympathetic woman who upholds general moral principles; who does not destroy unnecessarily; who is reluctant to kill but will when forced to; who is an outsider but who does not refuse human companionship when it is offered; who abjures sexual morals for whatever feels good but who is responsible for her actions; who uses but does not abuse people; who judges all according to her standards; who rejects the double standard for sex and for power; who resists slavery of any sort as death to human spirit; who retains her autonomy despite the struggles of her society to remove it from her.

Many of these women authors have created several picaras: Jo Clayton has created Alyetys of the Diadem series of nine novels, Skeen with three novels, Brann of the *Drinker of Souls* series with two, Serroi of *Moonscatter* with three. Sharon Green has created Diana Santee of the *Spaceways* series with two novels, Jalav the Amazon warrior with five novels, Terrilian with five novels; Inky in *The Mists of Ages* series of two novels. Marion Zimmer Bradley has numerous picaras in her many novels of the Darkover planet as well as her Lythande of the short stories and her Zygydiek of the warrior stories. Other authors have one or more: Elizabeth A. Lynn has many picaras in her three Tornor novels and several in other works. Ann Maxwell has Rheba in the three Firedancer novels. Suzy McKee Charnas has Alldera in her two utopian novels. Jan Morris has Estri in the three High Couch of Silistra novels. Joan D. Vinge has a mother/daughter set in her two novels of Tiamet; Pamela Sargent has one in *The Shore of Women* and several others in other novels. Judith Ann Karr has two novels about Thorn and Frostflower; Joanna Russ has Alyx in the Paradise novels and Jan in the Whileaway novels. Vonda McIntyre has one major picara in

Dreamsnake and lesser ones in *The Exile Waiting*. And there are many other novelists in the mainstream of science fiction/fantasy genre with others whose heroines are peripherally picaras.

As our investigation of the picaresque elements are defined, identified and classified, different aspects of these novels will be identified as being picaresque. No one single archetypal pattern flashes through every story but the persistence of the pattern in all the stories appears most often in fantasy. We shall trace important traits through the four steps of the picara mentioned—the early, the Puritan, the Victorian, and the fantasy—to attempt to establish the fluctuating presence of the picara. Even before we turn to the literary characteristics, the picara has accumulated her major traits of thievery, deception, disguise, sexual excess and avarice. She has become an autonomous, irascible, financially avaricious bawd who does not beget children nor nourish them, who does not align herself with anything but her own survival.

Autonomy is still the highlighting white which catches and disperses the light in the tapestry. The mix of traits provides a varied palette of colors to use, colors which are more freely mixed to enrich the personal identity of the picara. Restricted by the cultural or religious *mores* of male authors, the picara stands in her glaring yellow shade of the veil that the Renaissance courtesans had to wear. After the passage of time, the individual colors of the tapestry become more muted and more complementary and therefore harder to discern. Trying to explicate one strand of color from an entire tapestry involves touching all other colors forcing many levels of the picara to be discussed in each chapter; trying to give precedence to one color over another is a useless occupation. The patterns and combinations of colors may change but the primary colors of the picaresque blend into the subtle and complex tones of the picara's tapestry.

Each chapter that follows will try to isolate one or more colorful strands of the picaresque traits, identify its picaresque origins, trace its development in all levels of the picara—early, Defoe, novel, and fantasy. Because many traits overlap in time and emphasis, the order of the chapters is somewhat arbitrary as all the colors are needed to see the figure of the picara clearly. Each chapter will present picaresque color-traits which are either complementary or contradictory to each other but which are necessary shades to the tapestry.

Chapter Three
Literary Characteristics

The reason why the number of shades could be so limited was that the method of shading one colour into another by means of hachure—lines of one colour striking deep into the adjoining one, dark into medium and medium into light—created the optical illusion of an extra shade between adjacent hatchings, so that three shades of a particular colour could give the illusion of being five...In addition to the use of hachure to achieve a blending together of colours, such devices as mottling and stippling can also be used [or] done in such a way as to give a gradual transition from one colour to another. (Rhodes 69)

Tapestry-weaving terms—hachure, mottling, and stippling—can best delineate the outstanding literary characteristics of the picaro and the picara to show how each complements, contradicts, and contributes more traits to the tapestry of the picaresque genre and ultimately to the figure of the picara. For example, hachure gives the illusion of more shades. In picaresque literature, if we establish the entire genre of biography as a basic red, then the autobiography is a passionate crimson, psuedo-autobiography a pale pink, confession a cinnabar, memoirs a rose madder, and a criminal autobiography a plum-red shading into blue. As always, the picara's autonomy is the bright white silk that highlights her face and figure.

Another weaving technique is mottling which mixes shades in the same stitch or "pick" to make a smooth transition into the next color. In like manner, the characteristic mottling devices of the picaresque—episodic nature, verisimilitude, dialogue, and open-endness—are subtlety woven into the picaresque texture to provide gradual transition from the tale to the novel to the fantasy. Finally, the stippling process, which weaves "spots or flecks of one colour upon a ground of another colour [to obtain] intermediate shades" (Rhodes 71), adds a depth to the texture by contrasting the colors scattered throughout monotone shade. The special characteristics of the literary picara which differentiate her from the picaro—use of the confidante, her aging, her repentance, and her avarice—are so stippled onto the picaro's tapestry that they appear integral to the weave. As each process is revealed, each thread that contributes to the picara's figure can be unraveled for critical inspection.

Autobiography

"Well, first of all Your Grace should know that my name is Lazaro de Tormes, son of..." so starts Lazarillo's tale (25).

Just as a piece of flat weaving suggests some minimum texturing, even the simplest biography implies forms of research, selection of incidents, order of arrangement, audience, teller of the tale, and even a self-aware contemplation. Because an autobiography is told by the person himself, it is never the same monotonous color; its first-person narrator uses hachure when he darts forward into journalism, backtracks into his life, dashes into fictive imagination, or doubles back to historical biography. On the other hand, the creator of pseudo-autobiography always is an external craftsman behind the loom, spinning the tale of someone else's life. Most picaras are the products of pseudo-autobiographies "told, traditionally, from the first person, recollected point of view" (Miller 98). It is a truly personal recording of events and incidents which provides a sense of immediacy and veracity to any tale because "the sustained first person narration forces us to sympathetically identify ourselves more or less with the picaro" (Miller 98).

Because we are all seduced by the "let me tell you what happened to me" formula, Lazarillo's author addresses his "childish little story" to an unknown aristocrat so that it should not be "buried in the grave of oblivion" and that "somebody may read them and find something he likes and others may find pleasure in just a casual glance" (23). While formal biography and autobiography are relatively late developments, pseudo-autobiography, (especially memoirs) spiritual biographies, and confessions, are early signs of the need to tell a person's life story. The *Legenda Aurea*, that fourteenth century seminal collection of the lives of the saints by Jacobus de Voragine, used real and fictional confessions of saints as sources; if a story were efficacious, it merited retelling. Since the author's intent was to inspire emulation, there was no need to ascertain the truth of the saints' biographies. As literacy became more common, the emphasis of such spiritual biography shifted into the confessional mode of spiritual autobiography—a first-person, self-aware contemplation of past sins and the need for repentance. Works like the *Confessions* of Augustine kept alive the hero's quest in the confessional form; works like the Puritan spiritual autobiographies sustained the conversion as the center of the spiritual journey.

In contrast, the writings of the women mystics sustained the spiritual journal. This healthier and more balanced progression of the journey motif embodied the heroine's quest for spiritual awakening as a gradual process. For example, the writings of Teresa of Avila, a contemporary of Lazarillo and Cervantes, drew on her own life to warn others of her pitfalls and to console others with her joys. Hildegard of Bingen, Mechthild of Mechlenburg, Julian of Norwich, Bridget of Sweden, Margery Kempe, Therese of Lisieux, all wrote or dictated spiritual journals or memoirs. Each one uses the same spiritual "matter" but each one develops the "form" of the journey in her journal by stressing the intuitive over the rational, the creative journey over the reasoned pathway. For example, Domna Stanton in her essay "Autogynography" claims that the "existence of important but unexplored autogynographies, contemporary with or even predating the earliest productions of men canonized by literary history" (*Autograph* 6) has made the critics' views of autobiography disproportionately misgynogist. The neglect of women's autobiographies as valid studies occurs in the critics' not recognizing the diverse forms—memoirs, confessions, journals, diaries—as worthy of much scholarly attention.

The same neglect occurs when the story of the picara is told; the theory that "men's narratives were linear, chronological, coherent, whereas women's were discontinuous, digressive, fragmented" is being challenged on the basis that "discontinuity and fragmentation constitute particularly fitting means for...creating the rhetorical impression of spontaneity and truth" (Stanton 11). Thus, while the spiritual biography of the Magdalen is lauded as an *exemplum* of woman's need for chastity and the autobiography of Margery Kempe is ridiculed for her attempt at chastity, the confessions of St. Augustine are praised for their forth-rightness and logic. So also it is with the picaro and the picara: the autobiography of the picara is devalued because she offends sexual morals while the picaro's autobiography is praised for his cleverness in avoiding sexual entrapment. He is to be emulated; she is not. The telling of the picaresque tale is doubly difficult when the picara's tale is told by a man who may not choose to detail those problems with which women are ultimately or necessarily concerned. That is why this study must go back beyond the picaro's pseudo-autobiography to hear in the dim echoes of the past the continued cry of the woman deprived of her voice.

Psychologically, the autobiographical mode is keyed into the picara's autonomy: the assertion that she is bad prevents her from being a non-entity, a "non-self" that Peer Gynt fears when the Button Molder accuses him of mediocrity. The picara's pseudo-autobiographical narration is a combination of her need for deception and her need for spiritual confession through which she achieves autonomy. As Ian Watt notes, this emphasis on confession and autobiography allows Defoe to make the "total subordination of the plot to the pattern of the autobiographical memoir...an assertion of the primacy of the individual experience" (15). In the telling of her sins, the picara externalizes them for the reader's enjoyment, as if the act of writing itself atones for the sins because it establishes the picara as a sinner.

Where a confession possesses a sense of two times—the time in which the author is actually writing and the time about which he is writing—the memoir does not. For example, in a confession, the protagonist reminisces about his past offenses from the safe haven of his conversion. In fact, it is only from his vantage point of conversion that the protagonist assumes relevance. Before his conversion, he was a sinner blind to sins and a danger to good audience; after the conversion, he is able to see the extent of his sins and mourn the loss of his virtue. Still, for the sake of interest, the larger part of the confession occurs before his conversion. In contrast, since the memoir does not purport to be any more that an organized but casual reminiscence, it has no need for the conversion motif of the confession. What the memoir does provide is a framework (i.e. the unifying force of a central character) in which the pseudo-author can relate his or her adventures. The major difference between the memoir and the picaresque novel is in the control of the material by the writer: the memoir writer selects those incidents which are favorable and omits those that are deleterious, while the picaresque novelist the writer may construct a memoir form to tell his story. Defoe wrote two major memoirs *The Memoirs of a Cavalier* and *The Memoirs of an English Officer (Captain Carleton)* neither of which emphasize the picaresque form. Only in his novels did he produce two major picaras.

Spiritual autobiographies ultimately deal, however, with the process of sin, conversion, repentance, and reconciliation; the picara distorts the form to justify revenge. Autobiography as revenge, memoirs as vendetta, diary as blackmail, confession as a confidence game—all are familiar devices for the picara. For example, when Grimmelshausen's Courage recites her memoirs to her scribe, he questions her why "if you are not considering mending your ways, then why do you desire to tell your life story as if in confession and reveal to all the world your vices?" (34). Her answer is direct: "I am doing it to spite Simplicissimo because I cannot avenge myself on him in any other way" (34). Other picaras find excuses for their writings in their protestations of repentance: Moll intends to spend the "Remainder of our Years in sincere Penitence, for the wicked Lives we have lived" (343) and Roxana was "brought so low again, that my Repentance seem'd to be only the Consequence of my Misery, as my Misery was of my Crime" (330).

The repentance theme in the picara's story dovetails with her origin from the saints' lives. Since love was the topic of medieval romances and saints' lives, "the stories of extreme sin and extreme self-sacrifice or repentance were in fact stories of extreme love" (Ward 7) and none was more favored than that of the prostitute-turned-ascetic. Used as learning devices to teach that the mercy of God extends even to the worst sinners, pious monks or nuns who might think themselves better than sinners could be humbled by the example of the fallen woman who raises herself to God by a life of self-sacrifice. If the fallen woman became the symbol of the worst of sinners, then the story of a repentant woman could serve as moral instruction. On the spiritual level, the loss of virginity expressed by the prostitute's life reiterates the universal virginity lost when the soul separates itself from its Creator; it follows then that the reparation for such loss is of great value and the tears of repentance are valuable. "Only when they [harlots] had become aware of the force of this disintegration within themselves could they receive the gift of salvation which is Christ. In the later circulation of the harlot stories...this theme, fundamental to Christianity, was still the main reason for their popularity" (Ward 104).

From David and Bathsheba to Christ and the adulteress, the Scriptures accepted the prostitute as a didactic image. The courtesan, thus, became so stereotyped that Renaissance portraiture used contemporary courtesans as models for Salomes, Bathshebas, and Magdelen, giving the courtesans their own patron saints. Take, for example, the stories of Mary Magdalen. Excluding Christ's mother who epitomized all virtue, at least four other Marys blended into the one person of Mary Magdalen. Because the two reports of her (Luke 8:2, Mark 16) designated her as a "woman of the city who was a sinner" (Luke 7:37) whose "many sins were forgiven her because she loved much" (Luke 7:47), church fathers assumed that her chief sin was prostitution. By assuming that the woman who anointed Christ's feet (Luke 7:39) and the one who anointed his head before the Passion (Matthew 26:6-13, Mark 14:3-8) are the same, the silver tradition of church popular tradition blends Mary of Magdala with those Marys. Bendicta Ward suggests that the Magdalen's "identification as a prostitute lies deeper, in the imagery of sin throughout the whole of the scriptures [in] the image of unfaithful Israel, so graphically described by the prophets as a prostitute in relation to God...as unfaithful to the covenant of love between God and man" (15).

Further apocryphal stories about Mary's background were constructed out of Gospel allusions, making her picaresque if not a picara. For example, one legend portrays Mary's prostitution as a result of her abandonment by her new husband John the Evangelist at the wedding of Cana. Another cites her adventures following John to Ephesus, being buried in the cave with the Seven Sleepers, and having her relics translated to the church of St. Lazarus in Constantinople. Another legend details her sailing with her sister Martha and brother Lazarus to Marseilles and Aix where she lived her life of repentance. Her constant connection to Lazarus may have strengthened her aspect of prostitution since the physical decay of leprosy and the moral decay of prostitution were linked in the medieval mind. Thus, a hospital for lepers which might be "under the patronage of Lazarus, often had a corresponding house dedicated to the patronage of his sister [Mary Magdalen] for repentant prostitutes" (Ward 20). Where medical knowledge could offer no cure for the lepers, the church established several orders of nuns who not only specialized in rehabilitating in prostitutes but also accepted them as members of the community. Where the medical profession later accused prostitutes of spreading venereal diseases, the medical fears overshadowed the moral fears of prostitution.

Further literary sources of the picara are lodged in the city harlot-saints who fled to the desert for salvation. Connected with port cities, i.e. Alexandria, Jerusalem, Rome, Marseilles, the courtesans "had achieved a freedom from the control of father or husband, and from the domesticity inevitable for a woman of good reputation." (Ward 63). When they left the city for their desert experience, they retained their autonomy. "Life in the desert, *anachoresisis*, was a practical demonstration of freedom from the limitations and responsibilities of society" (Ward 63). Even fleeing to the desert does not relieve the harlot-saint of temptation. Just as the progenitor of monasticism, St. Anthony of Egypt fought his devils daily, his female counterpart St. Amma Sarah was tempted by persistent erotic thoughts but never asked to be relieved of them, "asking instead for the strength to bear them" (Ward 6). The well-known sixth-century tale of St. Mary of Egypt tells of a young harlot of Alexandria who paid for her passage to Jerusalem with her favors and who was converted there, before fleeing to the desert to live a life of sacrifice for forty-seven years. Discovered by the monk Zossima who relates her tale, Mary died in the odor of sanctity and was buried by him with the help of a lion.

The flight to the desert often involved living in one of the caves which honeycomb the Middle East, substantiating the mythological concept that caves are primary feminine images of the womb—the sinner must reenter the womb to be reborn as a saved soul. Often caves are used as forms of the desert experience for the picara; in one version, Mary Magdalen retreats to a cave in France (Baume) where she is pictured with flowing hair, a skull, and books. In a similar manner, Pelagia fled Antioch disguised as a man and built a cell on the Mount of Olives; Thais was immured into a cell sealed with lead for three years, emerging just before she died. After her repentance Maria, niece of Abraham, stayed in a inner cell while her uncle stayed in the outer cell. However, the silence of Mary Magdalen's cave of repentance never enticed the picara; contemplation is not her scene anymore than inactivity is. The picara at the end of her career seldom leaves the city although she may seek repentance in other forms by living a quiet life. When Courage tries to retire to the country, she is pursued by billeting soldiers and easily slips back to her immoral ways. Moll leaves the "desert" of Virginia for civilized England while Amber is leaving London for Virginia; Roxana is in some Dutch "desert" city; Scarlett is going to Tara, fleeing Atlanta; Becky is in spa resorts of Bath and Cheltenham. All leave the city reluctantly to go into the "desert" of relative inactivity.

While the picara's flight to the desert replicates the picaro's hunger theme, her fasting gives her autonomy. In the tale of Mary of Egypt, the monk Zossima belongs to a community which left the safe confines of their monastery on the first week of Lent and returned only on Easter. Having no contact with each other, each man scrounged food from the desert itself: "If one did notice a brother afar off coming towards him, then he turned aside; each lived by himself and with God, singing psalms all the time and hardly touching food" (Ward 40). The picara's obsession with food becomes more than mere sustenance and implies the spiritual offenses of the deadly sins. Mary of Egypt was tempted by "irrational desires; when I began to eat, my desire was for meat; I longed for the fish that they have in Egypt, I even desired the wine...I used to drink so much that I got drunk" (Ward 49). Repentance of such immoderation allows the sinner to warn against worldly pleasures and to admonish the listener to be fed with the "incorruptible food" of salvation (Ward 50). Pelagia was so wasted by fasting that her friends did not recognize her; Thais nearly died of starvation and deprivation; their fasting gave them autonomy. Rudolph Bell in his *Holy Anorexia* cites later medieval saints' lives as examples of women who achieved autonomy by fasting. He claims that, to control their societies which would not empower them, women like Clare of Assisi and Catherine of Siena undertook so severe a fast that he speculates they suffered from the eating disorders of anorexia nervosa or bulimia. The fainting of the distressed damsel, the vapors of the Victorian picara, the headaches of the bitch goddess are signs of their struggle for autonomy.

The picara rises above mere hunger as a guiding principle, substituting avarice or the accumulation of wealth in its place. However, the desert harlots achieved as much picaresque autonomy by their abandoning their ill-gotten gains as by fleeing the city. Even here, the question of the prostitute's repentance hinges on money since money earned by them was "ill-gotten." In real life, prostitutes could contribute alms to the church only secretly to avoid scandal. However, since their stories were used for moral instructions, the fictional prostitutes had to surrender their possessions, which were then given to good use for the poor. Pelagia gave her wealth to her servants and to the poor while Thais burned hers in a public ceremony. While the loss of wealth seems contradictory to the picaresque avarice, it is actually complementary to her autonomy, if read on a spiritual level. While the saint has surrendered her earnings by renouncing her prostitution, she has also renounced dependence from individual man (her clients) and from men (mankind) in general, opting instead for the providence of God to sustain her. The woman who turned to religion was dependent upon no man and was, therefore, fully autonomous.

The picara's postponing repentance embodies her fear of renouncing the immoral but profitable life she leads. In speaking to the French Prince, Roxana argues so strongly against their sinful life together that "he began to receive the Impression a little deeper than I wish'd he had done;...for, *My Dear, say he*, if once we come to talk of Repentance, we must talk of parting" (82). Furthermore, the fluctuation of emotion the picara experiences in penitence is ruthlessly measured by an economic barometer. Courage, for example, declares that "what I lack is repentance and what I should lack but do not is avarice and envy" (33). Where avarice only protects the picara from physical deprivation, her promise of penitence is an extension of self-preservation. As a literary device, the picara's repentance is ostensibly her *raison d'etre*: "In the Manner she has told the Story, it is evident she does not insist upon her Justification in any one Part of it; much less does she recommend her Conduct, or indeed, any Part of it, except her Repentance to our Imitation" (*Roxana*, Preface, 2). John Cleland's 1748-9 Fanny Hill is a redeemed heroine, who repents her "scandalous stages of my life" (Preface).

Even more than as an autobiographical device does the passionate crimson of repentance theme serve to titillate the drabber parts of the book into implied excitements. As a picaresque tradition, the repentance theme allows the picara to reminisce over her sins without renouncing them. Courage ruminates on the possibility that "she might still be in time to set things aright, now that through the pangs of conscience that she is beginning to suffer hellish pain and torture which outweighs all the delights of the flesh she tasted and enjoyed during her whole life" (32). Much the same feeling can be seen in Roxana's attitude toward the storm scene, when her fear is for the wrong reason: "I had no Sence of Repentance, from the true motive of Repentance; I saw nothing of the corruption of Nature, the Sin of my Life...I had only such a Repentance as a Criminal has at the Place of Execution, who is sorry, not that he has committed the Crime, as it is a Crime, but sorry *that he is to be Hang'd for it*" (129). Like Steinbeck's mother in *East of Eden*, Becky is amoral not immoral; to defraud creditors, to appropriate unwarranted titles, to assume the mantle of respectability—all are accepted and adopted modes of action for Becky. Scarlett thinks she would be guilt-ridden but she is never repentant. Amber reacts much the same way; she never reflects on what she has done wrong because by her standards survival is never wrong, especially if it is hers.

The fantasy picara does not face repentance. Her sins are easily forgiven because the only sin she acknowledges is one against individual conscience. Bound by laws in created worlds, not real worlds, the fantasy picara has occasional bouts of self-doubt about saving a galaxy or kingdom or preserving wealth. Since she steals only from the wealthy, takes care of her own, murders only in war, never relishes killing, and seldom repents, she has no higher reality than her own standards. Since she has gone adventuring, she has no regrets about a life missed out on. The closure of the fantasy picara is that of the happy ending, open-ended, or in a temporary holding pattern with promises of the stars beyond.

With heady confidence in herself, the picara postpones repentance the way she disregards society's disapproval. However, in the background, her old need for security and stability press on in a chaotic world. Roxana's insistence that

"Necessity first debauch'd me, and Poverty made me a Whore at the Beginning" reinforces Defoe's familiar use of economic necessity as motivation. However, what established the picara in Defoe's money-motivated character is the phrase which immediately follows the quote above, "...so excess of Avarice for getting Money, and excess of Vanity, continued me in the Crime" (202). Vanity as a contributing thread will be discussed in a later chapter.

The stories of repentant picaras flooded the market as the number of spiritual biographies increased coincidentally with the Puritan commonwealth and with the better printing facilities. As chronological panoramas of the protagonist's life, they "updated and concretized biblical themes and offered Puritanism a kind of substitute for Catholic oral tradition" (Hunter 78). An additional source for such spiritual autobiography is found in the common criminal ancestor of the Elizabethan drama convention of the overreacher's confessing or bragging about his success. For example, Defoe with his Dissenter background used autobiographical techniques to good advantage in his criminal biographies, where, once he is caught and repentant, the criminal can take pride in revealing his crimes. (Interestingly, today most minor criminals are discovered because they bragged to friends about their successes.) Where there is a reluctance on the part of the picara to detail the graphic reality of her life, the use of confessional autobiography overcomes some of this reluctance; the memoir provides an ever better medium for the picara to establish her own personality.

The Criminal Autobiography

Just as the lives of the saints provided morally acceptable subjects for literature, so also did the lives of criminals provide source material for the picaresque tales. In England, in particular, the criminal biography was prevalent in pamphlets, broadsides, ballads and tales as well as in the translations of Continental tales.

So popular was criminal literature that Defoe himself translated in 1722 the story of Cartouche, the organizer of the Parisian underworld. His sequel in 1724, "A Narrative of the Proceedings in France, for Discovery and Detecting the Murderers of the English Gentlemen," strongly resembles the murder of Roxana's jeweler husband near Paris. Supplementing the three-part pamphlet, "The True, Genuine, and Perfect Accounting of the Life of JONATHAN WILD," Defoe's interest is Wild began as lengthy journalistic bulletins in *Applebee's Journal* as early as June 6, 1724, and continued through Wild's trial, execution, and body-snatching of May 1775. Part of Defoe' fascination with Wild was in his organization of "the criminal world like a capitalist" (Novak 44); another subject, Jack Sheppard and his escapes, appears in no less than sixteen articles in *Applebee's Journal*. How Defoe's mind was transforming criminals into picaros and picaras is shown in his connecting of the historical Sheppard with his two fictional picaras, Moll Flanders and Mrs. Betty Blueskin. This latter picara was "born in *New gate*, the famous Moll Flanders was my aunt...I have been so deeply in Love with your Friend Jack Sheppard, that I have been quite distracted...For as he was the most dextrous Housebreaker in England: so I pretend to be the cleanest-handed shop-lift, and the nicest Pick-Pocket in Europe" (Novak 44). In addition, Jane Jack suggests that Defoe used the life of the forger Mary Butler as a primary source of Roxana (*Roxana* 332, fn.164).

The criminal background of the picaro is integral to any early picaresque work but the level of criminality to which the picara descends differs with her society. Thackeray can only hint at Becky's involvement with unsavory characters like Lord Steyne and the Bohemian students; her pursuit of a life on the watering-spa circuits and gambling casinos of Europe put her as far into the underworld as a social critic like Thackeray could go. Scarlett deals with equally unsavory characters when she engages convict labor for her lumber mill; Amber is bailed out of prison by Black Jack and Mother Redcap to join them in their blackmail and robbery tricks. The fantasy authors gleefully plunge their picaras into galactic criminal activities on both sides of the law; sometimes the heroine is a special governmental agent, sometimes she is outside the law, but she is always autonomous. Each author immerses his or her picara only to the level which her society will tolerate; how realistic that society is depends on the literary characteristic of verisimilitude.

Verisimilitude

The pseudo-biographical form laced with verisimilitude provided Defoe with the perfect answer to the Puritan dilemma—how to write convincingly without writing fictitiously. The device of the pseudo-autobiography or pseudo-biography, told by the protagonist himself and recorded by an interested scribe, distanced the author at least two degrees from his history. "I was born, as my Friends told me, at the City of Poictiers..." so starts Roxana's tale (5). Notice that her "Friends" told her; she cannot assert the fact herself. If such a fact, told by a subjective protagonist to an objective scribe, is somewhat altered from the truth, then the blame cannot be put on the author himself, since he is reporting from biased sources. Defoe's pseudo-autobiographical pose protects him from the charge of censorship as it protects the other picaresque novelists from the sins of their characters: Lazarillo, Guzman, Meriton Latroon, and Simplicimus may reflect the lives of their authors in some part yet no one could charge Grimmelshausen with prostitution in his writing of Courage, nor Defoe of theft in Moll.

In the same manner, the verisimilitude needed for pseudo-autobiography alleviates the problem of unwelcomed censorship. In keeping with the morality play's naming of Vice and Virtue, the early picara's physical attributes are never mentioned except as typifying names—Courage (guts), Moll Cutpurse (pickpocket), Long Meg (height)—just as the picaros are so detailed by their outstanding feature—Lazarillo (beggar), Simplicimus (simple), and so forth. The picaresque tale did not need truth-seeming details to give it substance since the charm of the tale was in its vagueness. Utopia is indeed no land and Lazarillo may live by the river Tormes but his subsequent wanderings lack the vital statistics to convince the reader. When the Spanish civilization was satirized in Lazarillo or in Quixote, it was a given and did not need to be described. Everyone who read either book knew that priests were knaves, that officials were corrupt, that women were faithless. In the romance and the tale, "once upon a time" was enough of a time line and "in a kingdom far, far away" was enough of an aesthetic distance. As writing became more accessible, the need to rely on fact rather than on myth and oral tradition developed; as trade and industry grew, the need for specific numbers rather than generalities increased; as the picaresque accrued verisimilitude, the tendency to be unspecific led to the tale's transformation into the novel and characterization became more distinct. In the early picaresque, the author does not have to detail what his heroine looks like. That she was a woman was enough; she was already stereo typed, categorized, and condemned.

Aphra Behn is the first novelist to make significant use of that particular sort of detailing known as verisimilitude in her novel *Oronooko*. In her history of this Royal Slave, she does not seek "to entertain my Reader with Adventures of a feign'd Hero, whose Life and Fortunes Fancy may manage at the Poet's pleasure" but rather she will send forth the truth "recommended by its own proper Merits, and natural Intrigues; there being enough of Reality to support it, and to render it diverting, without the addition of Invention" (Behn 1). Her "reality" lies in the specifics she mentions. While controversy still exists over whether Behn actually visited Surinam as an "Eye-witness to a great part of what you will find here set down" (1), her careful recording argues that she could distinguish between romance and reality. For example, she describes Oronooko, in the most romantic of terms: his face was "of perfect Ebony, or polished Jett. His Eyes were the most awful that cou'd be seen, and very piercing; the White of'em being like Snow, as were his Teeth. His Nose was rising and Roman, instead of African and flat" (8). But the relating of Oronooko's death is so realistic that her verisimilitude convinces critics that she was an eyewitness to the event. Even the use of the hero's name Oronooko connects several disparate strands in literature. According to Lore Metzger, the editor of the Norton edition, "Like Columbus, she was certain that the earthly paradise was bound to be discovered near the Orinoko River" (xii), the Amazon. This same river which gives the name to her hero is the river Orinoco at whose mouth lies the island on which Robinson Crusoe is shipwrecked some forty years later. Behn's specificity extends to small details: for example, when they visit Oronooko for dinner, he "dress'd Venison and Buffalo for us; and, going out, gather'd a Leaf of a Tree, called a Sarumbo Leaf, of six Yards long, and spread it on the Ground for a Tablecloth; and cutting another in pieces, instead of Plates, set us on little low Indian-stools" (56).

The strongest argument for her verisimilitude lies in the specific use of the feathered gown as a means of seduction in later drama and novels. When she visits the Indians upriver, she describes the clothes she wore: "my own Hair was cut short, and I had a taffety Cap, with black Feathers on my Head; my Brother was in a Stuff-Suit, with silver Loops and Buttons, and abundance of green Ribbon" (55). In her description of the articles traded by the Surinam natives, Behn notes that

we trade for Feathers, which they order into all shapes, make themselves little short Habits of 'em, and glorious Wreaths for their Heads, Necks, Arms and Legs, whose Tinctures are unconceivable. I had a Set of these presented to me, and I gave 'em to the King's Theatre, and it was the Dress of the *Indian Queen*, infinitely admir'd by Persons of Quality; and was unimitable (2).

Normally the early novel does not encourage interest in the intimate details of woman's physical attributes or wardrobe. Notice, for example, Defoe's self-description of Roxana:

I was (speaking of myself as about Fourteen Years of Age) tall, and very well made; sharp as a Hawk in Matters of common Knowledge; quick and smart in Discourse; apt to be Satyrical: full of Repartee; and a little too forward in Conversation; or, as we call it in English, BOLD, tho' perfectly Modest in my Behaviour. Being French Born, I danc'd, as some say, naturally, lov'd it extremely, and sung well also...I wanted neither Wit, Beauty, or Money. (6-7).

There are no specifics, only generalities. Even the beauty is tucked into the last grouping as if it counted for nothing when indeed her whole career depends on her combining beauty with her wit. Roxana's self-awareness is explained away in her disclaimer: "to give my own Character, I must be excus'd to give it as impartially as possible, and as if I was speaking of another-body" (6).

Only when the picara slips into the romantic or historical genre does the heroine collect physical description; only when the tale matures into the novel does she become physically real. That Scarlett has red hair and green eyes places her in her time period as an Irish-French woman in southern United States during the Civil War. Except for the prejudice against red hair, the physical attributes do not determine her character any more than Becky's sandy hair and pale eyes form a blazon in Thackeray's novel. The authors of fantasy picaras who must give enough detail to locate their heroine within time and space are often dependent upon descriptions of futuristic clothing and exotic colorings to set the scene and convince the reader of the created world. For example, the deformities or peculiarities which set the heroine aside also make her a picara; a clan mark on her cheek or a different colored skin or the power to cause fire from her body will ostracize her from her society and set her on the path to picarahood.

Still, what the male author of a picara's tale would stress is far different from what the picara herself might stress, if she were writing her own autobiography. The early author of the picara can afford to make her seem fickle by jumping from episode to episode without expansive narration; he can boldly sketch plot lines and neglect fine detailing required by later third-person description. The major advantage of the women fantasy writers is that their picaras are the result of conflicts already solved. It is not strange, then, to find the re-emergence of the picara in fantasy nor to discover that the writers of fantasy picaras are, for the most part, women. Their approach to the problems of women may take futuristic answers but the problems are the same to all women—autonomy, survival in a hostile world, injustice. The answers proffered by women authors rest in their constructions of their characters who surmount these problems by rejecting society's norms, by asserting autonomy, by preparing for battle, and by accumulating adventures.

The Episodic Structure

While the journey motif is not limited to the picaresque genre, tales of travel both provide a unifying force to a series of disconnected episodes and serve as a religious symbol of man's pilgrimage in life. Just as myths cluster about a central hero like barnacles, the episodic action clusters about the picaro's travels where the apparent disorder of the independent tales is not important to the picaro's development since he never matures as a novel hero does. Where the realistic novel shows the causal relationship of probable events and the romantic novel shows a less probable world controlled by chance, the picaresque world order is chaos.

The episodic technique of expanded incidents often appears within a larger framework device, like sausages on a link: the isolated tales are only expanded incidents connected by a thin webbing of narrative tissue. For example, Ovid's *Metamorphosis* has about fifty expanded stories and two hundred less expanded stories or allusions and Lazarillo has only the thinnest connective phrases. In place of the clumsy "meanwhile back at the ranch" technique, the novelist learned short cuts—foreshadowing, retrospection, linearity—to introduce the incidents and to move the plot expeditiously. Yet the journal or memoir base of the picara's reminiscences lends itself to the accordion-like development: connective but mundane incidents are compressed while central and fascinating incidents are expanded, since those events which are central to development of the main character are in need of greater detailing than those which merely unite. When Erich Auerbach in *Mimesis* speaks of the "fluctuation of intensity," (8) he sees the necessity of compression and expansion within the picaresque novel. Often this framework aligns itself with the journey motif as in Apuleius' *Golden Ass* and Chaucer's *Canterbury Tales*, while Boccaccio's *Decameron* uses the country house as a motif for story-telling. Unrelated interpolated tales appear in authors from Henry Fielding to Jo Clayton in her Skeen series because they are good stories, although such digressive tales intrude into the novel's structure.

Another reason for the episodic nature lies in the nature of the confessional aspect of the novel. Peter Axhelm in *The Modern Confessional Novel* notes that "the confessional novel presents a hero, at some point in his life, examining his past as well as his innermost thoughts, in an effort to achieve some form of perception" (fn. 64). This shifting from action to introspection is not a characteristic of the picaro; rather, if an action works, he does it; if it does not work, he abandons it. Never learning from past experience, the picaro never seeks an objective view of himself because such a view might disclose unsavory facts. The picara follows suit in this. The confession motif in literature supplies a sense of two times: the time in which the author is actually writing and the time about which he is writing. For example, the protagonist reminisces about her past offenses from the safe haven of her conversion. Before her conversion, she was a sinner blind to her sins; after the conversion, she is able to see the extent of her sins. Still for the sake of interest, the larger part of the confession occurs before her conversion. Who wants to read the story of a converted sinner when he can read the sins of the unconverted? As one critic of Defoe cites, he was "acutely conscious of the fact that the fertile period of a converted sinner's life for the storyteller's purpose is the sinner's career before his conversion" (Stamm 45).

The Confidante

When the picara presents an incident in her life, her version is one-sided; she does not have a verbal antagonist unless she invents one. If the picara does invent one, the antagonist is still an agent of her creator and, therefore, questionably effective. The creation of a scribe alleviates the problem somewhat, but, in the memoir, the problem still exists. The creation of a female confidante solves the problem.

Here the picaro and picara disagree. The only confidante needed by the picaro is the scribe or reader who becomes the listening board. Because he is a man, he is less likely to need the cover of respectability to mask his tricks since his skill lies in the one-man trick. Lazarillo learns from each of his masters but he would be reluctant to confide in them or, much less, to entrust them with either his wealth or his future plans. The picara, on the other hand, needs a protective mask of respectability, one usually provided by another woman. The protection offered by this second woman is not that of the soubrette or convenient maidservant; she might be too young and pretty and might detract from the picara's glitter. No, she is old and unattractive, either virtuous because of her age or scorned because of it. Here again the various levels of prostitution intervene as the picara adapts to circumstance: when the picara is the courtesan, her confidante serves as the procuress in good times; in bad times, when the picara returns to being a common prostitute, her confidante becomes the bawd, often engaging in prostitution herself.

More often, though, does the older woman provide a smoke-screen of respectability behind which the picara performs her scam. Thackeray declares such a lady's companion to be "an article as necessary to a lady in this position as her brougham or her bouquet...an exceedingly plain friend of their own sex from whom they are almost inseparable" (391). For example, when Becky seeks to assume gentility, she associates with a "sheep-dog...a *moral* shepherd's dog...to keep the wolves off me" (392). It takes Becky some fifty pages to find her but the hapless Briggs becomes that "inevitable woman in her faded gown seated behind her dear friend in the opera-box" (391).

These are the respectable companions. Scarlett's use of Melanie as a companion and Aunt Pittipat as a proper chaperon is noticed by Rhett. At Tara Mammy as a black woman house slave is truly Scarlett's confidante and conscience, warning her of the pitfalls of improper behavior at the party, with Ashley Wilkes, as a young married woman, and at the impropriety of the strange menage at Tara after the war. Although Mammy is symbol of the antebellum society made real to Scarlett, and of the mother whose care she had to leave, she is a confidante only in the first few chapters. Aunt Pittipat in Atlanta provides similar respectability with her black coachman. Amber has slightly different experience with her confidante. The older woman Sally Goodman, her paramour Luke, and her young maid Honour who befriend the pregnant Amber bilk her out of her money, setting the pattern the Amber herself will imitate as a schemer. Roxana has her Amy, Moll has her foster mother as confidante but nowhere does any picara truly trust another human being; for example, Celestina may brag of her success to her clients and her servants but she keeps the money herself.

So also in fantasy literature, the picara keeps journals or records but seldom trusts fully. While the urge to confide is a plot exposition, it may also be a form of negative confidence. For example, since the picara usually has some reason to conceal something about herself—her psychic powers, her witchcraft, her heritage—she is reluctant to reveal any details to anyone. The exception occurs in a committed relationship such as between female lovers where the mutual revelation of inner fears is needed to further the relationship. Bradley's heroines, Madga and Jaelle, learn each other's secrets and secret fears; when they absorb enough of each other, they commit to a "freemate" marriage in which two women agree to raise each other's children without the help of men. In the third book of the Tornor trilogy by Elizabeth A. Lynn, Sorren confesses her psychic powers to her lover, the older warrior woman Paxe, as "the only person she trusted enough to tell about it" (12). In P.C. Hodgell's *Godstalk* the heroine Jame confides in Cleppetty, the motherly cook at the tavern. Seldom do such relationships go beyond the early picara's nurse/bawd, perhaps because of the moral censorship against homosexuality imposed on earlier writers.

As a woman also, the picara often finds herself in the dual role of the maid-picara. In the *commedia dell'arte*, the lower servant is the confidante of his *inamorata* mistress as well as being the bawd to her, performing the mundane tasks surrounding as assignation. In the later tales of the picara, the maidservant-picara role suffers a divisive break so that, from the one essential character of the picara, two complementary and agreeable characters emerge: the picara and her confidante. In spite of the confidante's lower status, these two work as one; their aims are the same, their methods are the same, their professions are the same. However, this convenient separation between maid and mistress is the basis of the mistaken assumption that the picaresque genre is closer to a tale than to a novel.

The division of the picara into two functioning components occurs in Courage's natural fondness for her nurse. From her paid positions as wet nurse to the Bohemian child, Courage's nurse protects the girl by having her masquerade as a boy; she later becomes Courage's "mother," serving as her bank, her blind, and her bawd. Defoe hesitantly establishes Moll's relationship with her governess as a prostitute to a bawd. With Roxana, however, Defoe firmly defines the respective roles of Roxana and Amy with so deft a hand that he is careful not to blur their outlines. For instance, while Roxana and Moll are attractive to men, they both establish good and continuing relationships with other women, differing from the usual practice of the picara in this. Moll is attractive enough as a child to secure the affections of her nurse and of the mayor's wife; she is charming enough to be a higher servant in the house of her first husband; finally, she is charming enough to invite the lasting relationship with her governess. Although she is more often in the company of men, Roxana establishes a more than satisfactory relationship with Amy and with the Quakeress; she is so well liked that her husband's cousin shares her sparse sustenance with her, intercedes her case with the relatives, and at last enters into the complex scheme to force the sister-in-law to take Roxana's children.

While the role of the confidante is usually subservient and parasitic to the picara, there is no sense of superiority or inferiority. Here is the crux of the division. Where the male picaro does not mind "doubling in brass" and completing his own adventures, the picara, who must maintain the facade of a lady, avoids the harsher realities of life. Courage has, for example, a nicety about the financial arrangements of prostitution and lets her "mother"-nurse arrange the details:

> She was much slier than a fox, much greedier than a wolf, and I cannot say whether she was more proficient in the art of making money or in the art of pandering. If I had a lewd plan of that sort in mind and felt a bit of apprehension (for I wished to be regarded as very gentle and modest) I had only to confide it to her and it was as good as assured that my wish would be carried out...Once I had a great lust to enjoy a young man of nobility who was a coronet at that time and had recently given me to understand that he loved me...because I had revealed my wishes to my mother, she arranged for this same coronet to be at hand. (110)

In the same vein, Moll cannot fence her stolen merchandise and Roxana lets Amy perform the more adventurous duties of the picara—selling the furniture on the jeweller's death contracting with errant husbands, getting rid of threatening daughters.

In return for these services, the confidante receives rewards that reflected the glory and partial wealth of the picara; however, she may also suffer the picara's decline in fortune. Nonetheless, Courage's mother is honored by the picara at her death:

> My Bohemian mother, or nurse, has the great good fortune to go the way of all flesh in the spendour of her assumed godliness and in this pious place, and I therefore had her buried with more spendour than if she had died in Prague at St. James Gate. (156)

So also Moll's governess is spoken of in high terms; she is an "eminent lady," a "grave matron," and a "mother" (144, 146, 151). Besides being Moll's governess and procuress, she becomes a banker in the manner of Courage's mother by holding Moll's money when she emigrates to America. That Moll had full faith in her is attested to by her comment: "The second year I wrote to my old governess [and] ordered her how to lay out the money I had left with her...which she performed with her usual kindness and fidelity" (194).

Of all the confidantes, Amy seems the most suited to the picaresque because she is so totally connected with Roxana. Granted that Amy has a literary existence only in relation to Roxana, her devotion and duties seem so exaggerated that it is possible to assert her basic complementary nature. She is the alter ego of Roxana on a lower level, an externalization of the worst tendencies of the picara: when Amy has an affair with the servingman of the French Prince, Roxana comments "*like* Mistress, *like* Maid...Why might not they do the same thing below that we did above?" (83). It is Amy who provides the "powerful motive...namely *Comply and live, deny and starve*" for Roxana's prostitution, and it is Amy who suggests that she herself will "starve for your sake, I will be a Whore, or anything, for your sake; why would I die for you, if I were put to it" (110, 28). Amy serves a further purpose; as the more passionate, she is willing to murder the problem daughter Susan to protect Roxana; she screams repentance during the storm on shipboard; she follows Roxana to Holland for reconciliation, even though Roxana is never certain if she killed Susan or not.

One of the main purposes of the confidante is to give the picara another viewpoint for story-telling without violating the artistic unity of the entire work; she preserves the continuity and measures the picara's progress in the novel. McIntyre's Mischa has a series of confidante/mentor of sorts. Kirillin was a "good friend" and "had been Mischa's teacher, from tricks of the trade of thievery to bio-control of fertility" (18). She provides an entry to the palace when Mischa needs it and risks her own life to obtain a death-easing substance for Mischa's brother. Jan Hikaru's journal is another confidante device in the same novel. Expressing an outsider's view of the strange world, even when he becomes Mischa's teacher, Jan becomes an accidental participant in it, almost losing his life in the process. While the good alien pseudosib also teaches Mischa, Val and the mutants teach Mischa how to survive in the underworld of the Center world. For example, her maimed sister's psychic cries for help deafen her until Crab, one of the underworld mutants, cuts the mind-link between Mischa and her sister.

The third reason why the episodic plot is particularly essential is lodged in society's perception of her flighty nature as a woman. The picara's life is supposed to be as changeable as her menses and, when her fancy is caught by something new and glittery, society judges her by harsh moral standards. Where the picaro travels from master to master with impunity, when the picara flits from lover to lover, she is perceived as being unfaithful, even though she is extolled as the courtesan. Where his lack of stability is the result of a disordered society, the picara's restlessness is a sign of the aggressiveness of the woman, trying to survive within a man's world. Where the picaro is judged anti-social for his erratic actions, the picara is judged morally diseased for the same actions.

What most critics overlook in their study of the picara is that her sense of disorder comes from her different reasoning system which critics condemn as having no order. Miller alone sees that:

There is no compelling reason to think of causal plot as more 'philosophic' than a non-causal plot. In our intellectual climate, with its notions of uncertainty, the fragmentation of reality, and the absurd, the older notion of order, predictability, and cause and effect may not seem very philosophic (in the sense of true) at all. The episodic plot may reveal a chaotic lack of order in the world. (9)

The episodic plot justifies and exemplifies the picara's feminine intuition; it is oblivious to order and reason because it operates on another standard—that of chaos.

Another aspect arising from this agreement of the picara and her plot is the manipulation of time within the novel: Lazarillo's life unfolds before the reader without the mention of time passing because he never changes or ages. In contrast, the episodic plot of the picara is basically chronological and sequential which emphasizes her aging. With the later picara's story, tinged by the confessional motif, the unfolding of the tale does not take a straight forward line but rather doubles back on itself; she thinks of repentance at the same time she commits her transgressions. Courage, for example, foreshadows her sins and her repentance within the first chapter while Grimmelshausen's chapter titles fulfill his introduction's intent. Roxana has no difficulty in jumping back to an earlier portion of her life with a casual "but to return to the Circumstances of our Wedding" (244). Even the titles of Defoe's novels are thesis statements of the contents, resembling the advertising blurbs on the covers of newer novels. The episodic nature encourages the blending of the dramatic induction with the confessional motif of repentance which in its turn blends with the dramatic structure of the confidante's dialogue.

Basically the episodic plot serves to create patterns which reduce the pejorative effect of pure episodic action. Miller suggest that one of these patterns is that of the dance: "This strange pattern may either soften or exaggerate the effect of chaos developed by the episodic plot and other devices" (13). The simulation of constant motion imparts a sense of adventure to the picara's memoirs. The leisurely rambling of the autobiographical genre allows the connective tissue to be compressed and the expanded stories to be stressed. It is not until the later stages of Roxana that a continuity of scene pushes beyond its barest outline. The next step beyond that is the novel, free from noticeable jointures which have been smoothed over to present a complete whole.

The Open-Ended Closure

The problem of ending a picaresque tale is simplified by having it not end. It simply goes on and on, begetting sequels, suggesting reader interpretation of future events. In this way, the picara of the fantasy literature finds a natural home in the ubiquitous trilogies and series. Bradley's Darkover series seems infinite. Green's Jalav has finished her fifth book and a sixth is implied. Clayton's Brann is in her second and headed toward her third while her Aleytys finished her story in the ninth book. The spirit of adventure never dies; and the horizon is only a star-leap away.

Critics of picaresque literature see its open-endedness as integral to the disordered nature of the picaresque world. The lack of a definite ending is a more serious charge against the picara than against the picaro. Other than the onset of senescence, there is no physical change in the picaro; he can perform his tricks at sixty as well as at sixteen. Generally, he is thought of as a young man, although he may be old by the end of the book: Lazarillo is ageless but Simplicius is an old hermit. The picara, on the other hand, experiences a physical change in menopause which limits her sexual attractiveness and sexual prowess even though she often turns bawd to maintain her economic usefulness. Still, aging as a process is one to be feared by the picara. Amber is forever worrying about her aging when she sees the youthful women at court attracting Charles' affections. Her chief rival for Bruce Carlton's love is his wife who is only five years younger than Amber. "But though the passing years filled her with terror and her twenty-sixth birthday was but two weeks away, she had never let herself think that he might know she was growing older" (666).

Where the picaro is only temporarily settled, the picara is usually in a relatively stable position at the end of the book. Courage travels as a gypsy; Roxana is a wealthy Dutch countess, Amber accumulates wealth, Scarlett has Tara, Becky has some financial security. Still, the picara has only a tenuous hold on security. "After some few Years of flourishing, and outwardly happy circumstance," Roxana falls into a "dreadful Course of Calamities" provoked by the possibility of exposure that Amy has murdered her daughter (329-30).

Moll survives transportation to Virginia and returns to England to "spend the Remainder of our Years in sincere Pentitence" (343). Scarlett is sure she can attract Rhett again and Amber follows Bruce to Virginia. In a similar way, many fantasies are left open-ended to accommodate a sequel or series. "The infinite possibilities of the picaresque plot express total openness. Since there are no limitations on probability, the door is left open to the fantastic, the improbable, and even the weird" (Miller 10). Only the tale of a picara like Moll can end with the hint of further adventure for the seventy-year-old woman who "liv'd it seems, to be very old: but was not so extraordinary a Penitent, as she was at first" (7).

The Colors Emerge

The bright threads of the autobiographical forms and its allied forms have blended into the picara's tapestry. Through the literary forms of the picaro and picaresque literature in general, the tale of the picara has modified those characteristics for her own story. Her tale is autobiographical in the telling, episodic in form, open-ended in closure, detailed in verisimilitude, criminal in content, and repentant on occasion, adding the confidante as a technical and emotional device.

And the picara persists in modern literature in so odd a form as the 1937 picaresque autobiography of Bertha Thompson who "told" her memoirs to Dr. Ben Reitman under the title of *Sister of the Road: The Autobiography of Box-Car Bertha*. In the grand style of the criminal autobiographies, Bertha's tale retains all the picaresque social and economic traditions as well as retaining the literary characteristics.

"I am," the narrator starts, "thirty years old as I write this, and have been a hobo for fifteen years, a sister of the road, one of that strange and motley sorority which has increased its membership so greatly during the depression" (7). Like most picaresque autobiographies, it is not a true autobiography because it was dictated to an intermediary, in this case, Dr. Reitman whose sociological interpretations flavor the text. Although the thirty-five page appendix substantiates the feeling that Bertha was a sociological assistant doing research, her detailing of the types of hoboes makes this a criminal autobiography. When Bertha spends sixty days in jail for vagrancy, she meets Lucille, a drug addict who undergoes withdrawal in solitary confinement with Bertha. Later studying Lucille and her gang of professional thieves, Bertha categorizes the drugs used, describes the preparation of each, and records her single episode of smoking marijuana with the aplomb of a social scientist. She notes the discipline of the mob, their moderate eating habits and even more moderate drinking habits, their loyalty to each other, their monogamous unions. Pickpockets, she assures us, sent money home faithfully to their families who knew nothing of the source of their income. As part of a thieves' gang, Bertha is instructed in various con games and scams, although she seldom takes part in them. Among the thieves is Otto, whom Bertha takes as a lover, despite fears for his criminal nature. When he is eventually hanged as a murderer, Bertha is present as his "wife" to see the event. This touch, whether true or not, is in direct imitation of Defoe's criminal autobiographies; although she profits from Otto's death and her own pregnancy through newspaper stories and lectures, her description is purely dramatic—the final jail confrontation during which she scolds her lover for murdering a working man; the gallows room crowded with witnesses; the hooded victims; the flop of the trapdoors; and, contrasting with the lack of movement of the hanged men, the "first movements of my baby...deep within my body" (208).

Bertha is a hobo primarily for economic reasons. Some of the wandering labor "agitators" leave home for economic or domestic reasons, some to escape from a dull life or for parental pressure, but others, she concedes "are just seized with wanderlust. The rich can become globe-trotters, but those who have no money become hoboes" (16). She freely admits to taking to the road "wanting freedom and adventure, such as they had" (17); at seventeen she and her sister take to the rails using the advice of one wanderer at union hall-cum-Hobo College to keep "your traps shut and your legs crossed" (33). While Bertha records that women travel in small groups because they had a better chance at hitchhiking and suffered less from unwanted attention, some sisters of the road, she admits, were lesbians, often posing as men to avoid disclosure.

Like the heteira before them, many female hoboes were formally educated or self-educated yet, rather like camp followers, the women trailed radical social reform lecturers from city to city. While most women vagrants did not fear the law, they shunned the welfare system because it divided families. To avoid church missions or welfare systems, the women took to begging as a means to sustaining life. Bertha is schooled in begging; she recounts the successful grocery shopping expedition in Florida where her teacher wangles some products out of generous merchants and shoplifts from less generous ones. Among these hoboes a code of ethics persists. One man refuses to steal gas from a car that costs less than two thousand dollars, reasoning that "those folks with Fords and Chevies are as poor as I am" (81). Most of all, curiosity motivated her: "All that I had learned in these fifteen deep, rich years was a little sociology and economics, types, classifications and figures...I had achieved my purpose—everything I had set out in life to do I had accomplished. I had wanted to know how it felt to be a hobo, a radical, a prostitute, a thief, a reformer, a social worker, and a revolutionist. Now I knew" (280). At one point she works as a housekeeper for a lawyer who classifies vagrants into three categories—hoboes, or those who occasionally work; tramps, those who are on the road for adventure; and bums, those on the road because of drugs or drink or addictions.

Rather than being abandoned by her mother, Bertha has a warm and loving mother whose belief in radical causes such as free love caused her to be jailed for producing a child out of wedlock. As a cook for railroad and construction crews, her mother traveled as a labor organizer, sometimes with Bertha, sometimes without. When Bertha reaches puberty, her mother advises her that "if a man wants you and you want him just take him...Men can't do you any harm. Nobody can hurt you but yourself" (29). Shortly afterward she takes her first lover, her mother's lover, living in that *menage a trois* for over a year yet admitting that he "never made romantic love to me" (29-30).

As a child, she is cognizant of the brothels in her hometown where the girls, restricted in their socialization, sought her mother's house for friendship. Some hoboes, she admits, are forced into occasional prostitution; when she succumbs, it is as much for the experience as for the necessity. In Chicago, she meets Bill Steward, a pimp, who has four women in his string, all of whom claim "he loves me. I'm his heart...I'm the only woman he really loves" (161-2). Bertha resists until she is seduced by his charm, even though it goes against her principles as an emancipated woman. Her curiosity wins out: "Thousands, millions of men the world over pay women for a few minutes of contact. Why do these men go to such women? What have these women to give them. I wanted to know. For a long time I wanted to know" (168). Bertha's detailing of her experience in a house of prostitution reads like a business audit sheet strangely similar to that of Amber and Moll; she lists her expenses—towels, protections, maids, clothing—and her assets. When the house's cut seems too high, she asks for and gets a further break down. What she does not expect is the exhaustion "as though I'd finished an unusually hard day's work" (180) nor does she expect the venereal disease she contracts or her pregnancy.

As a picara, children and commitment never enter her life. Her mother's advice burns deep: "Remember that I never made any sacrifice for you, nor did I give up any pleasure or good times for you. I never did anything different because I had children" (31). When Bertha has a child herself, she refuses to personalize her daughter by naming her "Baby Dear" and relegates her to her mother's care for eight years so that she can develop her profession as a social worker for social justice. Only when Bertha's mother dies in a house fire does she accept responsibility as a mother reluctantly: "I had never really achieved motherhood in the full sense of the word...I was just another woman who was being friendly to her" (270-1).

Bertha relates episodic tales in her expanded and detailed descriptions of individual stories of why men and women become vagrants. While her story progresses along a time line typical of autobiography, the interpolated and expanded episodes provide background, credence, and interest. Each story is complete in itself with the main character often telling his or her own story without Bertha's comments interfering. No judgment is passed as if she were a sociological anthropologist recording data. In addition, Bertha is a repentant picara. When she turns thirty, she resolves her problems: "Suddenly I wanted to be out of New York...I bought some clothes and a first-class ticket to Chicago, to what or whom I did not know" (256). She ends the book with this open-ended certainty that will be well because she has knowledge and experience of all that life might deal her and she has only to play her cards to be secure. "Everything I had ever struggled to learn I had already surmised. Before I had ever hoboed a mile I knew what it was like. All my experiences with the vagrants, criminals, sex variants, radicals, and revolutionists merely clarified that which I had always know or felt" (279). There is no indication as to what happened to her eventually.

If a picara as current as Bertha can capture the imagination, how much more easily can the figure of the picara be seen to emerge from the folds of the tapestry of literature when her autonomy is highlighted by the white silk thread. The next six chapters will explicate other colored threads of the picaresque traits that further delineate the figure of the picara.

Chapter Four
Hunger, Avarice, Criminality

The method of working one section of a design—one area of colour—at a time, and gradually building up shapes as one goes, brings certain limiting factors into the technique of tapestry weaving. The design tends, as it were, to dictate to the weaver which areas should be woven first...as that they can support the new weft. This entails building up certain sections of the design before other over-lapping sections can be woven. (Rhodes 77-8)

Three critical colors which overlap in the picara's story are the gray-red of hunger, the green-white of avarice, and the blue of criminality. While "money does not become for him the single consuming end to which all means are subservient" (Alter 69), the picaro's immediate hunger lapses into gluttony, the consumption of excess food or pleasure. The picara, on the other hand, is somewhat distanced from this immediate need; she would rather accrue money to buy food than hoard the food itself. Thus, she transforms the picaresque hunger/survival theme into the sin of avarice which then subdivides into gratitude and into vanity, the corollary to pride. The first half of the chapter will detail the progression of the criminal element in both.

Hunger

The first recognizable picaro, Lazarillo, is constantly linked with food, especially bread: his mother gives birth to him in the mill; his father is a miller who leaves home when he is caught cheating in his weights. The boy notices early that his family eats better when his mother's lover visits them because he "always brought bread with him" (43). Lazarillo's pursuit of bread takes on such a sacramental character that Alter speaks of the picaro's living in a "desacramentalized" (15) world where bread itself is worshiped as God. When he seeks the sacraments on his own, he finds them flawed: his baptism is in a mill stream, his marriage is a farce, his reconciliation is achieved by his "confession" in his autobiography, his adventures have ordained him into the "holy orders" of thievery, his blind beggar has confirmed him into vagrancy, his anointing of the sick is achieved by his very name. Only in the actual bread and wine denied him by his early masters does Lazarillo find the sacrament of bread and wine, the food of spiritual life; only in the Archpriest's ironic gifts does he receive the sacrament of bread and wine. And the gifts are always connected with a feast. For example, Lazarillo is content with self-deception that his marriage entails as long as he is protected from hunger by the archpriest who gives Lazarillo's wife, his mistress, "a bit of wheat now and then—in the course of a year it must add up to four or five bushels. And at Easter...and from time to time there are a couple of loaves of holy bread" (149). Lazarillo concludes his tale with a ironic oath to the "Sacred Host" that his wife is "as good as any woman in Toledo" (78).

Whether the hunger motif is the result of socio-economic conditions or literary demands, the theme of hunger pervades the book. When Lazarillo is in the employ of the reckless hidalgo who believes that "stuffing oneself is natural for pigs but decent people eat with moderation" (51), he finds that he must beg to feed both of them. The hidalgo questions the propriety of eating Lazarillo's begged bread:

'...This bread looks pretty good...Where did you get it from? D'you think it's been kneaded by someone with clean hands?'
'That I can't tell you,' I said. 'But when I taste it it doesn't make me feel ill.'
...
He put it in his mouth and began to tear chunks out of it just as wolfishly as I did.
'It's very tasty bread, by God,' he said.
...
He went into a little side room and picked up a jug that had a broken lip and looked very old. When he'd had a drink he invited me to do the same. I wanted him to think I was a teetotaller so I said:
'I don't drink wine, sir!'
'You can drink this,' he said. 'It's water.' (51-2)

In addition to hunger, thirst becomes a religious symbol in the wine used as the most common antiseptic, anesthetic, and healing agent. Lazarillo experiences this when the blind beggar, who has smashed his face with the wine bottle for stealing the wine, uses the same wine to dress the cuts: "The wine that caused all the damage is now making you healthy and well again," the beggar comments (Alpert 31). Even when Lazarillo discovers that the first deadly sin of pride caused his employer's poverty, his own pride makes him feel insulted because "masters are usually left by their servants, but with me it was the opposite: he left me; in fact, he deserted me" (65). While the picaro skips over avarice to settle on gluttony as a major sin, he does not hoard food or accumulate wealth; what money he gets above his sustenance goes into clothes, the outward sign of his pride. The picara, however, bypasses pride to center on avarice, itself a form of immoderation; she also bypasses gluttony as a major fault so that over-eating and over-drinking have little appeal for her, except as avarice is a form of immoderation.

More often wine is used as a source of inebriation and of immoderation. Over-drinking to the picaro who can barely manage his survival is impossible: Lazarillo is never drunk simply because he cannot afford the price of wine. In a society where wine or beer was drunk in preference to dubious water, drinking itself carried no pejorative aspect. Many of the picaros were tavern-boys and the picaras were tavern-keepers or bar-maids such as Long Meg of Westminster; Celestina, a drinker in the manner of Falstaff, advocates the pursuit of pleasure at any expense. Courage many brag of her drinking as a soldier but the picara in her never loses herself in drunkenness because it would mean a loss of autonomy in conducting her affairs.

To later societies affected by Puritanism, any excess was untenable. Just when Becky thinks she has Jos Sedley snared, he imbibes Vauxhall's famous rack punch, which permits Thackeray to editorialize on "what is the rack in the punch, at night, to the rack in the head of a morning?" (57). Even though the text itself innocously alludes to bread, wine, and meat as necessary for sustenance, taken in combination and in suspicious situations, they are indicators of Becky's inevitable descent into loose living. The "rouge-pot, the brandy-bottle and the plate of broken meat" (689) are hidden under the covers when the naive Jos Sedley visits her in the Bohemian boarding house. When Becky sits on the bed, "the brandy-bottle inside clinked up against the plate which held the cold sausage," both being "moved, no doubt, by the exhibition of so much grief" the author assures us, just in case we missed the double entendre of the "broken meat" and the "cold sausage" (689-90). And just in case we missed the dubious status of Becky's drinking companions, they pop back into view as Becky regales them by "mimicking Jos to them as she munched her cold bread and sausage and took draughts of her favourite brandy-and-water" (691).

Becky's American counterpart, Scarlett drinks secretly despite the Southern concept that a woman's system is delicate and strong drink is reserved for males and that the women who drink do so "to the eternal disgrace of their families" (686). Scarlett's reluctance to drink her father's whiskey after her grueling return from Atlanta shows the custom of the day as strongly as Emma Bovary's putting her glove into her empty wineglass signaled that she wanted none. Later, when Scarlett develops a hangover from the brandy, it is because she has been half-starved, not because she over-indulged. It is not until her life is so unhappy with Frank Kennedy that Scarlett turns to the bottle for solace; she finds that a "drink of neat brandy before supper helped immeasurably...why were people so silly about women drinking, when men could and did get reeling drunk whenever they wanted to?" (686). Scarlett's drinking problem has forever been "made public" by the movie version which shows her swigging cologne to disguise the smell of the brandy.

The picara ignores society's criticism of over-indulgence until it limits her autonomy. When Scarlett wants to build a saloon in Atlanta, her husband and her community rebel against the idea that a woman would own such an establishment because of its inevitable connection with prostitution. While the picara in Scarlett chaffs at the business success of Belle Watling's brothel, she hypocritically denounces the bawd at the same time as she envies her. In this, she is closest to her picara ancestresses, although her Victorian society forbids her from participating in a similar success. Such social criticism found in early picaresque literature forced a major change in emphasis; where the picaro satirizes the foibles of his society by exposing its seamier side, the novel, as a consciously constructed fiction, highlights the value systems in which the picara is caught.

While the fantasy picara does not have to contend with Puritan-Victorian customs, she still retains a vestige of society's disapproval of women's drinking in her avoidance of over-indulgence. When needed, the fantasy picara shares the same sturdy head for liquor that the early picara did; drinking is part of her life and she can control it the same way she retains her autonomy. She seldom gets drunk; she often can hold her liquor better than braggart men; she frequents the barrooms and saloons associated with the picara figure. Green's

Sofaltis in *Lady Blade, Lord Fighter* is first seen drinking in a barroom with her male friends who comprise the elite fighting unit of the Fist. Bradley's Camilla is a hard-drinking soldier who is respected for her prowess in conquering a masculine pastime. Maxwell's Rheba the firedancer in *Dancer's Luck* destroys the hostile nightclub with her powers when she is thwarted. Green's Jalav and her Amazon warriors can and do drink stronger liquor than the male warriors.

Because each picara is so survival-oriented, she often is supercharged and cannot relax her defenses in social drinking. The maintenance of her constant alarm system can be undermined by excess of alcohol and, since any imbalance may cause her to drop her deception or disguise, she avoids drinking. This is particularly true of the computer-enhanced heroines. Goldin and Mason's Jade Darcy, for example, works in an end-of-the-galaxy casino/barroom as a bouncer because it provides safety in its anonymity, not because it provides free food and drink. Her computer-enhanced body does not tolerate alcohol well so that, when she does indulge, she does so for only the most desperate of reasons— to lose herself in despair or oblivion. Even in her lapses her control and self-discipline are proof of her autonomy.

The picara's over-indulgence sometimes hints at her aspect of the Terrible Mother who kills her children to preserve herself. Jo Clayton's heroine Brann (*Drinker of Souls* and *Blue Magic*) is reluctantly transformed into a vampiric force that consumes men by draining them and lesser beings of their life force. Akin to the passing of the "Ruah" or spirit of life from person to person, such "drinking" sustains the life of the Changer children who transformed her; it is an act so sacred that she is involuntarily rendered sterile by it as she becomes both a vestal virgin and a vessel to transmit life for the children. In a similar way, the picara's sexual excesses provoked by over-indulgence can be excused because they ultimately give life. Whereas Lazarillo compromises himself as a *cabron* or cuckolded man, the picara can use over-indulgence in drink as an excuse for promiscuity, like the romantic heroine who wakes up from a night of over-drinking to find herself in bed with a stranger who may or may not have made her pregnant. The picara can do the same thing. When Karr's Thorn awakens with a heavy head because of her over-drinking the night before, her nauseous stomach is caused by her pregnancy, the result of over-drinking several weeks earlier. While immoderation in any form is dangerous to the picara, such excess can lead to an imbalance which has no polar opposite to balance it. For example, when no female support system is present for the fantasy picara to vent her feelings, she takes the masculine way out by getting drunk. While the picara has a long and hard struggle to autonomy, which any immoderation will endanger, the picara seldom drinks heavily for two reasons: the readers will not identify with a heavy drinker and the morals of the society decry immoderation and gluttony. Although gluttony is a minor sin, the picara is never accused of over-eating, because readers do not want obesity in fantasy novels.

For similar reasons, the fantasy picara relies on alcohol rather than on drug use for her immoderation. What drug abuse exists is seldom voluntary. Green's Terrilian is injected with aphrodisiac drugs and inhibiting drugs to block her mental powers and to condition her to accept her sexual slavery; at one point she is painted with a liquid which causes great pain without doing damage but at no time is she a willing drug user. Drugs inflicted on others can be humorous also. When Green's heroine Jalav and her Amazons capture a man, they feed him an aphrodisiac drug to increase his virility. Once he is wise to their actions and avoids food, they put it in his drink. Drug excess is used only occasionally as in Elizabeth A. Lynn's Tornor trilogy (*Watchtower*, *The Dancers of Arun*, and *The Northern Girl*). After a few mild references to a drug called heavenweed in the first two books, Lynn has a lengthy description of a "House of Pleasant Dreams" modeled after an opium den with its hot, stuffy, shadowy, cubicles which "gave the illusion of privacy [where] the air was heavy with heavenweed...the strong, sweet scent of the drug...Paxe preferred heavenweed as an intoxicant to wine, because it heightened the sense in a way she liked" (192-3). P.C. Hodgell's *Godstalk* has the character of the dancer taking a drug called "dragon's blood" (28) because it restores youth temporarily while causing swift aging in between doses.

Poison is associated with the Terrible Mother aspect of the nourishing mother gone wrong; medieval literature used the spider as a symbol of a body's producing poison to kill in opposition to the bee whose body produced honey which nourished. Traditionally, poison is a woman's weapon because it is ironically associated with woman's function as nourisher. For example, poison is the weapon suspected in the death of Jos Sedley when Becky takes care of him. Amber doctors Samuel Dangerfield's posset with poison so that she can tend him but her later attempts to kill an enemy by the same method are thwarted. Barbara Hambly's *Ladies of Mandrigyn* has the resourceful women poisoning the warrior and withholding the antidote until he agrees to teach them warfare. Where poison is ingested in most societies, the fantasy world used technological devices like injections, inhalation, or contact to transmit the poison. Such conventions echo the poisoned princess theme where the presence of the woman contaminates people around her, especially her lovers. In her aspect of a prostitute, the picara contaminates men with physical and moral disease. In her aspect as a witch, the picara faces accusations of practicing black magic with her potions and of white magic with her herbal medicine. Either way, she is often cast out of society for her knowledge of drugs.

Avarice

The picara in later stages has risen economically so that the gray specter of hunger has been substituted by the leprous green-white of the excessive ambition of avarice. In a hostile world, with its lack of security or stability, the picara sees the accumulation of wealth as her only salvation, literally and actually. Courage asks who will convince her to "hate my ducats, when I know from experience after all, that they can save me from want and be the only consolation on my old age" (33). It is significant that the picara departs from the traditional male picaro in this respect: the picaro must provide only enough food to sustain his life; the picara, in a more sophisticated society, needs more permanent goods to sustain her. Her autonomy both encourages and supports her avarice as a decaying corpse provides phosphorescence.

The early picara is forced to settle for material goods (food, clothes, shelter) in place of food; Celestina accepts "a piece of bacon, or some wheat flour or a jug of wine, or any other sort of provisions they [serving girls] could steal from their mistresses" (37). The later picara demands actual money, which represents buying power and capital. Even within a picara's life span, a similar shift in avarice occurs. Courage is satisfied with her silk gown from Vienna as a gift from her first love; however, by the middle of the book, she is demanding both clothes and money from a lover, claiming "he would not have succeeded if he had not sent me, right after I took off my widow's weed, a piece of dove-colored satin with all the trimming for a new dress, and more important, if he had not presented me with a hundred ducats for my household" (55).

What is Fortune's whim to a Renaissance picara is more correctly translated as opportunity to a Puritan picara. Defoe had touched on this theme earlier in *The Compleat English Tradesman*: "Necessity tempts the poor man; Avarice tempts the rich" (Shinagel 58). The avarice of the early picara towards hoarding food and money shifts in later ones so that when Roxana's jeweler husband dies in Paris, she claims that she almost "cry'd myself to Death for him" while in the next breath she concedes that "the first thing I did upon this Occasion, was, to send a Letter to my Maid...I order'd her to convey away...things of value...and then to sell, or dispose of the Furniture of the House" (54-5). Her seizing of opportunity is a combination of her picara's use of chance and her economic heritage from Defoe. Forced into prostitution by the "dreadful Argument of wanting Bread" (43), Roxana lands on her feet when the landlord provides shelter, a rent-free home, the restoration of her impounded furniture, food, wine, and a "silk Purse, which had three-score Guineas in it." (42). So also does Courage abandon pride when she "began to be on short ration and Hunger had no trouble persuading me to gain my daily bread by my nightly handiwork" (146). By the time her tale is ended, however, her motive for theft is less than that of hunger than of joy in deceit when she steals the peasants' feast: "My mouth watered for the food, and the idea that the peasants were going to eat it all by themselves vexed me greatly" (221).

Two subdivisions of the picara's avarice are the magenta of vanity and the cloying mauve of gratitude. While the mauve of gratitude is a pale disposable item, it tinges the white silk of her autonomy and, after the first flush of gratitude, the picaro and picara abandon its pretense. Lazarillo is grateful to his blind beggar/master for showing him the reality of the world; he is never naively grateful after that and his gratitude to the archpriest for giving his wife food is self-delusive irony. While Celestina is obsequiously grateful to her clients for their business, Courage shows the splendor of her gratitude to her nurse by giving her an "imposing burial...as if she had died at the gates of St. James in Prague" (198). However, Courage's concern for her household smacks of exaggeration:

Even had it meant that I myself would have to go hungry or naked and shift day and night under the open sky, I would have seen to it that my mother, my Skipinthefield, my other servants, and my horses had at all times enough food, drink, clothing, and fodder. (164)

Luckily, such effusion is never tested and we are left wondering how much of it to believe.

Like hachure, gratitude provides a transition from the clinging dependence of the embryonic picara through the period of dependence on the ravisher into the final stage of independent agent—the picara. However, the white of the picara's autonomy is not stained by the mauve of her gratitude any more than the white of her virginity is stained by her devirgination. Courage, for example, in her first affair with her captain-lover uses her gratitude as an ironic buffer; when he first seduces her, she expresses only relief at being rid of her virginity. The exaggerated gratitude with which Roxana thanks her landlord from rescuing her from poverty and starvation is such a colorful hachure or bridge to ease her shift from being a deserted wife into a picara. Moll's initial sense of romantic devotion to her first lover, the older brother, is quickly submerged in her gratitude to her husband, the younger brother.

In the more recent picaras, this gratitude shifts to the companion Amelia when Becky tries to snare her brother into a safe marriage. Emotionally faithful to Bruce Carlton, Amber is forever grateful to his friend Almsbury for his constant support but she does not love him in a sexual way.

What is pride in the picaro is vanity in the picara. In the same way, the magenta of vanity is an essential complementary color to the purple of the picara's pride because her body is her chief economic resource and its deterioration threatens her livelihood and money. In her profession as a courtesan, so excessive is the picara's vanity that it threatens her avarice as the dominant capital sin. Roxana acknowledges that, when avarice is no longer sufficient justification for her sins, vanity is.

Necessity first debauch'd me, and Poverty made me a Whore at the Beginning; so excess of Avarice for getting Money, and excess of Vanity, continued me in the Crime, not being able to resist the Flatteries of Great Persons; being called the finest Woman in *France*; being caress'd by a Prince; and afterwards I had Pride enough to expect, and Folly enough to believe, tho' without ground, by a Great Monarch" (202).

Roxana's insistence that "Necessity first debauch'd me, and Poverty made me a Whore at the Beginning" reinforces Defoe's familiar use of economic necessity as motivation. However, what established the picara in Defoe's money-motivated character is the phrase which immediately follows the quotation above, "so excess of Avarice for getting Money, and excess of Vanity, continued me in the Crime" (202).

The picara's vanity rests mainly in her own charms rather than in a vanity of her material possessions. It is not until later in Roxana's career, when she has already accumulated some money, that the importance of clothes intensifies her role as a picara. The French count gives her three suits of clothes and Roxana uses these spoils of her profession as an additional erotic enticement. Certainly her retaining of the Turkish dress becomes a theme in her relations with the King, with the Dutch Merchant, and finally with her daughter. In a way, the retention of this dress, in itself both an avaricious and a thrifty act, does strengthen Defoe's moral stand on avarice, for the dress continually endangers Roxana's happiness and security.

There seems to be a recognizable pattern in the picara's fortunes: striving from poverty to attain the minimal necessities for survival, the expansion into more lucrative prostitution, the worry of investing accumulated money, the voracious accruing of money beyond a reasonable amount, all lead to the picaresque threat of an uncertain future.

With usury no longer a sin, the Puritans transmuted the pursuit of Mammon into a virtue and the accumulation of capital into a duty. This avaricious habit of collecting or hoarding is integral to the picara figure and is, in fact, one part of the theme of self-preservation. Roxana's picaresque avarice even extends beyond the accumulation of money for its own sake. Traditionally, one's life can be extended by fame, infamy, or children. The usual picara, being barren, cannot depend on children to carry her memory into the future and so substitutes money which increases as progeny does. When Roxana finally does send money to her son by the jeweler, her maternal pride is aroused only when that son increases his wealth; when he chooses a wife, she approves his choice because such a wife will be an added benefit and a protection of his future fortune. So also does social status count for wealth. Critics have seen the picara's switching of lovers as a form of the picaro's switching of masters. The rank of lovers is an economic barometer of the picara's financial state; the higher the lover, the more avaricious the courtesan. Courage fluctuates from high to low in her choice of lovers, yet her wealthiest period is not when she is at her social zenith of lovers (i.e. her captain-lover) but rather at the midpoint when she is engaged in trade. Even Roxana's choice of lovers reflects a growth of vanity and of avarice as she claims title after title, first that of Countess, then as an English Lady, until she speaks of herself as a "German Princess" (271), referring to the early English picara, Mary Carleton Moders and her habit of assuming false titles. Roxana experiences a similar fluctuation in her wealth and popularity. When she is mistress to the king, her wealth increases by the clever investments of Sir Robert Clayton without expenditure of her own effort; as the mistress of the jeweler and the French Prince, her wealth increases by her compliance and charm. Nevertheless, it is her marriage to the Dutch merchant that establishes her greatest wealth.

The picara's avarice and her autonomy emerge simultaneously in her role as an entrepreneur and coincides with the rise of mercantilism. As a business woman, the picara is both merchant and bawd. Whereas the early picara avoids all economic responsibility, the picara, since she does not deal with the problem of immediate hunger, is distanced from the need to obtain food. Her concern is with the money which can buy food and all her energies go into that effort to the exclusion of emotions and relationships. As both the prototype of the *homo economicus* and the Great Goddess, the picara becomes obsessed with her need to acquire money or its equivalent; as the courtesan, this obsession appears in the use of gold jewelry as ornament and investment. Thus, Shakespeare's courtesan in *A Comedy of Errors* demands the disputed gold chain for her favors; Renaissance courtesans are pictured with golden chains, reminiscent of the Latin *carpe diem* poems extolling the powerful golden chain-bond with which the poet's mistress controls both him and her pet sparrow. Celestina knows the value of her services and is killed because she demands the wage she contracted for. Courage is a sly merchant who profits on selling items in the war as well as on her marriages. Becky knows the value of marriage; her greatest defeat is in losing Sir Pitt because she opted for the safety of marriage with Rawdon Crawley, banking on the imminent death of his aunt. When the inheritance does not fall to Rawdon, she abandons him for richer men like Lord Steyne. Amber is less consciously a businesswoman, but Scarlett prides herself in her business acumen.

The picaras know the value of cash money. Courage is the first woman to make use of the international banking system when she speaks of sending bills of exchange from city to city. Furthermore, Courage uses "money which I kept here and there in large cities to loan to bankers and merchants from time to time, for which I made such honest little profit that I was able to live pretty well from it and was not obliged to touch the principal at all" (73). Roxana is also conscious of the banking circles; when she arranges for one son's welfare, she apprentices him to a "Turkey-merchant," the word for international businessman. She sends her son to Italy to learn the business and to the Indies to profit in it. Roxana learns the basics of capitalism from as eminent an authority as Sir Robert Clayton, a seventeenth-century economist who "took frequent Occasion to hint, how soon I might raise my Fortune to a prodigious Height, if I wou'd but order my Family-Oeconomy so far within my Revenue, as to lay-up every Year Something, to add to the Capital" (167). How far this is from the easy-come, easy-to attitude of the picaro demonstrates the path which the picara takes. Periodically she takes account of her wealth, detailing its growth with actual figures with as much glee as she records in the acquisition of wealth and husbands.

The best example of financial independence of the picara is in Defoe's two heroines. Robert Alter claims that Moll's living in "the criminal milieu of the novel is in some important respects simply the capitalist milieu writ large" (71). Her thievery is toward the progressive accumulation of wealth and the means she uses are those of a prudent businessman. Much has been written about Moll's middle-class morals, but it is in the character of Roxana that Defoe creates his best business person outside of Robinson Crusoe.

Roxana never loses. Each move she makes enriches her rather than impoverishing her. Even the dissolution of household goods represents some increase for her in good will if not in cash. Thus, Roxana hedges about the amount of dinner service she possesses, explaining,

My meaning was, about the Box of Plate, a good part of which I gave her, and some I gave to *Amy*, for I had too much Plate, and some so large, that I thought if I let my Husband see it, he might be apt to wonder what Occasion I cou'd ever have for so much, and for Plate of such a kind too; as particularly, a great Cistern for Bottles, which cost a hundred and twenty Pound, and some large Candlesticks, too big, for any ordinary Use. (254)

However, when she deals with normal household goods, they often turn into a tangible threats to her safety and the only household good she mentions are those which represent portable wealth or which are immediately convertible into cash: gold, jewels, silver-plate service, Holland bills for credit, and the investment with her banker.

Similarly, while Amber details her household plate for its monetary worth, she also accrues her wealth through the means of a financier, Shadrac Newbold, the founder of the firm still in existence as an investment house. When Amber's lover leaves her with five hundred pounds to see her through the birth of her child, he advises her "to put in with a goldsmith...Shadrac Newbold is perfectly reliable and he'll allow you six percent interest at twenty days call, or three and a half if you want it on demand. He lives at the Crown and Thistle in Cheapside" (75). When she gets her first substantial amount of money from Rex Morgan, she "hunted out Shadrac Newbold—whose name she remembered, Bruce Carlton had told her—and put it with him at six percent interest" (189). When she wishes to deceive the older businessman Samuel Dangerfield into believing she is a rich widow, Amber asks him to advise her on her financial matters; she captures his approval by referring to her "goldsmith and when she mentioned Shadrac Newbold's name was glad to see how favourably impressed he seemed" (279). Samuel subsequently is wise enough to place the gold he wants her to use as her inheritance with Newbold (343) so that when the fire hits London in 1666-7, Newbold is able to "inform her that not one of his depositors had lost a shilling...almost all the goldsmiths had saved what was entrusted to them (498). However, when the 1667 plague and attack by the Dutch navy undermine the confidence of the nation in their economy, Winsor invents an exchange of dialogue between the fictional Amber and the real Newbold, explaining how bankers and financiers work. "Your money is safe, but it is not in my possession, but for a small sum. The rest is out at interest, invested in property and in stocks and in the other ventures of which you know. I do not keep your money lying idle" (558). Although Amber is satisfied with this answer, Winsor uses the modern understanding of investment rather than the earlier picara's hands-on approach to her wealth. Amber is a further step in the progression of the picara's avarice.

As a businesswoman, Scarlett readily uses banks and bankers to suit her purpose; her most famous dealing with money is in her immediate need for cash to pay the taxes that forces her to try to deceive Rhett when he is imprisoned. That she fails is only a sign of her embryonic picara state because later she is able to outwit less astute men with her confidence schemes. Land poor she may be but she marries Frank to insure retention of Tara. Her fertile brain makes her husband's store in Atlanta a thriving enterprise at the price of her marriage and her children's health; the saloon she starts has an equal success, binding her closer to the picara's image as a tavern- or brothel-keeper. As an experienced business person, Scarlett engineers the sawmill into a financial success by using convict labor when the proud southern men refuse to work for a woman. The sawmill becomes a symbol of her self-defeating maneuvers; it serves to retain Ashley near her while it destroys Frank; it endangers her relationship with Rhett when she uses his loan to support the sawmill which employs Ashley. When Rhett has become her banker and not her lover, their conversation revolves around financial terms.

'Just remember, my precious little cheat, the time will come when you will want to borrow more money from me. You'll want me to bank you, at some incredibly low interest, so

you can buy more mills and more mules and build more saloons. And you can whistle
for the money.'
'When I need the money I'll borrow it from the bank, thank you,' she said...
'Will you? Try to do it. I own plenty of stock in the bank.'...
'You were a good risk, my dear, an interesting risk. Why? You didn't plump yourself
down on your male relatives and sob for the old days. You got out and hustled and now
your fortunes are firmly planted on money stolen from a dead man's wallet and money
stolen from the Confederacy. You've got murder to your credit, and husband stealing,
attempted fornication, lying and sharp dealing and any amount of chicanery that won't
bear close inspection.' (771-2)

Not a bad description for the picara who finds her identity, not through the
usual channels of marriage, children, and society, but through her work. Scarlett
has no scruples about acquiring money once she realizes that the social status
of those engaged in trade has shifted so that money, not breeding, dictates the
new society of Atlanta. While she admires those who "carried their losses with
an air that she could never attain, would never wish to attain," she convinces
herself that "you can't be a lady without money" (609). Immediately after that
realization, she marries Frank to keep Tara and she marries Rhett who as a
picaro himself admits that his money was "honestly made with the aid of honest
Union patriots who were willing to sell out the Union behind its back" (624).

In fantasy novels, the picara is often more idealistic, preferring to save the
galaxy rather than to preserve the economy. Many of the picaras are mercenaries
who sell their military services; many are prostitutes or bawds who sell their
sexual favors; many are queens or princesses who rule countries; many are
sorceresses who sell their magical powers. In science fiction, many picaras are
itinerant but skilled workers—pilots, navigators, starships' captains—while some
are pirates, scavengers, or thieves. Few are honest business women although
they all possess skill in haggling, preferring a shady deal to an honest one.
Unlike the picaro who never profits from his learning experiences, some picaras
learn their business as they go along. Morris' dream dancer Shebat falls heir
to an intergalactic business she does not know how to handle it; she learns
slowly but well. Clayton's Brann is an artist who learns discipline to create
and sell her pottery. Clayton's Gleia in *A Bait of Dreams* designs embroidery
on fabric and ends up with a profitable sideline selling the designs. But on
the whole, the fantasy picara is not a business woman.

If the gray of hunger and the green-white of avarice have been woven into
the picara's design, the next color to be added is the blue of criminality which
arises when her basic needs cannot be satisfied.

Criminality

In investigating the origin of the word "picaro," critic Joan Corominas
"correctly reminds us that implicit within this semantic shift is a change in
emphasis from the *picaro*'s social situation to his immoral and delinquent
behaviour" (Sieber 6). If, as she suggests, the word "picaro" comes from the
verb "picar" to bite or nibble, then grey-red of hunger pangs separate the picaro
from this tapestried background. As an outdated reminder of the medieval
wandering rogue, the picaro always retains a certain criminal flavor. While his

criminality is less serious than that of most professional criminals, society measures his offenses with an economic barometer. Critic Frank Chandler's limiting of the picaro to a petty or occasional criminal whose "typical crime...is theft" (4) clarifies the level of the criminal world to which the picaro usually descends. As Sieber traces the changing emphasis of the picaro through the centuries, he notes the accruing of elements of delinquency, of autobiography, of journey, of satire. Avarice also distinguishes the picara by forcing her into criminal behavior. However, the picara retains her autonomy through theft and prostitution for, as a prostitute, her life is lived on the edges of criminality and, as a thief, she raises the craft of theft to an art.

A serious criminal offense in one society may be less serious in another society; for example, in a society where there is little material property, theft is a serious crime because that which is stolen—usually food—might make the difference between life and death. As towns became more complex, the survival crime of stealing to eat evolved into stealing the means to buy food to survive. The later and more sophisticated picaro, dealing with a more materially wealthy society, turned from direct theft to indirect theft, not by stealing what he immediately needed, but by stealing the means to obtain what he needed. Picaros such as Lazarillo had no scruples about stealing food nor did later picaros worry about stealing money or goods to obtain that food. When the picaro makes this transition, he often becomes a con-man or swindler rather than an outright theft.

The origin of the thief motif in the picaresque stretches back into the trickster archetype where the theft provides an amusing and intricate tale. Such intricacy involves labyrinthine deceptions in jargon or thieves' cant with which story-tellers and authors pepper their works, almost as if the hidden signals of such vocabulary evoke a glamorous spell of secrecy. In England, the popular *liber vagatorum* and the conny-catching pamphlets combined with the jest and criminal biographies to form an underworld language in itself. For example, Thomas Harmon's 1567 "Cavueat or Warening, For commen Cvusestors Vvulgarely called Vagabondes" specifies the different types of criminal women:

a Dell is a yonge wench, able for generation and not yet knowen or broken by the ypright man [leader], a doxe be broken and spoyled of their maydenhead by ypright men and then they haue their name of doxes, and not afore. And afterwards she is commen and indifferent for any that vse her, as *Homo* is a commen name to all men. (Viles and Furnivall 27)

Best of its type is Richard Head and Francis Kirkman's *The English Rogue*, the 1665 tale of Meriton Latroon, a not too distant cousin of the 1554 *Lazarillo* and of Thomas Nashe's 1594 *The Unfortunate Traveller*. Meriton, whose last name suggests his thief background (ladron) while his first name contradicts it, provides the reader in Chapter five with a detailed five-page index of thieves' cant, including the pedigree of some words. This need to list and categorize extends down to Box-Car Bertha in the 1930s, who provides the same type of list, carefully divided into sociological classifications such as transients, vagrants, bums, migrants.

The fantasy picara makes use of such jargon also. Authors imitate the secrecy of criminality by creating unusual names for their characters, replacing vowels, consonants, syllables with a mixture of apostrophes and capital letters. Some authors use derivative words or names which, while still understandable without a glossary, may suggest other literary echoes. One of Bradley's heroines carries three names: Magda, the name by which she is spoken of in the novel; Magdalen Lorne, the name given her by her Terran father; and Margali n'ha Ysabet, the Darkovan name from her mother Ysabet (Elizabeth). Even this is not as simple as it seems. Magda is named after a Darkovan heroine Margali who entered a "freemate" marriage with another woman to protect her unborn son's inheritance just as Magda enters a "freemate" marriage with her friend Jaelle to protect both their daughters. With the Terran form of her name, Magdalen Lorne, suggesting her "forlorn" or "lonely" aspect, Magdalen also is an echo of the Biblical Magdalen, the woman from the "Magdala" or "fish towers" or "dried fishes" of the Hebrew origins which may, in their turn, relate her back to the sea goddesses of the Mediterranean basin myths. Like her Biblical ancestress, Mary of Magdala, Magda finally is released from her seven demons of sexual and religious passions when she accepts entry into the mystical Grey Sisterhood.

While it is in the nature of fantasy to create worlds and languages, most authors limit the number of invented words and most of them are easily understandable. An author like Charnas limits her invention to a few obvious words like "fem" for a woman or "Holdfast" for the city of the men while Vinge transforms the base word "mer" for the sea into the word "mers" for the helpless sea animals slaughtered for their life-sustaining fluid. On the other hand, Clayton constructs an elaborately different set of languages for each of her series; within each language world, there may be invented words for new species who talk in asterisks and new words for common early objects. Some authors extend this practice to include new names for old earth animals or for newly created mixtures of animals serving the same function as an earth animal; a four-legged biped used to carry people or burdens is still a horse although he may have any number of odd characteristics. What he is called does not affect his function. Within those languages there are specialized words for the criminal categories such as appear in her *Skeen's Leap*, which details the categories of criminals (8).

Another form of language manipulation occurs when the author appends glossaries, maps, time lines, or summaries to the novel. Clayton's final work in the *Drinker of Souls* trilogy has three glossaries before the main story, each one with complex names and nicknames of imaginary beings or characters and their relationship to each other. Her Skeen series has a summary of the action to date and helpful chapter headings. Her last Diadem adventure, *Questers Endgame*, has a seven-page summary of the characters. Such detailing adds to the verisimilitude of the science fiction and fantasy genre as it did to the beginning novels.

Criminal language is not the only criminal adornment. Unlike the picaro who steals so regularly that he must name each action, the picara is only an occasional thief who steals only when her other resources fail. Once started, however, she continues her thefts because her avaricious nature demands it and because she is good at it. Her autonomy allows her to be an independent thief.

Moll Flanders, for example, begins to steal when she is nearly fifty and accumulates so much money in her twenty years or so that she can retire and support a husband. Sieber sees that "the nature of crime itself was redefined in *Moll Flanders*. For Moll it is more 'criminal' to be poor and insecure than to be a criminal in the ordinary sense" (54). The picara then sees that it is more of a crime to be a beggar than to be a thief. Especially in the Puritan times, when trade was valued over aristocracy, the crime of theft was only slightly worse than begging. As A.A. Parker notes, "by the Puritan times dishonesty had become not so much a sin as an activity that undermines the merchant's credit and so leads to bankruptcy" (98).

To be a beggar was to lack the Puritan virtue of valuing work. A thief "worked"; he went to school to learn techniques; he belonged to a guild or gang; he sold his "goods" to a middleman; he profited by his labors; he risked his "capital" in his brushes with the law; he expended his time in the pursuit of gain. In short, a thief was a working capitalist who took risks and as such could not be faulted that he worked outside the law. The beggar, on the other hand, was a non-worker. Where the trickster/picaro earned his keep in early literature by amusing and diverting the populace with his antics, the beggar contributed nothing. The Poor Laws with their restrictions grouped all apparently non-productive people into the classification of vagabonds and tramps, needing the protection of a lord who would swear for them such as Elizabethan theatre groups who had to ally themselves with a member of the aristocracy. Where the religious houses had absorbed the poor as part of their acts of charity, when those houses disappeared after Henry VIII's dissolution of the church lands, the poor became the burden of the parish or town. The situation was even worse in the Puritan days as the picara makes plain in her complaints about the restrictive parish workhouses and Poor Laws. For example, the opening of *Moll Flanders* compares the Continental system of caring for the children of criminals by putting them

into an Hospital call'd the *House of Orphans*, where they are Bred up, Cloath'd, Fed, Taught...plac'd out to Trades, or to Services, so as to be well able to provide for themselves by an honest industrious Behaviour [and she castigates the English society for leaving] a poor desolate Girl without Friends, without Cloaths, without Help or Helper in the World. (8)

Because her autonomy resides in her thieving skills, the picara/thief considers herself superior to a beggar. She possesses verbal skills and disguises which enhance her craft but she never descends to humbling herself as a beggar because her pride forbids it. This is particularly true in the fantasy. For example, Vonda McIntyre's Mischa in *The Exile Waiting* is a thief openly scornful of the beggars, not for their deformities or infirmities but because they did not beg for themselves, but rather

for the people who owned them, deigned to feed them, further disfigured them if they grew too healthy, and beat them if they made no profit. Mischa could have pitied them if she had ever seen any one of them defy a master or try to escape, but she could not pity an unthinking acceptance of degradation. (13)

Even when her two brothers and sister are sold by her uncle into the slavery of begging, she feels disgust but only slight compassion and disgust. To her, the beggar is lower than the pick-lock.

Vinge's *Snow Queen* incorporates the thief motif also in several secondary female characters. The first is Tor Starhiker, who precipitates the hero Sparks's downfall when she steals all his money and possessions after she has conned him into watching a sporting event. Eventually, she is used by Sparks as a contact with the "offworld criminal subculture" (199) as the hostess in Persipone's nightclub, hinting at the Hecate aspect of the Great Goddess. The other thief is Elsevier, the interplanetary smuggler who becomes the heroine Moon's confidante and who provides Moon's escape from imprisonment. Moon herself must leave her home planet to find herself as a sybil through suffering before she can return to rescue her lover Sparks from the underworld of Persipone's nightclub, a reversal of the Orpheus-Eurydice theme.

Besides the use of thieves' cant and the distinction between begging and thievery, picaresque criminality extends to the education of the young into the fine art of thievery. Lazarillo's first theft is for food for survival but his later ones are for his master who is equally hungry. What looks like nobility is actually a satire on the inability of the Spanish aristocrat to provide enough money to feed himself or his servant. Even when Lazarillo progresses in skill, his motive—food—remains the same. The English rogue Meriton, for example, first bilks a woman of her basket of cherries and steals apricots from his tutor until he progresses to trying a "picklock of my own invention" (17-8). Along with the stealing is the beating which accompanies it, a beating more typical of all young tricksters when they start their pranks. The trickster Diccon in the mid-sixteenth century English folk play *Gammer Gurton's Needle* counts his mild beating small payment for his joy in the pranks he has pulled on the townspeople. Seldom does his first attempt into theft condemn the male picaro to a serious punishment.

Most male picaros have their start in the child's gang, overseen by a Fagin-like teacher. In one sense, this school for thieves replaces the education or learning skills that are needed for survival when a child is abandoned as the picaros are. Stuart Miller cites "the stone trick by the blind man in *Lazarillo*, the inn tricks in *Guzman*, the inn and university tricks in *Buscon* all represent the same rite of passage...where innocent youths are turned into worldly tricksters (61). In Clayton's *A Gathering of Stones*, the young slave Davindo is given a choice of livelihood by his owner Maksim. When he shows surprise that thieves have a guild, Maksim elaborates

They don't put it about, but they do take apprentices and they have teaching masters who'll work your tail off...if you don't have a Family here to back you, you'd better have a Guild or you're fair game for the Pressgangs supplying meat to the pleasure House and the Whips who run the childgangs and anyone else with a taste for boys. (57)

In contrast, where the boy must have a school, the girl picara thief often has only one person as a tutor. For the early picara, that person is usually her confidante or bawd since her fall into thievery happens when her beauty starts to fail; in the novel picara, however, the historical novel adopts criminal life to provide color and obstacles for the picara. Amber, for example, is taught how to be a thief by Mother Redcap and Black Jack who recruit her from Newgate when she is pregnant and friendless.

To the fantasy picaras, the tutor to crime is often an older man who takes the paternal interest in them that their own fathers did not or an older lover whose interest is both monetary and sexual. For example, a modern picara like Peter O'Donnell's Modesty Blaise has her Chief of Operations Tarrant as her mentor when she turns from her criminal Network to working for the government. Like a typical picara, Modesty grew up on the streets of the Near East, formed her own Network in the criminal underground before she was twenty, and retired to right the occasional wrongs brought to her attention by Tarrant, working with an unspecified government undercover agency. With her male counterpart Willie Garvin, Modesty's forays into crime-fighting involve the subtlety and inventiveness expected of master thieves. Unlike the picara, however, Modesty seldom steals for her own gain because she turns the money over to a good cause. Such Robin Hood ventures are not truly picaresque but, since Modesty already has accumulated more money from her Network than she will ever need, her generosity offsets the avarice expected of a picara. With this necessity for money removed, the picara can concentrate on the beauty of her scam in re-establishing a primitive justice and in patriotically bringing law and order back to her society. The means she uses to do so involve her constantly in picaresque disguise and deception: for example, Modesty and Willie have a pre-determined set of signals to throw off suspicion if they are caught; their captors may think they have the upper hand but the wily duo manage to "sting" their enemies repeatedly because of their carefully plotted crosses, double-crosses, and triple-crosses. However, Modesty is seldom autonomous. She lacks the driving force of the picara in her constant returning to Tarrant and the other males for approval, part of her heritage as the female counterpart of Ian Fleming's James Bond. Where Bond is a lonely and independent agent in the novels, his movie persona is dependent upon the paternalism of his superiors in the British Secret Service and his raffish ways with women. Modesty's autonomy is diminished by this paternal head-patting and sense of loyalty she feels toward Tarrant, Garvin, and a few other friends. Interestingly, she is crippled sexually until a friend works with her, and the only other significant women in her life are either blind or crippled.

A fantasy picara does not have this crippling need for approval. For example, the autonomy of McIntyre's Mischa permits her to shut off draining emotional experiences, even to recognizing that she is better a thief than her brother Chris who "had taught her to pick locks so early that she could not remember the lesson. He had been a good thief; she was better" (57). The craft of picking locks is so much a part of her survival mode that, when she is asked to rejoin the thieves' gang, Mischa refuses, claiming that "I work better alone" (15).

Once she is trained by her male tutor, the fantasy picara retains her autonomy by supporting herself through her thefts. Sharon Green's *Mists of the Ages* presents a typical picara thief in Dalisse Imbro (Inky because of her black hair, Smudge to her teasing lover). Like the juvenile picara, Inky has had a master thief Seero as tutor and foster father: "I was raised by him. If he hadn't kept his word to my mother to look after me, I would have ended up in one of those orphan shelters after she died. He forced me to go to school, bribed me into learning something...he was always there for me." (13). Seero's philosophy of thievery which pervades the novel is a form of Robin Hoodism.

There were people who worked hard for what they had and others who tried to take those things away from them, but not all of those who took were arrested, tried and put in a cell...That made the bad people think they were something special, that they had the right to keep stealing from innocent people and getting away with it. Seero said he didn't blame them for thinking that but he didn't agree...No matter who the targets of our stroking were, it was still stealing and against the law...we stole from those who had no legitimate claim to what they had. Seero refused to start training me until I proved to him I understood the point. (149-50)

Later, when she has been deserted by her lover Serendel (notice the similarity of names), she still feels so close to Seero that she contemplates suicide "to find out if there really was a place we would meet again. I needed him very badly to cry out my hurt against him and have him show me how to bear it for the rest of eternity" (311).

Because Seero was set up and murdered by the gambling houses, the Twi Houses, Inky sets out on a complicated course of revenge which, unfortunately, forces her into being blackmailed by Steller Intelligence to participate in their own scam by claiming that "you are a *thief*, young miss, and we have enough evidence against you in your dossier to keep you in a cell until long past the time the designation 'young' is no longer appropriate" (34). Her assignment is to penetrate the Mists of the Ages recreation area to retrieve some document to prove that the Mist is actually a murderous company. To this end, she is given a plan and team members, each of whom has a specialty which divides the picaresque traits into separate characters. Inky's shadowy ability to sneak into places without detection so that it becomes "more of a game than a necessity" (27) and her skill in deception is complementary to her teammate Lidra's skill in reproducing invisibility screens. Chal, the health-food enthusiast, is a medical genius whose survival skills are needed while Serendel, a galactically famous gladiator who seeks revenge for his sister's death in the mists, provides the warrior image.

The point at which the fantasy picara and the picara diverge is in their approach to love. A fantasy picara like Inky must meet the needs of her sword-and-sorcery genre and that involves a love interest. Green incorporates the necessary tension of having the lovers love, then part, to carry out her larger themes of the loner thief. For example, while Inky never feels a part of any society, much less loved, she is a full romantic heroine when she finally falls in love with Serendel, despite their initial required hostility and her valiant fight against love. However, the romantic complication of parting the lovers occurs when he discovers she is a thief:

Seren, my love, what I am is a thief...Seero raised me and trained me to do what he did, to get back at all those who think they're above the law, and that's who I steal from. I'm very good at my profession, as good as you are at yours....

"You're a *thief?*" he said, sounding and looking utterly repelled..."You pretended to be someone decent, but you're actually a *thief?*"

"...I only steal from those who deserve it, those who are bigger thieves than I could ever be...I'm still the same person I was..."

"How can you say there's nothing different about you?...You steal, don't you, no matter who it is you steal from? Stealing is stealing, which means you're nothing but a dirty *thief!* I wish to hell I'd never laid eyes on you!"

Part of his repulsion is explained by the fact that his sister was killed by a thief; the rest is integral to his gladiator's code of fair play, a particularly masculine one which contrasts with the more flexible feminine one of Inky and the other picaras.

Minor picaresque traits are neatly used within the fantasy. The novel starts with her breaking into an enemy's office and using futuristic criminal cant: stealing is "stroking"; she has to overcome a "complex maze lock," "diddle box," "scanners," and a "security force board instead of a dead-end panel"; she tosses her "prowling suit, tools, and belt" into her "jump-around" (5-7). The resort of the Mists of the Ages specializes in disguise and magical illusions as its base. Inky and her teammates constantly change clothing, rooms, and lovers much as the picara travels among lovers and lands.

Autonomy is not dead even in a romance fantasy. Inky has always depended on herself. When Serendel misjudges the illusionary giant monster and his sword crumples, she is left to her own devices. Much as she might contemplate "envying the old-fashioned sort of book heroine, the kind who handled nasty situations by fainting, thereby leaving it to the broad-chested hero to get her out of the soup," Inky realizes that her "own broad-chested hero was down in the shadows somewhere" and that she "still had this need to do something to protect myself" (257). She frees herself, climbs up on a chandelier, garrotes the monster with her discarded chains, and saves herself and Serendel.

Even here Green employs a picaresque trait incorporated in a romance-fantasy. The romance demands that, although her disillusioned lover may rescue her from her torturers, he must immediately leave her to the ministrations of Chal, not even stopping "to look at me long enough to see if I was going to live. He just disappeared through the door" (310). The picaresque demands that in the final scene Serendel show only a "careful neutrality" (316) when she is almost coerced into undertaking another assignment. To underline her autonomy and her separation from love, Inky forces an agent to restate that she is a thief, that "your talent is stealing, young miss, and you're nothing but a thief" (316). Ironically this statement of her essential nature precipitates her arrest "for action damaging to the general public" (317). While the novel apparently ends with two men hauling her away to prison, the reader can scent the whiff of more adventures of Inky and her teammates. No sword-and-sorcery novelist would leave a heroine without her love; no picaresque writer would leave her heroine without a future adventure. And the tale goes on.

Jo Clayton's trilogy on Skeen also presents a typical child picara thief. Like most picaras, Skeen "stopped being a child somewhere around her sixth birthday" (*Leap* 12) and her "being broken repeatedly as a child and badly mended" (*Return* 262) led to her caution in dealing with people. The victim of her uncle's incest, she kills him when she is nine and flees to the city's streets as a thief because she'd "far rather steal than whore and, preference aside, I haven't the temperament or physical qualities for that line of work" (144). She describes her life on the streets as "the miserable days of her teen years in a youth labor pool, swept off the streets with hundreds of others by a labor pressgang" (*Leap* 48).

In a lengthy description, she explains how she has no illusions about herself: she killed her uncle when she first realized that she might become as vicious as he was. She admits to Timka that she is on the "Scum Team. The ones respectable types sneer at and stomp when they can...Pit Stoppers aren't a sweet bunch, Ti; to say true, we're a godsawful collection of misfits, murderers, and thieves. The excrement of the universe" (*Return* 110). At one point, she asks if a tentative companion would be "morally outraged at traveling with a working thief" (*Leap* 44). As a thief who "if she had to, she could get some change by a little discreet burglary" (11), Skeen becomes a "Rooner: a specialized smuggler/thief/plunderer [who] deals in artifacts from (mostly) dead civilizations, a thriving and lucrative quasi-legal profession" (*Leap* 8). The invention of this word, derived from the "ruins" plundered by artifact hunters, ties Skeen tightly with the thieves' cant literature as does her constant knowledge of the galactic underworld of fences, shysters, con men, and gangsters. Given the fact that the names in any fantasy work are as imaginary as the characters, Skeen's use of her fellow thieves' names is strangely reminiscent of the *liber vagatorum* and conny-catching pamphlets of the early picaresque literature. "Swert the Mouth was sucking his fissatit and in two other worlds...Mala Fortuna solo knows what he managed to get out of him before Neep and Cleep pushed in beside them and shut the dribble down...I had a Sweep in and he rousted a pile...The Hound's hot after you, Skeen the Lean. You hear me, you call a Sweep for Picarefy every Pit you hit" (*Search* 32).

Clayton's Skeen is so consciously the fantasy presentation of the typical picara thief that the author names Skeen's spaceship Picarefy, which reflects the word *picaro*. The act of naming something gives power over it and Picarefy resents it when she must use a disguised name: "Picarefy was dryly sarcastic about the choice of AngelBaby" (*Leap* 8). The identification of the picara with her ship extends to Skeen's half-serious question "who owns who here?" Picarefy admits that "you've got the papers on me...but I prefer to think of us as partners. Neither of us can live without the other" (139). That Picarefy is a measurable reality is reinforced by Skeen's give-and-take repartee with the assertive ship: "Picarefy was far too complex and far too illogically arranged for the cleverish mind to understand her even in her parts" (138). When Skeen warns her that her increased complexity means that no one will be able to fix her, Picarefy takes her advice, "providing abundant redundancy and repair mice that scurried endlessly about the sprawl of the brain" (*Search* 139). The faithfulness of the ship is akin to the western hero's horse but serves the picara more as a confidante. For example, in the last book, Skeen and Tibo retire to the sonic cleaner, safe in the womb of Picarefy who nags them in a motherly fashion that the time limit is "one minute off, don't hit the sonic till we transfer" (*Search* 299).

While many of the fantasy picaras are not maternal, they are often left with the companions on a quest whose ultimate care depends on the picara; that care may involve theft. Amber and Scarlett have the family and households to look after; when Scarlett "steals" Frank from her sister Suellen, she justifies her action on the grounds of having to preserve her family. Maxwell's Rheba has a shipful of galactic misfits who want to be returned to their native planets. Throughout the three books, Skeen supports a varied crew of mixed races and personalities in quest of their homelands through her stealing efforts without letting herself become attached to any of them. Her life is controlled by the

uncertainties hammered into Skeen's soul during her rotten childhood [which] had surfaced and wiped away the certainties of her mind; her trust was betrayed time after time by those who professed to care for her, who should have cared, her perceptions were constantly negated by such betrayal until she mistrusted her own judgment almost as much as she mistrusted the surfaces and professed intentions of those around her. (*Search* 258)

Even Tibo, the man she has stayed with for five years, is suspect. Interestingly, he is pictured as smaller than she, just as the lovers of the Great Goddess are pictured in hieroglyphics as being smaller and of lesser importance. Each of her adventures turns into an episode of the picaresque fantasy with the lengthy chapter headings providing the linking transitions between separate episodes. The interpolated tales told by Tibo and Skeen serve as another form of the later proto-novel form of the picaresque. The ending of the three books is open-ended and contradictory. The chapter heading of the blank page after the final episode declares that "that's it. Story's over" (300) while the optional "epilogue of sorts" is followed by another blank page stating, "So, there you are. Cycle complete, a new cycle begins" (303).

Just as the picara Courage has a spinoff novel in the Simplicimus cycle, Clayton links spinoff novels from the Diadem characters; for example, Swardheld Quale, a spinoff from Clayton's Diadem series where he had been imprisoned in Aleytys' diadem, is the major character in the *Shadow of the Warmaster*. As a man attended by an eclectic group of ancillary companions, he is "a violent brute with a strong skilled body and enough intelligence...to acquire a ship," the Slancy Orza, which, like the Picarefy, is the best transport in the galaxy (44). While he acquires precious "rosepearls and the rewards" (396) so great that his financial future is secured, he prides himself more on being "set for a decade of lazing about, taking the commissions we liked, not jobs we had to do" (396). In the best manner of the white knight detective like John MacDonald's Travis McGee, Swardheld keeps his options open for "it won't hurt having a stash of rosepearls in the basement that we could dip into should Luck turn mean on us" (398).

These spinoffs are not just a fantasy aberration. Many literary characters are directly interlinked by blood ties as well as by the nature of the repetition of characters in trilogies or series. Such relationships provide the reader with identification ties which imitate the crime "families" such as the Hollands in Elizabethan England. Simplicimus and Skipinthefield are cousins; Moll Flanders and Mrs. Betty Blueskin are related. So also are Rostico Burn and Skeen "shirttail" cousins, since Burns comes to her planet "with Imperials on his tail, not unlike another skinny kid I knew some half hundred years ago" (*Search* 14), as a fellow thief comments to Skeen.

Occasionally a picara will have an older woman who teaches her thief's tricks without encouraging her to be a prostitute. Courage's nurse is her banker and fence. When Moll accumulates some stolen goods, she discovers that her governess is a pawn broker who has "a Sort of People about her, that were none of the honest ones that I had met with there before" (200). She warns Moll about the perils of Newgate and encourages her to steal:

She Laugh'd and told me I must go out again and try my Fortune; it might be that I might meet with another Peice [sic] of Plate. O, Mother! *says I*, that is a Trade I have no skill in, and if I should be taken I am undone at once; *says she*, I cou'd help you to a School-Mistress, that shall make you as dexterous as her self...by the help of this Confederate I grew as impudent a Thief, and as dexterous as ever *Moll Cut-Purse* was...

The Comrade she helped me to, dealt in three sort of Crafts, (*viz*). Shop-lifting, stealing of Shop-Books, and Pocket-Books, and taking off Gold Watches from the Ladies Sides....(201)

Even after this "Comrade" is hanged, Moll is fueled by her avarice which, she admits, forced her to "still get farther, and more: and the Avarice join'ed with the Success" (207) until she has no more thoughts of repentance.

Vonda McIntyre's Mischa in *The Exile Waiting* is a thief in the manner of Moll Flanders. After Moll's initial foray into theft by pilfering the bundle of childbed linen from the neglectful maid servant, her second attempt is done by daylight when she risks stealing the valuable necklace which a child is wearing. She is even tempted to kill the child "that it might not Cry" but refrains when "the very thought frighted" her, insisting that "meer Necessity" drove her to it (194-5). Mischa, on the other hand, is also under "necessity" to get her brother Christopher off the planet to save his life. When she sees a "child in a gilded kilt and a collar" emerge from the Stone Places, Mischa uses the child's "memorized route" back to the Palace. And, just as Moll uses her governess as a fence, Mischa calls upon her confidante Kirillin to set her up with a delivery job, although she complains that "it would be a shame to distract such a good thief" (22) among the Palace riches. As a clever thief and a bad delivery person, Mischa is "annoyed to have taken a job of manual labor with no result. Thieves did not have to work with their backs, but with their hands and minds" (22).

While the picara as thief has been transformed in popular literature into the charming cat burglar or seductive spy, she never loses her identity in even so slim a volume as Truman Capote's *Breakfast at Tiffany's*. Capote's picara Holly Golightly is what her name suggests—a light-fingered thief, a casual thief who encourages the narrator to steal Halloween masks from Woolworths and to wear them blatantly on the street solely because "successful theft exhilarates" (55). When she visits her lover in Sing Sing and delivers the bogus "weather reports" to his accomplice, she does so because each visit nets her a hundred dollars. She refuses to become attached to anyone and skips the country to escape prosecution. Like the picara, she overlooks what is moral when it is convenient to her and her picaresque laziness keeps her always on the periphery of crime, never at its center.

Russ's Alyx is also a thief because, when her belief in her religion failed, it was easier to become a thief than to live by prostitution: "Alyx—with a shrug of contempt—took up a modest living as a pick-lock, a profession that gratified her sense of subtlety. It provided her with a living, a craft and a society" (2). She deviates from picaresque avarice since "much of the wealth of this richest and vilest of cities stuck to her fingers but most of it dropped off again, for she was not much awed by the things of this world" (2). Criminality often subdivides into specialized thieves: Skeen is a smuggler and art thief; Mischa is a pick-pocket, Moll is a shoplifter, Gleia is a jewel thief. Roxana, Becky, and Scarlett, however, specialize in deception in business affairs, a white collar crime ignored by the increasingly mercantile society.

Often the picara's thievery results from her basic sin of pride as much as from her avarice. Even though a picara like Courage can claim that she "stole not from necessity or want, but mostly in order to avenge myself on those I found hateful" (186), she finds safety with the gypsies because they are beggars and thieves, skilled in misdirection and distraction. Although the picaro derives from the Hermes-Mercury trickster, the confidence woman stems from the soubrette of the Greek and Roman stages and from the Columbina of the *commedia dell'arte*. Moll Flanders has an ancestress in a real-life thief and con artist, Moll King or Godson who flourished in Defoe's time; at one point, Moll refers to herself as a "Moll Cutpurse," a well-known thief on the Elizabethan era. Roxana takes advantage of the adventures of Mary Carleton Moders when she adopts the guise and the title of a German Princess; critic Jane Jack claims that Defoe based his character on Mrs. Mary Butler who had been convicted of forging bonds of Sir Robert Clayton (*Roxana* 332, fn. 164).

A good part of the thief's role in fantasy is in misdirection and disguise. Vinge's Arienrhod plans to save her own life by substituting her look-alike and drugged daughter in her death ritual, a deception involving masks and costumes and elaborate preparation. When Ann Maxwell's Rheba the Firedancer (*Firedancer, Dancer's Luck*, and *Dancer's Illusion*) needs ready money in her Firedancer series, she arranges to cheat at a chess game where cheating is expected; she puts up a smoke screen by rearranging the energy in the chess pieces and the cheaters are cheated. While Rheba is not by nature a thief, she has no compunction in the second book in using the talents of her group of assorted former slavers to outwit the villains on the inhospitable gambling planet of Onan. Intending to rob only those who can afford it, Rheba the Senysan Firedancer and her Bre'n mentor Kirtn suggest that the two illusionists traveling with them would make

"...crackling good thieves. Would you?"
"...What kind of thieves?" asked f'l'Tiri neutrally.
"Ummm...ordinary," said Rheba helplessly. "What other kind is there?"
F'l'Tiri's voice was patient. "Are we to be *yimon*—"
"—electronic thieves—" whispered Fssa to Rheba.
"—or *s'ktimon*—"
"—armbreakers—"
"—or *mnkimon*—"
"—kidnappers—"

"Wait," said Rheba desperately, wondering what kind of culture named its thieves so formally. "Kirtn and I will do a little act on a street corner. When the crowd gets big enough, you'll go through and take whatever you can get you hands on while the crowd is watching us."
"Pickpockets," summarized Fssa in Universal.
"*Liptimon*," said i'sNara and F'l'Tiri together. (11-2)

In just a short passage the author has implied the existence of a criminal language, a complicated galactic species, and the intent of her picara.

Jo Clayton's novels of the Diadem start out with a thief and most of the characters are thieves in some way but they soon assume the role of the confidence man. The first thief Miks Stavver steals the diadem to precipitate the heroine's problems in escaping from her native but hostile planet. He rescues her stolen son Sharl from powerful witches and the duo keep turning up as thieves, smugglers, and con-men throughout the novels. Clayton blends several concepts together in one scene in *Ghosthunt*. Stavver and Sharl are posing as a mother and daughter to gain entry to a planet for their latest theft when the boy encounters a hermaphroditic thief:

The boy felt a series of touches across his back and buttocks, twisted his head around to glare at the Lazone...he (or she, Lazonen didn't go in for sexual dimorphism)...stared with blank innocence at the boy until, fuming, he turned his back on the creature and moved up until he was closer to the thief [Stavver].
Stavver looked down...'She wasn't groping you loveling.' His voice was lighter, higher, quavering. 'Just practicing her trade to past the time.'
'Trade?'
'Dip.'
'Oh.' The boy thought a minute. 'She?'
'Odor,' the thief murmured. 'Going into heat, she is.'
'Oh.'

Sharl is one of many young boys forced into thievery by circumstances of his birth; he is trained by the abusive thief master who "taught him the finer points of thieving" (120).

Quest novels involve some form of theft, always for righteous reasons: the sword must be returned to the rightful king, the kidnapped child must be reinstated as heir, the treasure must be taken from the dragon. Such theft is "honest theft" because it is righting moral wrongs and fantasy often falls within this category. The early picara does not bother with such niceties but the fantasy picara does. For example, throughout Maxwell's *Dancer's Luck*, the thieves win with the ultimate theft being the salvation of the planet; with Rheba's help, Daemon, who is the "Luck" of the planet, is able to "steal" enough of the alien food-producing entity, the *zoolipt*, to save his city from starvation and to assure the continuation of the original function of the *zoolipt*. Rheba is gifted with a smaller version of the healing *zoolipt* organism which, while it saves her life several times, also endangers it because the protective *zoolipt* renders her unconscious when she reaches a state of exhaustion. The third book *Dancer's Illusion* deals with Rheba's trying to outwit the organism's defenses, to convince it that her exhaustion is sometimes necessary to save her life and to reassert her autonomy.

Often theft is that of Prometheus' stealing of knowledge. Since her survival is dependent upon her autonomy, the picara must know. If education is denied, she obtains it by experience. Tarr's Frostflower so longs for knowledge that she endangers her life to read the farmers' books. Rheba seeks knowledge in understanding and restoring the stones in *Dancer's Illusion*. Another form of this search for knowledge occurs in the picara who is a spy. Lynn's Tornor series deals with messengers whose observations make them into spies. The quest for knowledge is one of self-identity but in the picara it becomes a practical need for immediate survival even if it leads into criminality.

While the picara's criminality is usually confined to theft and prostitution, sometimes she may be suspected of more morally heinous crimes like murder. In picaresque literature, the picaro is so close to the trickster that he seldom comes close to murder; rather than skill of the novelist is tested by the ways he makes his picaro avoid direct confrontation which might lead to battle. Lazarillo will play a trick on someone to embarrass them or to show up the foibles of society; he will not put them out of life to ease his life, even for his hunger. In one sense by taking the bread from the priest and beggar, he is in effect risking their death by saving his but, since that is not his intent, he cannot be called a murderer. The picara does not hesitate at murder, although the murders committed are done for the "right reasons," i.e., to protect herself, to revenge herself, to keep herself in existence. For example, Goldin and Mason's Jade Darcy is thirteen when her family is killed; after "two years as a guerilla, learning the hit-and-run tactics" (214), she enlists as a specially adapted bionic guerilla who thinks nothing of killing in self-defense.

Each author must walk a fine line in having her heroine kill only those who threaten her autonomy. If an enemy comes at her, she strikes back. As the archetype progresses through the phases of literature, she acquires the skills of self-protection and self-preservation which sometimes take her into grey areas of murder. The picara often murders for political reason: Judith killed Holofernes the tyrant threatening her people, Esther condoned the murder of Haman. Sometimes she does it for misguided love: Salome caused the death of John the Baptist; Medea slaughters her sons and brothers for her lover Jason. In addition, the picara has a long history of murder connected with her role as the Great Goddess who slays lovers and children alike to satisfy her needs. However, more typically mothers preserve their sons in favor of their daughters, as occurs in William Styron's *Sophie's Choice* and the picara, an indifferent mother at best, seems to prefer and to preserve the sons over the daughters. Becky neglects her son while Amelia dotes on hers; Scarlett particularly dislikes her daughter.

Roxana may or may not be a murderess; Amy most certainly is. Roxana admits that she hardly saw her one son "four times in the first four Years of its life, and [she] often wished it wou'd go quietly out of the World" (263). Two of her original five children by her brewer husband which she left with her sister-in-law are dead, leaving two daughters and a son whom she sets up in Roxana's household, she pieces together enough of Roxana's history to be a threat to her. (At this point, Defoe begins the longest episode in the novel, devoting nearly sixty-five pages to it and framing it in a series of dramatic dialogues with even the dialogue form being assumed.) The progression toward the girl's murder is bulwarked by Roxana's usual negations and musings over her state.

While she claims no knowledge of the murder, "Amy was so provok'd, that she told me, *in short*, she began to think it wou'd be absolutely necessary to murther her" (270). Roxana at this point is so upset that she threatens to murder Amy if she persists: "I...as well as I love you, wou'd be the first that shou'd put the Halter about your Neck, and see you hanged...you wou'd not live to be hang'd I believe, I shou'd cut your Throat with my own Hand" (270-1). When the girl follows Roxana on to Holland, she tentatively identifies the similarity of Roxana's morning dress to her famous Turkish dress. Roxana only alludes to the actual murder with ambiguous phrases, "*as I may in time relate more particularly*" (302) and "of which I cannot enter into the Particulars here" (328). She never really says that the girl is murdered but twists her language around to obfuscate the truth:

the wicked Jade [Amy] shou'd make her [Susan] away, which my very Soul abhorr'd the Thoughts of; which however, *Amy* found Means to bring to pass afterward; *as I may in time relate more particularly*. It is true, I wanted as much to be deliver'd from her, as ever a Sick-Man did from a Third-Day Ague...But I was not arriv'd to such a Pitch of obstinate Wickedness, as to commit *Murder*, especially such as to murther my own Child, or so much as to harbour a Thought so barbarous, in my Mind: But, *as I said*, *Amy* effected all afterwards, without my knowledge. (302)

. . .

Amy was provok'd to the last Degree at her, and yet she thought it was not her time to present, because she had a more fatal and wicked Design in her Head, against her which indeed, I never knew till after it was executed. (311)

Roxana has to disengage herself from the murder and she does so by dismissing Amy after thirty years of service. This distancing, so familiar in the substitution of the stepmother for the natural mother in fairy tales, serves to remove Roxana from the direct murder yet the guilt remains and her life is changed by the "injury done that poor Girl, by us both" (330).

Becky's involvement in murder is foreshadowed in the charade in chapter fifty-one where she plays the part of Clytemnestra "like an apparition—her arms bare and white,—her tawny hair floats down her shoulders,—her face is deadly pale,—and her eyes are lighted up with a smile so ghastly, that people quake as they look at her" (537). Her final episode is where Jos Sedley is in such fear of her that he cannot meet Dobbin in her presence: "she'd kill me if she knew it. You don't know what a terrible woman she is" (726-7). Jos's death three months later cannot be laid directly at her feet, although the insurance lawyer "swore it was the blackest case that ever had come before him; he talked of sending a commission at Aix to examine the death; and the Company refused payment of the policy" (727).

Amber is also guilty of the suspicion of murder. When the businessman Samuel Dangerfield almost eludes her matrimonial clutches, Amber feeds him mushrooms which act as a mild poison to his system, forcing him to be nursed by her. At the end of the novel, she pretends to go along with a plot to poison a political enemy but instead arranges a "harmless sleeping potion to stir into the Baron's sack-posset" (719). Her final scene where she confronts Bruce's wife with his infidelity has her wanting to "grab her by the hair, tear at her face, destroy her beauty and her very life." When Bruce denounces her, Amber's "lust for revenge was so powerful she would have killed him if she could" (714).

The fantasy picara is less fussy about murder. Because she is a warrior, a rival's death in battle is never wrong when her own survival is in question. Off the battlefield, the picaras kill only when necessary, such as in self-defense or in revenge. Clayton's Skeen kills her incestuous uncle, "chopping his face into hamburger" (*Leap* 151) to prevent further abuse; her Aleytys in the Diadem series become a Hunter, a hired detective who kills when necessary to survive; her Brann, the Drinker of Souls, kills only those who are unworthy of life and only to keep her Changer children alive. Vinge's Arienrhod not only kills the native "mers" on her planet to obtain their anti-aging juices but she also condones the death of innocent people. Green's Terrilian who abjures all violence kills the men who destroyed her child. Bradley's Free Amazons kill only in battle or in self-defense.

Murder is not outside the picara's spectrum of colors but it is always limited by the risk to her survival or her autonomy. Avoidance of troubling situations preserves her autonomy and, unless she is driven by a revenge to cleanse her spirit, the picara seldom kills. The grey-blues of her criminal association are seldom shot through with the red of murder. The picara is content to slip in and out of the shadows of theft, of prostitution, of criminal language and of the underworld to have the white silk of her autonomy heightened by the contrast.

Chapter Five
Sexuality and Children

The principal textural effects in woven tapestry are caused by the occurrence of ribs in the surface when the warp threads are covered by the weft. These effects vary according to the direction of the ribs in the finished panel and also according to whether they are crossing areas of light or dark colour: the ribbed effect becomes much more noticeable on light areas and tends to be obscured on dark ones. Hatchings, which are lines or spires of color used for shading from a light colour into a darker one, or vice versa, create middle tones. They usually cut across the ribs of the warp at right angles and so form a strong contrast of flat colour against their round relief. (Rhodes 52)

The picara's concerns with her chief economic resource—her body—are like the crossing of warp threads with shots of color, "flat colour against their round relief," which build up her design without any specific color being dominant. The green of her fecundity as the goddess figure, the yellow of her prostitution, the pale rose madder of her abandoned children, the crimson of her abortions, the marbled gray of her marriage: all color her design. This chapter will center on the picara's physical concerns of sexuality—virginity, barrenness, contraception, miscarriages, and abortion. The next chapter will consider why her sexuality leads her away from marriage and towards prostitution.

The archetypal pattern of the Great Goddess myth encompasses her nourishing and protecting presence at the same time that she is "also the death of everything that dies...the womb and the tomb: the sow that eats her farrow" (Campbell, *Hero* 113-4). Jo Clayton defines her Great Goddess as "She whom the men call variously Maiden, Matron and Hag, She who was implicit in the alternation of death and birth, in the cycling of the seasons, the complex circling of the moons" (*Moonscatter* 9). As the life-giver, the goddess is the sexual playmate who brings the pleasurable "little death" of the Renaissance; as the death-dealing mother, she is the sorrowful mother who eases her children into death. As a courtesan, the goddess retains the right to refuse her sexual favors to anyone she wants. As a mother, she retains the same rights whether to bear children or not and whether to support them financially. As an emanation from the Great Goddess, the picara possesses her paradoxical attributes of being both virgin and mother, both fertile and barren, both life-giver and death-dealer. This binary aspect further subdivides into the triad of classical goddesses—the wife (Hera), the virgin (Diana or Athena), and the love goddess (Aphrodite)—and subdivides again into a quaternity where the hag goddess (Hecate) incorporates the role of wisdom or Sophia to her attributes. Because the nature of an archetypal pattern is as fluid as a hologram, the archetype of the picara shifts emphasis from one aspect of the Great Goddess to another to suit her story as easily as one color "hatches" into another in tapestry.

Virginity

The first attribute of the Great Goddess is the paradox of her virginity: she is the fecund mother of nature, bearing children to many lovers, at the same time that she remains a virgin. Just as man's perception of the face of the moon changes, the face of the goddess "changes" as she is viewed in her different aspects as mother/virgin/lover/hag. Along with most mythologists, Lederer claims that

"Ishtar was called 'the Holy Virgin' or 'the Virgin Mother' because she was unwed and untamed, and that the virgin and the prostitute are two of a kind. The hierodules or 'sacred virgins,' and the veil of the goddess—behind which she remains impersonal and free in pursuit of her purpose—is worn by virgins and prostitutes alike." (119)

The picara's autonomy appears in her being "untamed" and "impersonal and free in pursuit of her purpose"; she is "unwed" in that she is not committed to a single man but to a series of lovers as were the hierodules. The paradox of the term "virgin-mother" then is not contradictory in goddesses who are associated with the moon and her monthly cycle. Thus, Aphrodite has her virginity restored each month with the moon's cycle and her ability to bear children is asserted each month with her menses; she is both virgin and mother. In Catholic tradition, Mary, the mother of Jesus, is accorded the title of virgin and mother. Tales of saints' lives suggest this dichotomy; the letters and writings of foundresses or superiors in religious communities refer to their double roles as the "mother" of their community and as the virginal bride of Christ. More specific is the case of Margaret of Cortona, a thirteenth century Magdalen figure, who had her virginity restored by Christ when she repented of her immoral life. According to her revelations, the mystic argued that since Christ is the source of purity, only He could "give it and maintain it." He agrees that "because you have attained a dove-like innocence and purity...and because of your love for chastity, I will place you among the Virgins" (Hiral 61-2). Interestingly, all these women are involved with the image of doves.

Modern literature equates virginity with integrity rather than sexual innocence and modern romance often make the length of time between sexual encounters render the women virginal. In fantasy literature, restored virginity allows the heroines to appear repeatedly in sexual situations without promiscuity. For example, when they are made slaves, they are kept in a constant state of arousal imitative of the voracious appetite of the Great Goddess and the experience of defloration is ever new, ever available. In fantasy, such as Green's *Mind Guest*, when Diana Santee is given the body of a teenager, she immediately faces a sexual encounter to prove that she can control Bellna's body: she "hadn't expected to be matched to Bellna to the extent of being turned into the next thing to a virgin!" (112). With the emphasis on sexuality in modern literature, if there are few virgins in the beginning of fantasy books, there are even fewer at the ends of the books.

In her drive toward integrity and autonomy, the Great Goddess' virginity represents both potentiality and kinetic strength of such virgin mothers. The word "virgin" itself suggest that the word "vir" or strength is combined with the word "gyn" for woman in much the same way that the Renaissance concept of *virtu* meant strength more than manlihood. In addition, virginity (or its appearance) gives power and autonomy in certain societies: in saints' lives, the preservation of virginity justifies excessive physical disciplines; in picaresque tales, virginity is a renewable resource. When necessity demands physical proof, the bawd resorts to a major stock-in-trade in her ability to restore virginity; consequently, Celestina repairs some maidenheads "with bladders and others with a few stitches. She kept a stock of fine furrier's needles and waxed silk thread [and] she sold one of her girls three times over as a virgin" (39).

Where romance uses virginity to serve as an enticement, in fantasy novels, virginity preserves the powers of sorceresses. Bradley's Callista and Karr's Frostflower believe that they must remain virgins for their powers to work. While their magic powers are not harmed by their loss of virginity, the prohibition links them with the poison princess myth whose love is fatal to men. The fear of defloration transfers itself to the image of the veiled woman and is easily transferred to the harvest goddess whose face is too terrible to see, the most distasteful aspect of the Great Goddess. In her role as the Terrible Mother who, fearful for her own immortality, gobbles up her children as they are born, she is the Pig Goddess or sow who eats her farrow. In this aspect, her reputation has some physical basis in fact since mammals (first time mothers in particular) occasionally devour their young at birth. This seemingly unnatural act takes its place among the four great social fears which concern mankind throughout the ages—incest, suicide, polygamy, and cannibalism or its corollary—child sacrifice.

Child Sacrifice

To understand how the picara's sexuality turns into child sacrifice and cannibalism, we have only to look at the original Lamia, Zeus's lover, who had her children devoured by a jealous Hera; in return, Lamia ravaged the children of other women by cannibalizing them. Another primal archetype devouring children is the Hebraic myth of Lilith whose blood-thirstiness is a convenient explanation for early cannibalistic child sacrifice which is never far from the human experience. As the first wife of Adam who argued for autonomy with him since they were created at the same time, she was set aside in favor of Eve because she refused to be submissive to Adam. Lilith was punished by having her fecundity limited to producing demons rather than human children; consequently, Lilith is accused of killing children in retribution.

Often this charge is cannibalism arises from legends like those of the Celts of the cauldron of life as the source of all matter and the restoration to life of the dead or wounded. Patriarchy transformed the cauldron into the witch's stewpot or oven, like that in Hansel and Gretel, where children are sacrificed. Lederer claims that the prohibition "Thou shalt not seethe a kid in his mother's milk" (Ex. 23:19, 34:26, Deut. 14:21) is not a "dietary but a religious precaution" (61) against child sacrifices to the Great Goddess Astarte. While the picara avoids cooking and therefore any direct connection with child sacrifice, the literary picara does involve herself with dubious acts. For example, Medea slaughters her brother and scatters his body on the waves to distract her father from pursuing her; she murders her children to revenge herself when Jason is unfaithful. Courage "sacrifices" her maid's child by forcing Simplicius to care for it; Brecht's Mother Courage "sacrifices" her three children to the Thirty Years' War. Roxana and Moll abandon their dozen or so children while Amber and Scarlett emotionally neglect theirs. For the most part, fantasy heroines protect their young, although they are seldom involved in the direct care; Charnas' Alldera is not typical in wishing her child dead.

The picara as the Great Goddess sacrifices everyone, children included, who stands between her and her survival. Not all the measures a picara takes lead to so drastic an action as child sacrifice. The ease with which the picara rejects her children would seem to come from the early belief that the *homunculus* was delivered *in toto* by the male into the body of the nurturing, but not the creating, womb; the child, therefore, was in the woman but not of the woman. The Great Goddess preserves this same distancing—her children are expendable as long as her survival is assured. Lederer claims that the "prenatal act of hostility toward the child which is exceedingly common in any culture [results in] the induced abortion" (63). The picara takes advantage of such beliefs in her choice as to whether to keep a child or not; she shows few maternal instincts. While the picara may bring an unwanted child to term, she will abandon him or her within a short time. However, as the social *mores* change, the picara changes her attitude toward her children.

In fantasy, although the sacrifice of any life is always reluctantly undertaken, the loss of energy—any energy—is the modern equivalent of death. Thus, when Rheba in Maxwell's *Firedancer* trilogy must rob power from beings, she uses only energy sources which are atomic or chemical, not organic; she literally resonates with the sufferings of inanimate and animate beings. So also do witches and sorceresses invoke death chants over those they have had to kill while most women warriors avoid the unnecessary taking of life. Even the killing of lower life offends: McIntyre's Snake apologizes to small animal she must kill to have the cobra Mist swallow to make the necessary antidote she needs. Clayton's Brann is an unwilling nursemaid to two young Changers who need the sentient life energy until they are mature enough to tap directly into the sun's energy. Known as the Drinker of Souls, she is so "sickened at what she had to do," that she "quiets her soul by choosing thieves and slavers, usurers and slumlords, assassins and bullyboys, corrupt judges and secret police, anyone who used muscle or position to torment the helpless" (*Gathering* 30). In doing so, she equalizes the balance of power in Clayton's created world as other fantasy heroines maintain the harmony of nature by judicious use of it. Nevertheless, the picara is an emanation of the Great Goddess in her most virulent aspect as the death goddess.

Tanith Lee's *The Birthgrave Trilogy* is an example of the Great Goddess legend made fantasy. In it the heroine seeks knowledge of her identity by pursuing a quest which has a mixture of picaresque and mythological aspects; she takes three lovers/mentors who die; she can convert energy for good or for evil; she has no need for mortal food or love; she is identified with an erupting volcano; she destroys her lovers, abandons her son; she wears veils to hide her whiteness in her aspect as the moon goddess; like her fish-serpent ancestresses, she bears her son "in a tent on the Snake's Road" (311). Although her real name Karrakaz is withheld from her son until the end of the first novel, she is known as Uastis, a form of Astarte. In the second and third novels, her son Vazkor, switched at birth with the dead son of a chieftain, also seeks knowledge of his birthright and parentage; on his quest, he gains the power to raise himself from the dead after he has been betrayed by the hag Lellih (Lilith?). At the later time, he commits incest with the goddess, now known as Ressaven, thinking her his sister, only to discover that she is actually his mother and his goddess Karrakaz. He admits that she is victorious over his father in a tribute worthy of the Great Goddess's victory songs over her sons/lovers as the son related how the original Vazkor subdued her:

Me, he put in her like a beast in a stall, both to chain her and to ensure his kingdom. When she would be a warrior he reduced her to a womb, and when she would be a lover he showed her she was a garment hung on the wall for his occasional wearing. Some women are such things, but not Karrakaz. He overreached himself with her...Thus, she killed him with Power, as sometime one with Power must have done, as I should have, I believe, if I had lived as his son and he had set such lashes on me... (312).

Disillusioned by his incest, Vazkor tries to flee his mother/lover's influence but the traditional symbols of her goddesshood follow him; he sees her in the sea waves, the moon, the silver bird, the spring waters; he becomes blind and impotent until he rejoins her where "the blue sky, the blue mountaintop behind her, the blue mantel about her that leaves bare her white girl's shoulders [becomes] the end of this chaos, the horizon of the wilderness, which open on another land" (316).

While the Great Goddess encompasses all stages of a man's life as father, lover, son, brother, husband, in all of these her autonomy demands that he be an expendable entity, a separate and distinct being from her emotionally. This separation is the one major difference between the isolated picara and the romance heroine who seeks the masculine to complement her own feminine so that, in marriage, the two become one entity. The picara, in contrast, is an integrated being already, albeit an incomplete one; she never finds her soul-mate because she is functioning as a completed individual who has incorporated the masculine side of her nature into herself in her autonomy. In this sense, the goddess *figura* is a good one because the goddess may need the male for ritual fertilization but she is quite capable of sacrificing a particular male to her greater need. Where the romance heroine depends on someone other than herself, the picara does not.

The sacrifice demanded by the Great Goddess often includes the picara's lovers as well as her sons because the two are often interchangeable: "she needs no husband, but she glories in lovers" (Lederer 119). Often lesser in strength than the female, characters like Ashley Wilkes are typical of the son/lovers of the Great Goddess, as Erich Neumann defines them: "'These flower-like boys are not sufficiently strong to resist and break the power of the Great Mother. They are more pets than lovers...victims, dying like adorable flowers...They have no individual existence, only a ritual one'" (Lederer 121). When Becky's husband Rawdon Crawley becomes an expatriate, he assumes the role of a victim, literally going to a hot outpost of Hades on an undisclosed island, significantly named Coventry, where "the climate's so infernal" the governors "don't enjoy it long" (579). While Rhett Butler seems to be the perfect "rogue scoundrel," he too becomes a victim, a "swarthy sodden stranger disintegrating before her eyes" (1004), the tired man "too old to shoulder the burden of constant lies that go with living in polite disillusionment" (1035). Here the novel picara begins a change; the hero is such a rogue scoundrel that he almost turns the novel from a true picaresque into a maudlin romance; Scarlett's final decision to return to Tara for consolation saves the novel from this fate. In contrast, Amber's lover Bruce Carlton is "unfaithful" to her because he returns to Virginia with a healthy and pregnant wife, only to be pursued by the resilient and persistent Amber. Even Charles II is as much the victim of the picara as he is of fate because he experiences the death of his beloved sister Henrietta Marie.

The victim/lover of a picara is not confined to novels. For example, Blanche DuBois in Tennessee Williams' *A Streetcar Named Desire* is such a picara who devours her children. Although she seems to lack the resiliency to survive (a common phenomenon of the modern literature), her attempt at integrity results in her obsession with the sexuality of her son/lover Stanley. Blanche's last name DuBois signifies her role as the Great Goddess of nature as she tries to retain the family estates of Bellevue (ironically the name of New York city's chief mental hospital). That Blanche maintains her virginal attitude despite a succession of lovers links her with the lunar aspects of the goddess *figura* in her fragile and changeable personality. But, because the modern Blanche is so entrenched in her autonomy, the violence of Stanley's phallic power apparently overcomes her frailer psyche and she succumbs to the role of the goddess of death in returning to the underground, escorted by her white-coated attendants. The picara's modern emanation flees to the madhouse, so that the patriarchal Stanley can fertilize a submissive wife Stella who belies her goddess name of Star Mother. Lilith has been replaced by Eve once again.

The repetition of sacrificial images in picaresque literature prove that the picara's autonomy will sacrifice anyone who stands in her way. In trying to secure the survival of her own mother/child *figura* archetype of Tara—the land— Scarlett embodies her Irish father's love for the land and matches her mother's resilient knowledge that the land—power, money, prestige—will suffice even if romantic love will not. Her original bonds with her own nurturing mother and her Mammy are built up on false assumptions and only when she realizes that Ellen died calling the name of her cousin Philippe and not Scarlett's father is Scarlett able to separate from her ideal mother fixation. In essence, Scarlett and her sisters have been "abandoned" and rejected by their mother; where Ellen is the Great Mother sacrificing herself for her children, Scarlett is the Terrible Mother, the Hecate, who sacrifices her children to preserve herself in the hellish cauldron of the Civil War, a fact stressed by the impact of the burning of Atlanta scenes in the movie. Scarlett repeatedly refers to the eleven people dependent upon her in a war-ravaged land as "parasites" and to Ashley as her "other child." In this, she returns to the configuration of the Earth Mother who will sacrifice some of her children to insure growth of others.

In her insistence on autonomy, the picara is restricted from her pursuit of personal survival by children and lovers and husbands; although children and lovers may be proof of her fecundity, they remain obstacles to her potentiality and must be removed. It can be argued that the early picara is not overly concerned with fecundity because her stories were written by men whose interest centered on the pleasure of the sexual act and not with its result—children. Like the Great Goddess, the early picara is a life-giver who destroys life through child-sacrifices and a death-dealer who restores life in her pursuit of new adventures. Her fecundity is lodged in her tales, not in her children.

When the Chinese say that women must "open the door" for the new generations, they are referring to the sons, not to the daughters. Since the girls who marry out of the family cannot be of later economic value as farmers or as sons who will ultimately take responsibility for aging parents, some cultures like the Chinese practice female infanticide. In the picaresque tales, however, since the heroine is a woman, infanticide and abortion are not stressed for two reasons. Induced abortion was a procedure unfamiliar to the male writers and the social code within the writer's society might be offended. For example, despite the fact that Margaret Mitchell and Kathleen Winsor wrote within ten years of each other, Mitchell's Scarlett of the 1860s never considers abortion while Winsor's Amber of the 1660s accepts it as a common practice. In a like manner, romantic and realistic literature employs the convenient miscarriage or spontaneous abortion as a guilt-free way of ridding the heroine of responsibility; the early picaresque tales seldom delve into such issues. If an infant brought to full term dies in these stories, it is usually through natural causes and not by an action of the picara.

Such social pressures are not unusual in literature; prior to the AIDS epidemic of the 1980s, the romance novels never concerned themselves unduly with protection against pregnancy; after 1980 or so, frank reference to the use of contraceptives was mandatory as a sign of social responsibility and personal health. Even though the early picara is the center of her tales, her feminine aspect of motherhood is never mentioned, save for her sexual peccadillos. This changes as the picara changes. If she is not barren, the early novel picara abandons or neglects her children; the later one emotionally neglects them; and the fantasy picara prevents them or distances herself from her children. Seldom is the early picara considered as a woman with a woman's physical problems for nowhere are the problems of menses, pregnancy, and abortion discussed. Even the issue of spontaneous abortion or miscarriage is seldom acknowledged while sexual initiation is stressed for its salacious quality. To get a grasp on sexuality and its implications for the picara, we must look at how the production of children through virginity, barrenness, contraception, miscarriages (induced and spontaneous) affects the picara.

Children

The picara, we have claimed, insists on autonomy over her body and its uses. Sometimes that autonomy is dependent upon the production of children. In desert societies, where a person's "whole commitment is to the society which is protecting you" (Campbell, *Power* 101), the women must bear sons to achieve autonomy. Thus, the persistence of barren women in Scriptures to be granted a son to relieve their "reproach among men" (Luke 1:25) is a form of autonomy achieved only through the birth of a son. When Hannah, the mother of Samuel, implores God so often that He "remembered" her and gives her a son, she gives the son back as a first-born offering. When Hagar, Sarah's handmaid pregnant with Abraham's first son Ishmael, is insolent to her mistress Sarah and she must flee to the desert, her autonomy is restored when she bargains with the Lord for her own way. Only when she is promised that her son will inherit land equal to that of his younger brother does she return. Later, when she runs into the desert with Ishmael, she asserts her autonomy again. Although Abraham and Sarah may have had daughters, the birth of a son is necessary to establish Sarah's autonomy; when the angelic visitors say she is to bear a son and she laughs, one suspects, for the first time because she has gained autonomy. In contrast, barrenness in the Scriptures was often reserved as a punishment for God's enemies. For example, when the Philistine king Ablimelech took Sarah as a concubine, God "tightly closed every womb in Ablimelech's household, on account of Abraham's wife Sarah (Gen. 20:18) until Ablimelech surrendered Sarah to her husband.

While the Scriptural picara pesters God until a son is guaranteed, the hint of child sacrifice lingers in the vestigial substitution of the lambs or doves to effect the "buying back" of the child from the Temple. At the circumcision of Christ, when Mary presents the Child to be "sacrificed" as the eldest son, the aged Simeon is balanced out by the aged prophetess Anna. She serves as a symbol for Israel whose barrenness is relieved by the virginal fecundity of Mary's producing the Messiah. Even her name "Anna" harkens back to the Great Goddess' title of "Inanna." The Scriptures also use unlikely pregnancies to further their religious ends. For example, the genealogy of Joseph in Matthew's Gospel includes four women whose actions breached the Israelite moral and sexual codes: Tamar posed as a temple prostitute to insure being impregnated by her father-in-law Judah; Ruth's marriage to Boaz was instigated by Naomi under the Levirite law; Bethsheba, the mother of Solomon, had an affair with David who had her husband killed; and Rahab, a non-Israelite tavern keeper and possibly a prostitute, saved the Israelite spies.

Each culture and each reader shapes his or her own perception of the picara's ever-changing form. The early Continental picara is an infertile womb because she never matures emotionally to accept responsibility for anyone's survival other than her own. In this way, she is either a juvenile delinquent, as Parker claims of the picaro, or an emanation of the love-goddess figura of the tripartite Great Goddess, dependinng upon how she is viewed and who is viewing her. Stuck in the masculine outward quest of the hero in her thirst for adventure, she never develops the feminine inward quest of awakening to responsibility in accepting motherhood. Her spiritual side is deadened. Unlike the picaro Simplicius who finds peace in the inward quest represented by his hermitage, the picara never makes peace with her spiritual side.

Autonomy always demands that she retain control of her body. Voluntary virginity is one way. The virgin has always had worth and power in society up until the Puritan times when her economic worth as a single worker was devalued along with the rest of women's work by mass industrialization practices. Smollett's Tabitha Bramble is cited as the first old maid because only in post-

Puritan times was a woman considered useless (Utter and Needham 221). While such critics claim that no primitive or feudal society ever found an extra woman useless, the *Fraufrenage* in Northern Europe found too many single women a drain on society's resources (Utter and Needham 224). When economic responsibility rather than social cooperation or duty devolved upon the individual, the picara came into her own. As an autonomous entrepreneur, she could dispense or hoard her worldly goods. While the picara feels no urge to be virginal, the social effect is the same; she does not produce children and is not bound by laws of inheritance since she has no heirs or children. The picaras in realistic fiction tend to have children to complicate the plot problems: Roxana and Moll bear nearly a dozen children apiece but retain none of them. Later novel picaras like Amber and Scarlett revert back to their societies' customs; Amber, set in Restoration culture, feels free to abort while Scarlett, set in the American antebellum South, does not.

However it is induced, barrenness can become a convenient literary convention to free the picara for further adventures. Even though she may not use her uterus, the picara avariciously retains it as a possession. In short, the early picara is kept barren so that she can go on the adventures suitable to a wandering rogue. Moll tries to plead her pregnancy to escape hanging; Roxana uses her children as a way of extracting money from men, but none of the picaras use pregnancy to force men to marry them. Marriage and children are, after all, the ultimate restraint upon a picara's autonomy. For novel picaras, such outward sterility often becomes the symbol of inward moral death, an inversion of the shame that Biblical women felt. Becky does not conceive another child after the birth of her son, despite her hinted-at sexual liaisons with Lord Steyne, because his syphilis has made him sterile and has possibly infected Becky. Amelia is, of course, rendered doubly barren by the Victorian code of celibacy and her devotion to her dead husband; once she marries Dobbin, she gives birth to a daughter Janey who, in her turn, becomes the blinding object of delight to her father's eye as Amelia's son and dead husband have blinded her to Dobbin's fidelity.

In fantasy, barrenness or the sacrifice of fecundity is sometimes chosen for higher purposes. The need for sterility may be complicated by the additional factors of age, profession, or physical ability or disability. Voluntary sterility, temporary or permanent, is a logical requirement of space travel where long periods of confinement make the bearing of children impractical. So also, population control may force some women to forego pregnancy, for example, those who inhabit single-sex communities or who lack access to men. Age is also a determinant; if the woman is immature, she cannot conceive; if she is too old, she may not be able to conceive. Genetics itself may prohibit conception; if the woman is of a mixed species, she may be mature enough for sexual pleasure, but not for conception and child-bearing. Sometimes inability to conceive is part of the altered state built into the physical makeup of the character. Clayton's Brann is deprived of virginity and potential motherhood when her hormonal system and aging mechanism are transformed by the Changer children's need. True sterility appears in computer-enhanced or bionic individuals like Jade Darcy and Heinlein's Friday; their altered bodies cannot conceive at all.

Professions sometimes dictate sterility: McIntyre's Snake is rendered sterile because the snake bites of her chosen profession have produced anti-bodies which attack sperm. Nevertheless, the entire book is a handbook on sexuality and genetics: Snake teaches the mayor's son how to control his fertility by regulating his body heat at the same time she tells him about a mechanical means to do so; she discovers the secret of breeding the elusive dreamsnakes while she is protecting her adopted daughter from their dangerous bites; she counsels the horsebreeders as to why her horse cannot be reproduced because he is a hybrid. Certain professions are aided by sterility as the result of an operation. In Bradley's creation of Camilla in the three books about the Free Amazons, a young girl who was to have been a Tower priestess is abducted, raped, and made to watch as her child is ripped from her womb and killed. She turns from her own psychic powers and from her femininity to have the dangerous operation which removes her reproductive organs and her breasts to make her an *emmasca* or a neutered woman; as such she undertakes the life of a soldier, journeyer, and Free Amazon to retain her autonomy. Because she is never bothered by pregnancy and its complications, Camilla's wandering military profession renders her truer to the original picara who was barren so that she might adventure.

Occasionally, the picara is infertile because of infrequent ovulation; Morris' Estri expects to produce only several eggs and, when she wastes one giving birth to her captor's child, she is furious and rejects the child as a monster. Involuntary insemination occurs frequently, especially in slave narratives like Charnas' Alldera where women are forced to bear the children of their captors. In Clayton's *Irsud*, Aleytys becomes an involuntary surrogate mother to the hostile egg which will kill her as it comes to birth. Vinge's *Snow Queen* Arienrhod engineers the birth of her own daughter by having twelve drugged surrogate mothers implanted with her parthenogenetically fertilized ova to assure the birth of a daughter (87). Ironically, she has been rendered sterile by the same waters of life which prevent her aging. Arienrhod is a polyandrous picara, with her series of willing young lovers, the Starbucks, one of whom is her daughter's beloved. As the ruler of the frozen waters, she is still a "Sea Mother incarnate, [because] she had as many lovers as the sea has islands" (25) but none of them can bring her to fruition.

Artificial barrenness induced by contraceptive means becomes more prevalent in certain genres. The historical novel will often cite arcane contraceptive beliefs to create the illusion of reality; in *Forever Amber*, the heroine cites a country recipe that pregnancy could be avoided "by spitting three times into the mouth of a frog or drinking sheep's urine" (72). In fantasy novels, which lean more toward science fiction and where the created worlds are technologically superior to this one, the base question is the picara's immediate survival. Joanna Russ has her heroine in "We Who Are About To..." comment that "before we start any babies, we'd better start finding out what we can eat around here" (55). Most times, contraception is achieved by an electronic implant, by an invasive procedure of a chemical injection, or by naturally developed control and understanding of the system of conception.

Most often contraception is taken care of by some chemical injection. In Bradley's *Thendara House* Magda admits that she had been given treatment "to suppress ovulation and menstruation; it is fairly routine for women in the field" (44). In Clayton's Terrilian series, the heroine is caught on the primitive planet of Rimilia when her contraceptive shot wears off and she becomes pregnant with her lover's child. Her solution is not to abort the child but to have the fetus removed and stored until it can be re-implanted at a later date. Three books intervene before she is able to think about retrieving the fetus. By the fifth and last book, *The Warrior Victorious*, she is imprisoned as a sex slave on a colony where the villains are trying to breed empaths Primes by forced concubinage of both male and female Primes. Hiding the fact that she is superior in empathetic ability to all of them, Terrilian is nevertheless forced to submit because of the mental "block" her enemies have implanted, a block which enables them to secure her compliance through pain. The villains insure conception by aphrodisiac injections which both increase her sexual need and reverse the contraceptive effect of the prior injection. Only when she realizes that the villains have destroyed her frozen fetus, she becomes the Terrible Mother and, in an untypical act of violence, annihilates them all.

Because the fantasy worlds are often imitations of feudal or medieval worlds, some contraceptive devices tend to be natural ones, i.e. derived from a natural source such as a berry or an herb. Green's Sofaltis of *Lady Blade, Lord Fighter* had drunk "Blue Juice" which prevents conception until another dose reverses the process. One of her lovers who wants to marry her and raise children promises to give her the "Blue Juice" himself. In a similar fashion, on John Norman's patriarchal alternate universe Gor, the slave girls (essentially the entire female population of Gor), are forced to drink "slave wine" to keep them sterile. Their traveling from lover to lover, master to master, imitates the picara's love of change and adventure, which would be hampered by pregnancy. Norman suggests in a rare interview that, while his male utopian books produce "scientific verisimilitude within, of course, artistic latitude [and] take seriously things like human biology and depth psychology" (21), they also raise "serious questions about the intellectual superstructure of western civilization" (21).

In contrast, most fantasy picaras control their contraceptive means. While Elizabeth A. Lynn's heroine in *The Sardonyx Net* is more caring than most picaras, she is still autonomous. Rhani practices birth-control by taking a contraceptive pill weekly and tests herself for pregnancy by an oral thermometer which turns orange instead of pink when she is pregnant. Because she and her clan have children late, usually limiting them to one or two to ease inheritance demands and usually "extending artificially the period of fertility" (297), she fits into the aging category of picara. While Rhani's ruthlessness in ruling a slave-owning planet is delegated to her sadist brother Zed, her insistence in caring for the needs of her planet over those of her lover, the star captain Dana, makes her picaresque. While she looks forward to mothering her child conceived by the slave star captain, Rhani needs no one because the child will mature at fourteen and be given a choice of worlds on which to live. The planet itself is her child and needs her care. Lynn's *Watchtower* of the Tornor trilogy also has the biological functions of reproduction handled as normal incidents. The women prevent conception by drinking teas; they menstruate, they use sponges for the blood, they bloat and cramp; they wash out "blood rags." Clayton's Tuli in *Moonscatter* fears that "now she'd started her menses the danger was far greater [than before]" (23).

Suzy McKee Charnas' futuristic dystopia of Holdfast in *Walk to the Ends of the World* embraces most stages of feminine picaresque progress—autonomy from slavery through community to individualism but denies sexual autonomy to the picara at its beginning. Conception has been limited to the breeding pens where the "fems" or women are brought to be bred so that "breeding was a matter entirely out of the control of fems, who came into estrus as time demanded" (188). Any intercourse undertaken outside of the pens is illegal and dangerous for the man because the possibility of his "being robbed of his soul by the femmish void (through the medium of her body), [was] a risk that men spoke of running if they fucked a fem outside of the breeding-rooms" (167). When the man refers to the possibility of conception as resulting from such intercourse in Swiftian terms, "you haven't made a cub off me, have you?", the question sounds to strange to Alldera's femmish ears since "if a man intended to breed, it was assured that he did so unless interfered with by femmish magic" (188). The comparison of Swift's "Modest Proposal" continues in Holdfast's plan to use "downbred fems" as "flavor" for the main food of the male since "you can't run a Reconquest on a bulk-food like grain, so you use throwback fems as meat" (234). Like the medieval woman before her, Alldera reiterates the belief in the *homonoculus* when she feels "hollow in body, which was fitting in one who was merely a receptacle for the use of men...a man's usage conferred existence" (187). More serious is her feeling "hollow in mind...that she could have a mission, a direction of her own...was an absurdity" (187). Her autonomy is useless in the society where "any fem drifted helplessly, waiting their [men's] actions and desires until one of them inadvertently authenticated her" (187).

However, the perceptions toward conception change in the sequel *Motherlines* when Alldera escapes Holdfast after the destruction of the city of 'Troi; as a swift runner, she finds autonomy in her mission to find the women outside of Holdfast. When Alldera discovers that she is pregnant, she "cursed the fetus for a rape-cub, unwanted seed of the masters whom she has escaped" (12). Her maternal instincts are the same as that of the earlier picara—her own survival and in particular her need for food to maintain her own existence take precedence. Thus, "hunger made her bold...but is was never enough; how could she make milk for a newborn cub...an efficient little parasite, stealing from her the nourishment of whatever she could find to eat" (12). Driven by need for her own survival, she "chewed on roots and leaves...and she hoped that one of these painful episodes would kill the cub so that she could expel it and better her own chances of survival" (13). Later, after the Riding Women find her and nurse her back to health, she practically abandons the child to the care of the feminine community which is set up to care for children; they notice "how little interest she showed in the child, Well it was their child." (88). Each of the "sharemothers" who claim kindred, albeit artificial kindred, to the child provides a breast for feeding the infant and provides constant care for her. The children run wild in a "child-pack" with no attempt to nurture them, although notice is taken of any child who has the compassion to bring an ill child to the attention of the adults: "that child was generally discovered to have exceptional qualities" (64). When the individual reaches the physical maturity of menstruation, she is cast out by the child-pack and "that is the end of the free life. There's no place to go but to the tents [of the sharemothers] and sure enough there they are, all waiting to make you into a proper woman with a name or a family" (65).

In a society where children are "cubs," mothers "dams," and heredity is arranged along "motherlines," the women beget their daughters by semen produced by the controlled penetration by stallions, a scene reminiscent of Minos' wife and the bull. Essentially antithetical to the "free fems" who long to recapture Holdfast as masters over the men, the Riding Women are autonomous individuals who earn their own livings by capturing and taming wild horses. Living in "Tents" each woman from a different motherline shares in the raising of each other's daughters. For example, Alldera's daughter (who was conceived through male rape and is considered unusual for that reason) is "shared" by Nenisi, a black woman, Shayeen, a "shining being of smooth, red-brown metal" (41), Sheel, "thin and yellowed-haired and blade-faced" (28), and Bavaran, a large red-faced woman. Few motherlines exist so that each woman looks like the progenitor of her lines; her looks are replicated at all ages and even the personalities are the same. But, over the centuries, the women have developed intricate systems of relationships which cross motherlines and which establish other causes for relationships: tentmates or raidmates, who are those who help each other survive raids on enemy camps or lovers who are by necessity female.

Alldera is an excellent example of a picara. Even among the Riding Women of the plains, Alldera is a stranger; among the free fems, she is a stranger because she is feared as the first fem to escape captivity in over twenty years. While she encourages that fear by her position as a "runner" or messenger and she teaches these skills to the women, she never feels at home, although her young daughter Sorrel fits into the Riding Women with no problem. Even the tugs of affection she feels for her rescuer Nenisi—affections close to that of a woman toward her mother—fail to obliterate the distance she feels to all these women in general. While she is a pleased that Sorrel has adapted so well, she recognizes that she "was a messenger, and a messenger should know the importance of words without being told" (272). Her wanderings are similar to the wanderings of the picara from lover to lover, society to society, always restless, always homeless, always the picara.

While the picara usually retains her autonomous control over her body by using contraceptives, controversial pregnancies seldom end in outright abortion. When abortion is considered, it is seldom carried out. When it is carried out, it serves more to characterize the heroine than to explain the customs of the times. Moll's midwife assures her that "she could help me off with my Burthen sooner, if I was willing; or in *English*, that she could give me something to miscarry...but I soon let her see that I abhorr'd the Thoughts of it" (169). Sometimes it condemns the heroine. Amber, for example, is fully a picara, interested only in her own survival yet attached to the children whom her first lover Bruce Carleton gives her. Any other children who are the result of other lovers or casual liaisons are merely nuisances who interrupt her lifestyle. She aborts them without consideration but, in doing, so she represents the entire Restoration concept of pleasure as self-serving. Early in the novel, when she is in the bawdy house of Mother Redcap, she meets Mrs. Fagg, the local abortionist whose remedy for unwanted pregnancy consists of "a long ride in a coach, to be taken with her own special medicine" (269). Throughout the novel, she makes use of the abortionist's services, usually when she is involved in her theatrical career and in her quest for social prestige with the court.

In general, most fantasy writers uphold a woman's right to determine her destiny but few have created characters who have abortions. Tuli in Clayton's *Moonscatter* is a young girl on her way to be a warrior who has been seduced and who does not want the child because she fears that her temper might hurt the child. After her motives are "read" by a psychic, she is given a foul-tasting liquid which brings on a spontaneous abortion. Perhaps the most controversial example of an unwanted pregnancy is in Bradley's Darkover series in *Darkover Landfall* where the scientist Camilla finds herself pregnant after an orgy induced by the alien plant where she is stranded with other colonists.

"...The Chief announced the contraceptive failure a couple of months ago, and I seem to have been one of its victims. It's just a case of putting in for an abortion."
Ewen whistled softly. "Sorry, Camilla," he said gently, "can't be done."
"But I'm *pregnant*!"
"So congratulations or something...Surely you know that in the Colonies abortions are performed only to save a life, or prevent the birth of a grossly defective child...A high birth rate is absolutely imperative for at least the first three generations..."
"...But you know as well as I that women with advanced scientific degrees are exempt—otherwise no woman with a career she valued would ever go out to the colonies. I'm going to fight this, Ewen. Damn you, I'm not going to accept forced childbearing. No woman is *forced* to have a child!" (111-2)

Her argument is a familiar one to the autonomous fantasy picara: individual survival depends on the modern equivalent of inheritance—a profession—and child-bearing would take time from that profession. Defending her stance that "perhaps individual conscience should take a second place to the good of the majority" (*Chain* v), Bradley has Camilla required to bear the child to increase the colony's population.

The reasons why authors shy away from explicit abortions are many. Careless or selfish disregard of human life is not characteristic of a heroine with whom the reader must identify; indeed, most fantasy heroines are tolerant of and extra-sensitive to all forms of life in their nature as sorceresses or empaths. And authors strive to find new ways to skirt the abortion problem by inventing clever ways of handling unwanted pregnancies. Karr's Frostflower and Thorn series begins with the warrior Thorn nauseous with pregnancy looking for a " 'borter in this stinking town" and complaining that exercise had not dislodged the fetus because "the grub was so stubborn" (1-2). When the child refuses to abort spontaneously, Thorn stumbles across the sorceress Frostflower who manipulates time so that the child is born in one afternoon. The remainder of the book concerns trying to get Frostflower and the child Starwind back safely to the other sorcerers. At no time in that book or in its sequel does Thorn show any maternal interest in the child whereas Frostflower risks her life repeatedly for him. Also, when Frostflower is subjected to the rape which should remove her magical powers, it is noted that she cannot become pregnant since she has just had her period and the likelihood of conception is slight.

While the nature of fantasy itself provides escape from such decisions with its unusual devices to prevent conception, fantasy also uses that conventional solution to problem pregnancies, the ubiquitous miscarriage beloved of romance novels. For example, when Bradley's Jaelle has a spontaneous miscarriage of her child, it saves her from breaking the code of the Free Amazons because she no longer loves the father of the child. In contrast, such problem pregnancies do not occur as frequently to a picara because a miscarriage does not result in a product; as a pragmatic economist, only the children who are born can survived to threaten their mothers with financial status. All others exist only in that untouchable realm of "female problems."

In the later novel picaras, however, the story is different. When any pregnancy occurs, it affects the plot structure and, therefore, the picara. For example, the penultimate scene where Scarlett tumbles down the stairs after a verbal fight with Rhett ends in the miscarriage of the only child Scarlett professes to want. Not realizing that the child is a result of his drunken attack on her, (the one time she had thought he showed his love for her), he accuses her of infidelity with Ashley. She taunts him with the thought that "I wish it was anybody's baby but yours!" His response, "Cheer up...maybe you'll have a miscarriage," precipitates her fall and her immediate miscarriage. *Forever Amber* can dwell on abortion, spontaneous and induced, because of its historical setting. In fact, the novel is as much the book of Charles II as it is of Amber St. Claire because Amber's affairs are paralleled, chapter by chapter, with the love affairs and confinements of Charles' lovers Frances Stewart, Barbara Palmer, and his wife Catherine. With each birth and each miscarriage, history and fiction shift. Winsor creates a fictional moment when Queen Catherine, Barbara, and Amber meet during the Dutch attack when Catherine overhears herself called the "barren Queen." "Amber had sudden pang of shame; she wondered if Catherine knew that she was pregnant at the moment, with his [Charles'] child" (559). Each miscarriage of Queen Catherine both sets the monarchy on its path toward the Glorious Revolution and contrasts with the fecundity of Charles' mistresses.

If abstinence, contraception, and abortion fail, what does the picara do with the children she bears? The early picara bore no children so she could go adventuring. Few of the Continental picaras have children: Celestina, Justina, and Courage do not. (Those two sons and daughters of the tragic Mother Courage are Brechtian additions.) In fact, Courage brags about her sterility when she tricks Simplicimus into believing that the child left on his doorstep is hers and his. The later picara, however, is a true daughter of her economic system. She abandons the sense of tribal wealth as being in its children and adheres to the modern concept that material wealth replaces progeny as the means of survival. Just as the picara deviates from the norm in her avarice, so also does she see material wealth rather than children as the major source of security.

Although Roxana has a large number of children—ten or twelve—she is still in the picaresque tradition since she is separated from them the majority of their lives and does not concern herself unduly with their survival. In fact, her isolation from them strengthens her ties with the Continental picara since she rationalizes that she may be contributing to their delinquency. "I was terrible frighted at the Apprehensions of my Children being brought to Misery and distress, as those must be who have no Friends but are left to Parish Benevolence" (25).

Moll is the prime example of parish benevolence. Abandoned by her mother, who had pleaded pregnancy before being transported to Virginia for theft, Moll is turned over to a vague relative who gives her to the gypsies. At three, her natural repugnance at the gypsies' irregular life encourages her to have the parish officials of Colchester to accept her care "as much as if I had been born in the Place" (9). In placing her in Colchester, Defoe may have been alluding to two common beliefs about Colchester and children. If Colchester was the city of old King Cole of the nursery rhyme, then the king's calling for his "pipe and bowl" and for "his fiddlers three" are indications of his concern with his food, his wealth, and his merriment. The second allusion is that King Cole's alleged daughter, Empress Helena, became the wife of the soldier Constan and mother of the Emperor Constantine before she sought and found the True Cross.

With Moll, Defoe raises the expense of child-bearing into a sharp business deal. When the midwife proffers three different prices sheets ranging from thirteen pounds to fifty-three pounds, Moll can choose which one best suits her need; if the child dies, "the Minister's Article [is] saved; and if you have not Friends to come to you, you may save the Expence of a Supper" (166). Moll is "wonderfully pleas'd and satisfy'd" (167) with the arrangements whereas Amber is furious at being presented with a bill at all, a bill which Winsor compiles from Moll's three bills: "For these expense Mother Red-Cap had mentioned were not ones she had ever expected to pay. She felt that she had been cheated, and it made her angry" (151). In addition, Moll is made privy to the baby-farming practices: her midwife "has several sorts of Practise...that, if a Child was born, tho' not in her House,...she has People at Hand, who for a peice [sic] of Money would take the Child off their Hands, and off from the Hands of the Parish too" (168). Although she is assured by the midwife that the children are not "abus'd, starv'd, and neglected by the Nurses that bred them up" (168), Moll still is wary of the plan perhaps because of her own sorry start in life. While Moll's disposition of her children seems as careless as her mother's, such abandonment provides Defoe with several plot devices; namely, the incestuous relationship Moll experiences when she marries her own brother and her reconciliation with her mother in Virginia.

So also do Roxana's children provide additional plot devices for Defoe. Roxana's withdrawal from her remaining children of her brewer husband occurs when Roxana sends Amy to restore them to a higher rank in life. However, the picara's innate caution prevents Roxana from revealing herself; her fear is justified when Susan, her daughter and namesake, discovers that Roxana is her mother. Roxana has also estranged herself from her illegitimate children for fear that they would repudiate their mother: "If the Children are virtuous they doe their Mother the Justice to hate her for it [illegitimacy]; if they are wicked they give her the Mortification of doing the like, and giving her the Example" (152). Roxana also realizes that an irregular life is not conducive to the upbringing of children: "If she has any Children the Endeavor is to get rid of them, and not to maintain them; and if she lives, she is certain to see them all hate her, and be asham'd of her" (132). With the birth of each illegitimate child, Roxana regrets the drain on her economic resources which she must prevent by assuring the livelihood of each child before its birth. The concern here is not with the drain on her physical resources—indeed, she survives eleven childbirths remarkable well. Nevertheless, while she does not consider abortion as an alternative, she does express a desire to be relieved of the responsibility of bearing and raising the child.

I was brought to Bed very well...but the Child died at about six weeks old, so all that Work was to do over again, that is to say that Charge, the Expence, the Travel, etc...I brought him another Son...but it liv'd not above two Months; nor after the first Touches of Affection which are usual, I believe, to all Mothers were over, was I sorry that Child did not live, the necessary Difficulties attending it in our travelling, being considered...I wou'd willingly have given Ten Thousand Pounds of my Money to have been rid of the Burthen I had in my Belly (49, 104, 163).

Notice that the final state she reaches is that she is willing to surrender her precious money to be rid of the child as Moll was.

At the base of each discussion is the picara's genuine dislike of children. Some state it more forcibly than others but every picara can trace this hatred back to the disinterest of the Great Goddess in her offspring; in the later picara, the disinterest changes to child neglect while the fantasy picara are ambivalent about children because they do not want to surrender autonomy to raise the child yet they do not willingly abandon the child or abort it. The laments that Moll or Roxana make in leaving their children do not ring true. Becky's approach is at least honest; in using young Rawdon as a convenient tool in her disguise as a concerned mother, she is a prototype of the neglectful mother whose child's welfare is low priority.

By the time that the novel heroines emerge, there is only a vestigial sign of child abandonment which, in today's terms, would be called emotional neglect. Becky's consistent rejection of her son is pivotal in the novel because it contrasts so strongly with Amelia's over-protectiveness of her Georgie and with the mad son of Lord Steyne, that "brilliant dandy diplomatist...dragging about a child's toy, or nursing the keeper's baby's doll" (495). Thackeray limits both women to one son (and a daughter for Amelia) rather than burdening each with a number of children that Defoe's picaras seem to have. Becky's literary daughters, Amber and Scarlett, differ. Amber is a softer mother than Scarlett or Becky; she provides some affection for her children by insisting that they accompany her. Only when she wants to be alone with their father does she banish them to the care of governesses or nurses.

Scarlett however neglects her children's development while providing for their physical welfare. To her, the oldest child, Wade, is a "spiritless little creature," (957) who "squirmed and twisted his feet in embarrassment" (956) when she tries to talk to him. Like Becky's young Rawdon, Wade is easily forgotten by his mother and made much of by his stepfather, Rhett, and his other relatives. Like Amelia's doting on her only son Georgie, Melanie centers her life around her one son named Beau but, unlike Amelia who is a foolish mother, Melanie becomes mother to everyone; she defends Rhett, babies Ashley, protects Belle, nurses the sick, rehabilitates criminals, raises Scarlett's children without prejudicing them against their mother. On the other hand, Scarlett never pretends that she likes children. When she is pregnant with her second child, Ella, Rhett taunts her about her hatred of children, insisting that he likes babies. "Aren't you proud to be having a child?" he asks. Her reply is decisive: "I hate babies...anybody's baby" (683); her description of her daughter Ella by Frank is equally decisive—a "small bald-headed mite, ugly as a hairless monkey" (745) whose birth conflicts with Scarlett's business at the mill. She admits that "during the babyhood of each child she had been too busy, too worried with money matters, too sharp and easily vexed, to win either their confidence or affection" (956). When her third child, Bonnie, Rhett's beloved child, is killed in a riding accident, as Scarlett's father had been, Scarlett is unable to reach Rhett in his sorrow; only Melanie can.

Sexuality

While the picara must occasionally worry about pregnancies, she never worries about sex. She sees it as a natural function and enjoys it for what it is—a means to obtain money and a pleasure for which men are willing to pay. The early picaras bemoan the loss of salvation which sexual excesses may have deprived them of but they seldom deny its pleasure. Critics have long noted this double standard of the picara who protests her repentance while retaining the joys of her sexual excesses. Courage admits that it is only when "the gay times of her youth [when] her sauciness and wantonness have subsided" (89) that she looks to amend her life. Celestina convinces Parmeno that "love's invincible. It sweeps everything before it...Love is a sovereign delight" (43).

Only Puritanism found sexuality revolting and the development of the novel during those times reinforces this mystique, such as in Richardson's *Clarissa Harlowe* where death was a penalty for the innocent Clarissa and her seducer Lovelace. In this role, Clarissa assumes that mask of the death goddess when she designs her own funeral, shrouds herself in bridal white, selects the lily with its head broken off for her tombstone, haunts her letter-writing friends. In contrast, the woman denied sex can be equally devastated. In Dickens' *Great Expectations*, Miss Havisham is a death-in-life figure, seeking her vengeance, rather like Courage did, upon the man and mankind who deceived her. She has an adopted daughter in Estelle for whom she is the bawd; she has a son/lover in Pip; she accrues money and dirt; she is connected with food in the scene with her moldering wedding cake; she is "disguised" as a jilted Cinderella in her tattered gown and missing shoe. The perception of the picara's ever-changing form by nineteenth century child-lover pits the women who is not interested in children against Dickens' overly motherly figures of Esther Summerson in *Bleak House*.

While the fantasy picaras have few sexual prohibitions, all forms of sexuality and sexual excess are suggested in the picara's tale at some point. Sexual slavery does not appear until the modern picara expanded from erotica into a fairly narrow sub-genre of fantasy bordering on soft-core pornography. Since the word, pornography comes from the Greek word for harlot "*pornoi*," it is not hard to see the connection between the two ideas. A literature where autonomy is denied must border on fantasy and then it is limited to such works as Sharon Green's Diana Santee series and Terrilian series. Starting with John Norman's alternate world series of Gor, Green uses female slavery as an ironic comment on the independent woman whose autonomy is stolen by her being enslaved for sexual purposes. For example, Terrilian, a Prime Empath, is sent by her galactic secret service employers to a primitive planet where she must be disguised and banded as a woman slave to the barbarian leader she is supposed to help. Although her autonomy is compromised many times, she continues in her disobedience and is punished throughout five books until she discovers that the barbarian is a latent empath whose messages have been intensifying her empathy. Her slavery does not sit well on her; her autonomy is restored only by an increase in her control over her empathetic powers; her happiness is gained only when she and her barbarian lover are acknowledged as equal in all things, save physical strength.

Sexual slavery provides sexual adventures for the picara. In fantasy, the humbling of the picara to a sexual object effectively removes her autonomy for the moment but the nature of fantasy acts against this condition for very long and the picara's acceptance of sexual slavery is always tongue-in-cheek and temporary. She may pretend to be a sexual slave but she never accedes to it with any conviction. As a deceiver, the picara is used to masking her emotions; as a slaver, her autonomy must be hidden if she is to survive. Often the cardinal sins of pride and avarice appear to threaten her; the slave must be humbled, she can own nothing, and her autonomy must be limited until she learns obedience and trust. Her slavery is well pitted against her autonomy, just as the self-induced slavery of marriage is pitted against the autonomy of a single life. This balancing of autonomy and obedience occurs in other literature. For example, Chaucer balances his Wyf of Bath's knight granting of sovereignty to his hag-wife with his Clerk's Tale of patient Griselda and her faithful obedience. The interaction of these two extremes results in a balance of sorts of which the fantasy writers express as the Jungian balance of the integrated personality.

Since Teresias' time, people have asked who gains the most pleasure from intercourse. Despite her pious complaints to the contrary, the picara considers sexual activity as a natural function, one that she is good at and one which insures her survival. Since the picara is often outside the law, she is equally outside the bonds of marriage, although she never suffers from what Greenberg terms as "sexual anesthesia" (378). Indeed, the suspicion is that she receives as much pleasure as she gives, a pleasure doubled because she receives money for it. Nowhere in the early picara is there a suspicion of homosexuality because any connection between homosexuality and prostitution is a later development. Although social acceptance or tolerance of homosexuality fluctuates throughout history from acceptance to ostracism, most historians see that the increase in the growth of the complexity of town life forced the emergence of subcultures which identified themselves as homosexual. Where a single-sex milieu existed— the military, aboard ships, boarding schools—homosexuality became accepted if not desired. The death of the feudal society and the development of towns with its subcultures encouraged both homosexuality and the emergence of the picaro and the picara.

Often society's moral structure against male homosexuality considered the waste of male semen as a financial loss as well as the loss of new generation. So serious was this fear that Renaissance Venice hired prostitutes to lure young men from homosexual practices to heterosexual ones. Even linguistics substantiates this cultural fear. In England, the male counterparts of houses of prostitution were called molly-houses from the slang word for prostitute, a moll, which has come down to us as a generic term for a gangster's woman. Whereas earlier homosexual practices had not necessarily involved cross-dressing or transvestitism, the new sub-culture stressed effeminacy as primary in male homosexuality. For example, the subject of one of Defoe's criminal autobiographies Jonathan Wild attended a party at one where he saw "He-Whores...rigg'd in Gowns, Petticoats, Head cloths, fine lac'd Shoes, Furbelow Scarves, and Masks...tickling and feeling each other, as if they were a mixture of wanton Males and Females" (Greenberg 333).

Lesbianism had no such difficulty. Through the ages, according to Greenberg, lesbianism has been discounted and made less severe in penalty because it did not include penetration or the waste of semen. In days when the woman's womb was a receptacle only and contributed nothing to the making of a child, when the male implanted the entire *homonoculus* in a woman, then the sexual relations between women could do no harm. Women's lives were so private in so many cultures that their irregular sexual relations could not harm or change society because no children could result from such a union. The male prerogative of paternity was safe; the picara's autonomy was also safe.

In the early picaras, sexuality is limited to male-female relationships. Only in the background of the picaras can one see any "abnormal" tendencies. Courage is totally a woman dealing with the doubly harsh world of men and war. As Gilman contends, the three "central dualites underlined by medieval critics of Terence: rich against poor...old against young; and men against women" set up the opposition of Celestina as the "poor old woman" to Calisto's "rich young man...and that they meet each other as such is always taken into account" (58). Celestina does not hint at any abnormal relationships with her prostitutes nor with Melibea, nor does Courage suggest anything irregular in her relationship with her nurse. Only when the novel picara develops a dependence upon another woman as a friend, such Zola's Nana and Satin exhibit, does the hint of lesbianism appear. Where two women living together became an extension of boarding school practices where two in one bed was the norm, such practice became known as the "New England" or "Boston" marriage. For example, the lifestyles of Eleanor Butler and Sarah Ponsonby, two Irish aristocrats who eschewed marriage and lived with each other in Wales, became so famous that London itself was known as the center of lesbian activities with the suspicion of upper class lesbian clubs abounding. While so prominent a social doyenne as Hester Thrale inveighs against lesbianism, there is no record of any actual house of prostitution set up for women, either with male or female prostitutes. This lack of sub-culture prevented women from sampling or modelling lesbian prostitution for many reason: lack of money, lack of autonomy, lack of privacy, lack of "clubs."

Yet single sex activities have always existed. In the early classical times, for example, the original Olympics were not only performed in the honor of the goddesses but were also intended for female athletes alone. In professions like the military, women tried to emulate the male; in literature, however, the history of lesbianism has centered on two areas: the bawd-prostitute relationship and the male impersonators which includes Amazons and warriors as well as those fictional and actual women who chose to live as men.

It is in the woman who posed as a man to go to war that we must find one origin of the masculine aspect of the picara. While tomboyism is the first indication, it is a comparatively modern step, often shown by the girl's inordinate love of horses and the outdoors. Courage admits to it and even as lady-like a deceiver as Scarlett starts out as a tomboy. Fantasy authors use the same device: Bradley's Romily in *Hawkmistress* prefers her hawks to her needlepoint; so does Tuli in Clayton's *Moonscatter*. The sex of Lynn's *ghya* heroines is often indistinguishable as they present a warrior/messenger image. But it is the presence of war that first forces women into their male disguise.

Sixteenth century Continental sources begin to tell of women who left home, disguised themselves as men, found employment, and married women. Eventually their true sex was discovered and they, but not their gender-normal spouses, were executed. They called the women tribades, a term derived from the Greek verb *tribein*, "to rub," and carrying the connotations of masculinity. (Greenberg 373-4)

Often authors attributed tribadism to enlarged clitorises but later science proved that most lesbians were physically normal. However, the mannish lesbian image persisted in reality in such women as George Sand and Rosa Bonheur and in literature in Theophile Gautier's novel (1835) *Mademoiselle de Maupin* which was based on the opera singer Mme. Madeleine d'Aubigny.

Greenberg points out that *Gulliver's Travels* refers to "those unnatural Appetites in both Sexes, so common among us" (331). He cites in a November 1746 issue of *Gentlemen's Magazine* the story of Mary Hamilton "who had married fourteen wives in succession" and that one of them declared "that she had lived for three months with the defendant, 'during which time she thought the prisoner was a man, owing to the prisoner's vile and deceitful practices.' In addition to seducing women while disguised as a man, Hamilton picked up soldiers at the theater while dressed as a woman" (331). While this was an isolated instance in the legal records, it probably was not an isolated instance.

Although Greenberg cites John Cleland's *Fanny Hill* as taking "whorehouse lesbianism for granted" (331), it is only in recent years that the connection between lesbianism and the bawd-prostitute relationship has emerged. Greenwald and Krich in speaking of Cleland's *Fanny Hill* note that

it is fascinating too that he sees clearly the connection between homosexuality and prostitution which is so common this day that many analysts of prostitution believe that it is the homosexuality alone, pure and simple, which drives women to choose prostitution as an occupation. (17).

The picara would not agree with this. While her appetites for money and sex are insatiable, she is too independent to form a lasting relationship with anyone, male or female. Homosexuality does not appeal to her any more than marriage does because both demand emotional and financial commitment. Her confidante, however, may show such loyalty that the picara feels obliged to return the feeling, if not the full value.

For example, Roxana's ambivalent attitude in the scene where she entices the jeweler to ravish Amy emphasizes her close symbiotic relationship with her confidante. They are the same person in many ways, so much so that Amy identifies with Roxana so intently that she offers to "starve for your sake, I will be Whore, or anything, for your sake, why I would die if I were put to it" (28). Amy's reasoning against Roxana's conscience lets her offer to bed the Landlord herself if it will make Roxana's life any easier; she matches Roxana's promiscuity when she cuts short her own lower stairs liaison with the French Prince's gentlemen, commenting that it "ammounted to more than this, *like* Mistress, *like* Maid" (83).

What critics find offensive in the jeweler scene are the voyeuristic aspects yet it is those overtones of homosexuality and voyeuristic depravity in Roxana's reasoning process which ring true in the light of modern psychology.

With that, I sat her down, pull'd off her Stockings and shoes, and all her Cloaths, Piece by Piece, and led her to the Bed to him...and at last, when she see I was in earnest, she let me do what I wou'd; so I fairly stript her, and then I threw open the Bed and thrust her in.

. . .

Had I look'd upon myself as a Wife, you cannot suppose I would have been willing to have let my Husband lye with my Maid, much less, before my Face, for I stood-by all the while; but as I thought myself a Whore, I cannot say but that is was something design'd in my Thoughts, that my Maid should be a Whore too, and should not reproach me with it. (46-7)

The novel picaras imply homosexuality only in the background of the heroine. Scarlett becomes the son that her father never had. Like most picaras she found the "road to ladyhood hard" and grew up favoring boys and could "climb a tree or throw a rock as well as any if them" (58). Her mind was a reasoning one: her approach to men was "demure, pliable and scatterbrained" because such an approach worked on men's minds "like a mathematical formula [and] mathematics was the one subject that had come easy to Scarlett" (60). After the burning of Atlanta, Scarlett becomes the man of the family, the single autocrat to whom everyone must answer. Her financial activities border on the masculine; she uses slave labor in her lumber camp; she buys and runs a saloon; she becomes a hard-nosed business person, denying her feminine compassion to insure her household's success.

Neither Becky nor Amber show any sign of even liking another woman; they are scornful of women for their sentimental weaknesses. When Becky decries Amelia's over-sentiment, she also dislikes Lady Jane Pitt's genuine caring. As a user of people, Becky finds that she cannot manipulate many women and so disregards them. Amber does the same; she flatters the queen but insults Barbara Palmer and the other mistresses of Charles; she fights the actress Beck Marshall but uses her as a means to an end. The limit to the novel picaras' interest in homosexuality lies in their occasional wearing of breeches.

The fantasy picaras differ. Homosexual instances most often occur in the picara when she is in her warrior mode; Bradley's warrior women Zadieyek and Camilla are bisexual. Protectiveness which the warriors see as weakness often impels them to care for the physically weaker heroines. Thorn feels protective but not sexually attracted to Frostflower; she has heterosexual relations with several men during the two books but mentions some women warriors who are her lovers. Often the homosexual element is relegated to a secondary character to stress some character flaw; the more flamboyantly homosexual Free Amazons in Bradley's Darkover series are condemned for their juvenile excesses the same as some heterosexual characters are condemned for their excesses.

Some authors skirt the lesbian issue by not being explicit. Green's Jalav has been bred as an Amazon and can consider no other way of life; she is scornful of all sex which requires a commitment. Like the Amazons of old, mating to produce children is done at orgies but pleasure is taken from slave men whenever the woman warrior wants it. Jalav has a pleasure slave who becomes a nuisance; her society assumes that men are sexual objects to be used and discarded. When her warriors capture an attractive man, they force-feed him an aphrodisiac drug to increase his stamina before they rape him. To Jalav, pleasure is a natural event but not the prime directive of her life; too much pleasure can weaken a warrior's will and any pleasure she gets from heterosexual intercourse is fleeting. Nor is she lesbian. Rather, although constantly in the presence of her Amazon warriors, the relationship between them is one of sisters dedicated to a cause. Her primary duty is to her goddess Mida; she scorns anything which detracts from that.

In part, the bisexuality has its root in failed parental relationships. In the novel picaras, the role of the father as a moral and economic guide and protector is as insufficient as the role of mother. Whereas the picara has a substitute mother in her confidante, she either lacks a paternal guidance or she rebels against paternal authority. In each case, the father's authority forces the picara into autonomy. Described as an astute businessman who emigrated from France to make his fortune in London, Roxana's father arranges what he thinks to be a good marriage for her, securing her future to the best advantage. That Roxana's first husband turns out to be an improvident businessman who runs through her dowry is beyond the father's care. Becky's father is also French, although more of a rogue and con artist than a businessman; his inheritance is Becky's sly disposition and cleverness. Scarlett's father, Gerald O'Hara, who assures her that land is the only lasting value precipitates Scarlett's autonomy by his insanity after Ellen's death. Amber's father is also French, at least in his name, and does not know that he has a child. Each of the men are foreign to their cultures and each bears a daughter who rebels against the culture. In fantasy, fathers are elusive as befits the father of a hero. Morris' Estri's is a demi-god; Green's Jalav's father is revealed as a demi-god. Tepper's *The Gate to Women's Country* has a superior breed of compassionate men who donate their sperm to unknowing women while Sargent's heroine's father in *The Shore of Women* is some nameless man outside the wall and Charnas' Alldera's father is some unknown captor.

If her father figure is missing, the picara is constantly amazed that her lovers like her children more than she does. Like Dobbin's affection for Amelia's child and like Rhett's affection for Scarlett's children, Bruce Carlton's affection for his children by Amber exceeds her own. Although he admits that her son loves Amber he wants to take the young Bruce to Virginia where "he will never have to endure the humiliations of an unacknowledged bastard" (561). Since few heroines in fantasy have children, the relationship between father and child is not stressed. Clayton's Aleytys's son is raised by her lover, Morris' Estri's child is raised by his father.

Thus, the colors of her sexuality and her children are always muted in favor of the sharper white of her autonomy. The picara allows nothing to stand in the way of her survival, not even her children.

Chapter Six
Marriage and Prostitution

As the ribbed effect of the warp is somewhat obscured in the area of the darker hatchings, it is made more noticeable in the areas of high light, which appear in consequence to come forward in the picture. The combined effect of these contrasts created in the perfected medieval tapestries a remarkable illusion of great depth of form and richness of texture. (Rhodes 52)

In any consideration of the picara's attributes, the contrast between the stigmatizing yellow veil of her prostitution and the marbled greys of her marriage provides the "remarkable illusion of great depth" and rich texture in her design. This chapter will detail the picara's sexuality as it appears in her marriage and prostitution.

Marriage

"I knew no State of Matrimony, but what was, at best, a State of Inferiority, if not of Bondage," Roxana protests, preferring her "Life of absolute Liberty now, [where she] was free as I was born, and having a plentiful Fortune, I did not understand what Coherence the words *Honour* and *Obey* had with the Liberty of a *Free Woman*" (171). The picara's autonomy and marriage are not comfortable bed-fellows. The early picaras like Celestina are not married. Justina retires from picaresque adventures upon her marriage and Courage might as well not be married the way she collects husbands, loses them to war, or discards them. Long Meg provides an exception to this rule; Meg gives sovereignty to her husband in matters of marital obedience when she refuses to battle with him, although in matters of business, she retains autonomy.

While moral strictures might not have hampered Roxana, the legal implications of marriage make her re-evaluate her position. When she enters a marriage, she wants to be sure that it is a legitimate and legal one. When in her liaison with the jeweler, Roxana cannot enter into a legal marriage, she reluctantly accepts a pseudo-marriage, urged by Amy's protest:

'he calls you Widow, and such, indeed you are: for as my Master has left you so many Years, he is dead to be sure; at least, he is dead to you; He is no Husband, you are, and ought to be free to marry who you will; and his Wife being gone from him, and refuses to lye with him then he is a single Man again, as much as ever; and tho' you cannot bring the Laws of the Land to join you together, yet one refusing to do the Office of Wife and the other of a Husband, you may certainly take one another fairly.' (36-7)

Just as the marriage of the picaro fails to provide emotional or economic security, so also marriage of the picara does not provide security. Just as the picaros like Lazarillo, Colonel Jacques, and Simplicimus warn men from marrying whores, Roxana warns her reader to avoid her mistake of marrying her first husband whose only noticeable feature is that he was a "Handsome man, and a good Sportsman...and danc'd well" (7). The picara consistently turns so strongly from established marriage when she finds that it restricts her autonomy that Roxana has "no Inclination to be a Wife again [because] I had such bad Luck with the first husband, I hated the Thoughts of it" (132). Marrying beneath one's station is to be feared almost as much as entering into an unprofitable marriage. Courage quibbles about lowering herself to marry a mere musketeer after having been the captain's wife; Roxana hesitates between choosing the offer of the Prince or the Dutch merchant, rejecting the latter because he is a threat to her autonomy. Her picaresque autonomy asserts her economic individualism when she declares that "I thought a Woman was a free Agent, as well as a Man, and was born free, and cou'd she manage herself suitably, might enjoy that liberty to as much Purpose as the Men do" (147).

When her attempts at marriage fail to assure her of security, the picara is forced to choose between the alternatives left open to a woman unprotected by conventional marriage. The unmarried woman in early societies was welcomed as an extra set of hands in the household because she contributed to the extended family. As every picara endures an inferior position in society as a woman and as an unmarried woman, her temporary occupation as a servant assures her autonomy. The Columbina is a lady's maid; Long Meg is a tavern maid; Courage refers to herself as the "beautiful cook or maid servant whom mine host keeps in the loft to attract money guests" (115); Amber is first seen inviting travelers to her uncle's tavern. Even Roxana sees herself becoming an *"Upper-Servant"* on marriage (148), although the idea of being servant to a man is so repugnant that she openly declares herself a "full Agent" (147) in the conduct of her life, explicitly stating that "the very Nature of the Marriage-Contract was, in short, nothing but giving up Liberty, Estate, Authority, and every-thing to the Man, and the Woman was indeed, a meer Woman ever after, that is to say a Slave" (148).

The marriage of the novel picara also diminishes and restricts her. Scarlett's marriage lessens her ability to "wander" or flirt with lovers; she is trapped by society into mourning her young husband when she should be acquiring another one; her protests over wearing the black widow's weeds to the party when she craves the bright colors serve as a strong symbol of her unrest. The wings of her autonomy are further clipped when her second husband Frank denies her the use of the carriage when she becomes too assertive in her business dealings. So also when Amber marries the stodgy Puritan Samuel Dangerfield, it is "her last chance to take the world by its ears and climb on top" (280).

While entering a convent was another way for an unmarried woman to preserve her autonomy, it is never an option for the picara who values her freedom and her sexuality. Where the saints' tales held virginity as a cherished virtue, virginity, celibacy, and chastity are not much valued in later literatures: Hermia in *Midsummer Night's Dream* is warned against the cold unproductivity of the virginal life while Isabelle in *Measure for Measure* and Margaret in Greene's

Friar Bacon and Friar Bungay abandon their convents at the first sign of a valid marriage. Convents might provide refuge for some women but never for a picara who, while she remains essentially an unmarried woman, has too much zest to be considered an "old maid." While the archetype of the old maid can be traced back to England's awareness of Elizabeth's status as the virgin queen, Utter and Needham claim that the old maid is a social type which arose as a result of the Puritan economic concerns.

In all societies, the danger of the unmarried woman was that her intelligence might be mistaken for magic and that her presence as a chaperon might be a cover for her role as a bawd. Although the only security that the unmarried woman had was her fortune or her wits, the real danger of the unmarried woman was in her threat to a patriarchal capitalistic society where she represented a drag on the market. While Defoe recognized the economic and social plight of the unmarried woman in his essays on the old maid, he also links the lack of secure marriage with eventual prostitution. For example, in one essay "Satire on Censorious Old Maids" (*Applebee's Journal*, March 23, 1723), he has his Tea Table Court of vicious old maids pass judgment on a four-year-old girl whom they compare to Moll Cutpurse, "a very comely Jade" and who will be a "W----e, or it must be because no body will ask her the question." He projects three reasons for a woman's not marrying in another issue of the same journal:

[first] those who either by Religious vows, or by other private Engagement; by Choice, or Necessity, remain Single and unwed...[second] other humbled by South Seas adventures are sunk below the views they had...and will not...be Fettered to the Scoundrels...for the mere Satisfaction of being married...[third] being difficult and hard to be pleased, had rather live as they are, than Marry where they cannot Love; that is, in a Word, had rather be completely happy in the dear Enjoyment of themselves, than completely Miserable in the Bondage and Chains of unsuitable Matrimony, which without Doubt, is the worst condition in the world. (April 13, 1723)

In fantasy, marriage is not a popular institution either. Marriage and children restrict adventures and the heroine's marital fidelity is replaced by fidelity to her self-image or to a larger entity like the universe. Love, passion, and sexuality are not banished from the fantasy but often duty or a higher calling obliterates human marriage. Like the hero, the fantasy heroine follows her quest and abandons the laws and strictures of her world. In the primitive fantasy world, a marriage is arranged more for familial or social reasons rather than for romantic ones; for example, in Bradley's Darkover series, the ruling families marry to increase economic power and insure inheritance rights. Morris' Cruiser series has a political marriage turning into a real one, although the heroine Shebat is more married to her cruiser than she is to her husband. Often the marriage for political reasons hampers or encourages the fantasy heroine who must surrender her autonomy for the common good; the picara never does. Yolen's Jenna refuses to marry a man she does not love, even though it means denying her heritage as the Anna; she marries the right man later and lives with him sporadically for fifty years. (Jenna also has a mystical dark sister who is jealous of her husband's love. When Jenna is allowed to take only one of them with her into the afterlife, the author allows two endings—the tale told by the man has Jenna leave her husband behind while the tale told by the women has her take him with her, a tidy restatement of the Jungian triad.)

Since the nature of the picara is to be emotionally unstable, she never wastes time on unproductive relationships. What is characteristic is that her sexual encounters are based more on mutual pleasure than on long-lasting commitment. The picara's traveling from lover to lover turns into either polyandry or into serial lovers such as Green's Jalav and Terrilian have. Clayton's Skeen is affectionate to her lover Tibo but equally ready to kill him when she suspects he has stolen her spaceship. Her Brann is fond of her various lovers but equally glad to be rid of them. Karr's Thorn can't wait to leave her occasional lover Spendwell to return to her duties as a warrior while Frostflower rejects marriage to retain her powers. Often such marriages are turned into group marriages or loosely structured relationships based on affection and proximity rather than passion. While her first group marriage for Heinlein's Friday does not work out because of prejudice against computer-enhanced artificial persons, her second one is a success, perhaps because it is in a pioneer setting. Heinlein's Friday retires from adventure into marriage; McIntyre's heroine in *Starfarers* seeks refuge in a group marriage in a similar pioneer setting on self-sufficient space ship. Lynn's heroines find comfort in the dance groups of *chearas*; Green's Sofaltis in *Lady Blade, Lord Fighter* is part of a five-person fighting unit called a Fist. While marriage challenges the ingenuity of fantasy authors to create ways to make monogamy or moderate polyandry work, marriage to the fantasy picara is more often to be avoided or discarded. Russ's Alyx is married at seventeen, leaves her husband, after beating him, to go adventuring and never regards marriage as a viable option again.

The importance of marriage and the family unit as the stabilizing economic force runs contrary to the chaos of picaresque life. Peter Lazlett's demographic study of marriage, taken from the 1696 study of population of Geoffrey King and the 1706 *Review* of Defoe, sees the establishment of a family possible only when a "slot" opens up for them. Housing conditions were such that in some areas a marriage could not be performed until a family unit dissolved by death or other means because there was not living space available. Lazlett goes further to see that "nearly every activity was limited to what could be organized within a family" (8) where the woman was productive member whose earnings directly contributed to the income of the family. With the decrease of home industry and the increase of outside industrialization, the wife became less of a helpmate and more of an ornament, "a display figure on which her Lord draped the signals of his economic conquests" (Utter and Needham 59). Denis Donoghue goes so for as to state that to the average seventeenth century woman "a good marriage was the female equivalent of a successful transaction; it required the same 'virtues,' acumen, persistence, foresight, patience" (fn.60). Defoe has the Dutch merchant stress to Roxana that "where the Man did his Duty, the Woman's Life was all Ease and Tranquillity; and that she had nothing to do but to be easie, and to make all that were about her both easie and merry" (148), a forecast of the "marriage market" novels of Jane Austen. Socially, weddings had been formalized from the ranks of private ceremony when the Council of Trent demanded that the wedding ceremony be publicly performed in a church after a three-week proclamation of banns. As marriage came more and more under the control of civil and church authorities, the autonomy of the picara as a single woman was hampered by this Puritan ethos of seeing a family as an economically valuable unit.

The picara's autonomy always places her outside the family structure in her roles as a courtesan or bawd or as a widow or *femme sole*. Literature has long noted this progression. Chaucer's Wyf of Bath has had five husbands who met her at the "churches doore," a custom which guaranteed her a significant portion of her husband's wealth. Dame Alisoun acknowledges that she marries for money and power; widowhood provides her with the autonomy not only to sell the cloth she weaves but also to conduct her own financial affairs. Her tale confirms the picara's need for autonomy in marriage; when the knight returns to Arthur's court with his answer to the queen's challenge, he gives autonomy back to his hag/wife by letting her decide which she would rather be—young and unfaithful or old and faithful.

As a married woman, the picara seldom needs to practice her picaresque tricks but, when the marriage fails and she is again forced to gain her own living, the picara faces the additional problems of an unmarried woman in a society hostile to single women. When she is convinced that marriage will not work, the picara becomes a courtesan.

Prostitution

"I am neither wife, nor maid, nor widow. Who am I?" the old riddle goes. The answer is, of course, a prostitute.

Changing attitudes toward prostitution eventually affect the literature of prostitution. In earlier times, the prostitute was an accepted and necessary member of the society, although the adulteress was not because she violated the vows of marriage and threatened the paternal lineage of her children. In the Middle Eastern societies where temple prostitution was a sacred duty for young women, the occupation of prostitute was reverential; the Renaissance courtesan "had a 'sacramental' function for her lover" because the offering of her body united the earthly love and spiritual planes in a consubtantiation similar to that of the bread and wine of the Eucharist (Lawner 92).

As religious laws began to stress virginity, chastity, and celibacy as desirable virtues, the prostitute's occupation was threatened. Various civil and religious laws tried to control, abolish, or hamper prostitution; sometimes the bawd and her prostitutes were killed; sometimes they were outlawed; sometimes they were sent to houses of rehabilitation; sometimes religion unwittingly occasioned her occupation—some prostitutes were those "abandoned wives of those clergy [who chose] to follow the requirements of the Gregorian reform for clerical celibacy" (Ward 107). While some church fathers suggested that prostitution might be a way of sexual release for men so that they would not rape chaste maidens, it was not until the sixteenth century that the interest in the prostitute as a medical danger evolved. With the spread of venereal diseases—syphilis, in particular—the medical profession emphasized the medical danger and de-emphasized religious objections. In accordance with the double standard, this emphasis centered on the prostitute as an ill person, dysfunctional in herself and in her society. While Lazarillo's name suggests the white scales of leprosy, Courage's blackening her face suggests syphilis since medical science believed that the spread of venereal disease was caused by prostitutes alone; thus, the blackened soul of moral corruption showed itself in a blackened or darkened skin of physical corruption. In fantasy, where the fear of contamination by psychic forces is greater than by physical ones, some prejudice still exists; just as the blood of Grendel's mother is poisonous, so also, in Vinge's *World's End*, the hero fears that the Sibyl's "blood or saliva in an open wound could infect me" (32). More recent medical studies cite psychiatry as the proper science with which to study the prostitute; women's liberation and the sexual revolution have removed the economic basis of the profession; recent emphasis on child abuse may explain her choice of profession and the AIDS epidemic may affect its practice.

As Monteser points out, "the picara may enjoy sex but she is not a whore by choice and sheds the role as soon as the opportunity offers" (60). The ease with which the picara enters into prostitution is partially explained by economic factors. When socio-economic factors prohibited the establishment of new family units, when the cottage industries were replaced by capitalistic means of production, when the nuclear family rather than the extended tribal family became popular, the single woman became an economic burden. She could exert no force on the society to provide her with sufficient marketable skills; her survival depended often on a man to be the breadwinner. If that man were incapacitated, the entire family suffered because, according to many of the guild laws, the wife could not continue the business without a man as the owner. Some guilds permitted the widow and the daughters to retain the business but the same guilds severely cramped growth of such business by forbidding the passing on of the skills beyond the family unit even to sons-in-law. The daughters of widows often became prostitutes because there was no man to carry on the father's one-man business.

Such economic restrictions, coupled with the dearth of marriageable men at various times, forced some women to seek other forms of employment for survival. Some entered convents; since all convents had to be self-sufficient, dowries of the incoming women were needed to support the convent and not every woman could afford the dowry. Yet, there were few alternatives for the laywoman when the trades were restricted to her. The beguinal movement of the twelfth through twentieth centuries, for example, provided an alternative to dependence upon a male. The women earned their own livings, owned their own houses, conducted their own businesses in specialized groups of houses within the cities of Northern Europe. But they are the exception, since social commentators like Defoe decry the lack of economic possibilities for women.

The economic factors which make a prostitute also make a picara—autonomy, avarice, excessive sexuality, lack of marketable skills. Kate Millett's 1973 survey of *The Prostitute Papers* sees autonomy as the goal of all prostitutes, the "power over another human being, the dizzy ambition of being lord of another's will for a stated period of time" (56). In seeking economic and moral survival, the picara tries to avoid the dehumanization of selling herself as long as possible. Millett further agrees that

Prostitution is, in a sense, antique, a fossil in the social structure, pointing, as all fossils do, to an earlier age. But the correct metaphor must be social, not phenomenological; must remind us, as Levi-Strass emphasizes, that men have traded women throughout most of human history and have regarded her as currency in every country of the world, in societies where a monetary system was never arrived at. (56)

While the picara, like the picaro, has no family or wealth, she has one marketable resource he does not—her body. Courage complains that she is forced to earn "her day's bread by her night's wages" (37). This proclivity of the picara toward prostitution is usually detrimental in any world but that of the picaresque. To the early picara, the act of prostitution is a means of livelihood and, just as the picaro never gets himself hanged for his escapades, the picara never gets herself into serious trouble as a prostitute. The later novel picara participates in a limited form of prostitution or adultery and the sexually active fantasy picara seldom has to prostitute herself. To see the distinctions between the types of prostitution, it is best to categorize them according to the degree of frequency and seriousness into a hierarchy of four types: the fallen woman, the common prostitute, the mistress (the kept woman or courtesan), and the bawd.

Clarissa Harlowe and Tess Durbeyfield are the best literary examples of the fallen woman who makes one mistake and who pays for it by her death. Where a romantic heroine might expect suicide or a convenient case of consumption to atone for her stain by removing her and her offense from society, the picara refuses to die; she rejects only motherhood, never sexuality. She may reject the result of sexual actions—children—but she retains and enjoys the pleasure in begetting them. Since the picara fully participates in her defloration and seems to enjoy it, she has little sympathy for the outraged virgin.

The picara does not fall into the category of a street walker, either, for the same reasons that she is not a fallen woman. Both of these types are extremes of the spectrum because neither woman controls her own destiny. The raped heroine has no choice; the hapless and helpless common prostitute is held prisoner by her pimp. Because each is a captive and a victim of her deterministic society, the picara rejects her since her autonomy is threatened by such women. What characterizes the common streetwalker is that she often uses a procurer or pimp rather than a procuress or bawd while the prostitute is one of many women working for a man or in a house of prostitution. In contrast, a courtesan is "self-employed" and not dependent upon a man. Nor is the picara a concubine. Where a concubine is a privately established psuedo-wife, the courtesan is a public entrepreneur who can change lovers at will, who lives in a designated area, and who dresses in a particular way. Depending upon her culture, the courtesan's status is slightly lower than that of a wife and higher than that of a slave or concubine because she controls her own fate. Here again autonomy is the keystone of the picara. For example, in Renaissance Italy, the concubine's dress was heavily cloaked in black whereas the courtesan paraded in rich costumes and her distinctive yellow veil. Lynne Lawner in her *Lives of the Courtesans* notes that "in places where feudal and ecclesiastical traditions persisted, concubinage was still an accepted practice, but in Venice concubines risked being identified with the new phenomenon of the courtesan, far more threatening to society because of her high position and pretense to economic freedom" (115).

The picara participates in the two remaining groups of women—courtesans and bawds—depending on her age and stage of life. The highest form of picaresque sexuality is the mistress or courtesan. The origin of the word "courtesan" suggests that she is one who services the court; the *Oxford Dictionary* identifies a 1607 reference that "your whore is for every rascal, but your Courtesan is for your Courtier" (Seymour-Smith 93). Selling her favors to one man or to a limited number of men at one time, she is faithful for the duration of their liaison. As an independent entrepreneur who presents an economic threat, Lawner claims that she is "one of the first examples of modern woman achieving a relatively autonomous economic position" (4). In literature, the tricks of the picara match the flirtatious gowns and draperies of Renaissance courtesan portraits; the reflecting glass of literature captures this threat and transforms it into the virtue of autonomy. Defoe's tale of Roxana is aptly subtitled *The Fortunate Mistress*, for, descending as she does from a long line of courtesans and Greek *Hierodules* or *Hetairai*, she imagines herself united to her lovers in pseudo-marriage in a form of union sacrosanct as long as the money is there. Even a modern prostitute like "J" interviewed by Millett sees the trade as a source of money and autonomy. "The choice itself is a choice between working for somebody else and going into business for yourself...and hoping to make a lot of money...Prostitution on those terms is a kind of laissez-faire capitalism. But it's also slavery, psychologically. And it's also feudalism" (35).

When the "honest courtesan" became as recognizable a type as the courtier or the prince in Renaissance society, literature, and art, Lawner claims that the emergence of the courtesan came about by the need of the artist for a goddess of inspiration. In a society where wives were kept docilely at home, the courtesan imitated the *hetaira's* position as an intellectual stimulus and concomitant companion to the political mobility of the Roman men. She was held as the earthly emanation of divine beauty, especially in Rome where she reigned as a "female deity over an essentially celibate city, serving up her image as something at once august and delectable to be consumed but also conserved...as a revival of the ancient hetaera, the courtesan emerged in the Roman world, blessed, even partly regenerated by humanism" (Lawner 5). While the number of courtesans and their ancillary forces was estimated as low as one-tenth of the entire population of Rome, when Pope Pius V wanted to expel them from the city in 1566, he was convinced by the Roman city fathers that the city would lose half its population. Nor did literature neglect her. The most influential of the commentaries on courtesans was the production of the novel *Lozana andalusa* in which the wandering picara Lozana describes the Roman courtesan society. Lawner quotes a *Novelle* of the contemporary Mateo Bandello in which he describes the actual working conditions of the courtesan: "a courtesan take[s] six or seven lovers, assigning to each a certain night of the week when she dines and sleeps with him...Each lover pays a monthly salary, and their agreement includes the provision that the courtesan in allowed to have foreigners as overnight quests" (9).

While the courtesan has the economic advantage over the prostitute, both suffer disproportionate vanity. The myth of the happy hooker is just that— a myth. The restlessness of the picara, her disquietude and dissatisfaction with aspects of her life, contradict her French title of *la fille de joie* for her life is beset by numerous worries—loss of looks, age, disease, law enforcement for even the best of courtesans. In addition, her attitude toward aging distinguishes the picaro from the picara. While a picaro can begin his adventures at an early

age, the picara must wait until puberty to claim her only strong advantage—
her body. Lazarillo, for example, is a young pre-pubescent boy who was old
enough to "run errands for the guests to get them wine and candles" (27) when
he leaves with the blind beggar. His age does not matter but his agility does.
If he experiences puberty or adolescence, it does not appear in the tale. Once
he experiences the beggar's cruel trick, he feels "as if I had woken up and my
eyes were opened. I said to myself: 'What he says is true. I must keep awake
because I'm on my own and I've got to look after myself' " (27-8). His education
is complete; he becomes the trickster, not the tricked.

For the literary picara, however, the process is different. As a girl, she cannot
experience full knowledge of the world, especially in sexual matters because
that would smack of child abuse or incest. The isolation of the girl-child until
puberty is an unwritten necessity if only for the simple reason that no author
can resist recording the heroine's first affair, a scene which parallels the initiation
rites to the male picaro. Her defloration is relatively easy and always to her
advantage. Where the primitive picaro never profits from his experience, the
picara does. She learns early that she has a marketable attribute in her sexual
favors and this prowess leads directly to her obsession with its loss in aging
and in accumulating money as a substitute for her sexuality. Many times the
defloration of the virgin becomes the *raison d'etre* of the romance plot with
subsequent actions flowing from this central action. The rise of the novel,
simultaneous with the Puritan and Victorian cultures, made the fallen woman
both a victim and a heroine. Tess is caught in a technological world inimicable
to her best efforts to avoid it; Clarissa suffers a social death worse that her real
death. In contrast, neither Celestina nor Courage fuss about their defloration,
since it is a marketable commodity.

While the prostitute earns her living by her trade alone, the picara uses
prostitution as only one of her trades; she is equally adept at theft and deception.
Although Millett's other interviewee "M" followed the normal path into
prostitution, she swerved into stealing to support her heroin addiction: "And
I was stealing at that point. Compared to boosting, I was a lousy whore...I
was a good thief though" (71) and this stealing brings her into contact with
the underworld of fences and drug dealers. Another of Millett's interviewees was
a sociologist who concludes that most prostitutes are arrested not for prostitution
but for "petty theft and drugs...the two crimes prostitutes most often resort
to to supplement or to palliate their prostitution" (89). While the two categories
of picara and prostitute are not mutually exclusive, they are similiar in their
avarice, childlessness, and distrust of men. In commenting on the prostitute in
literature, Greenwald and Krich in *The Prostitute in Literature* see prostitution
as

the extreme form of a relationship in which the members are interested only in exploiting
each other, the man for his sexual release, the woman for her fee. This then becomes
the prototype of exploitive relationships in general.

The second problem perhaps as important as the first, is that the selling out—selling
out what we believe in, what we represent—purely for material gain. At what point does
economic security take precedence over our moral principle? (10)

Prostitution intensifies the picara's isolation and need for autonomy. In real life, the abandonment by her parents may be the deciding psychological impetus into that trade. In analyzing why women choose such a life style, Greenwald and Krich suggest that every prostitute they saw "had suffered from biparental rejection of the most severe kind. [That] the child was seen by her parents not as a fulfillment but always as an unwanted burden [is] the most important single fact in their later choice of the 'life' as a profession" (fn.54). Later in his analysis, Greenwald comments that the girls, despite their dependence upon the pimp, "were usually subject to painfully intense feelings of loneliness and isolation (7-8). Millett sees that "as a prostitute, you're alienated, isolated even not only from yourself but from the rest of society because you can't talk to people about it" (41).

If such autonomy causes isolation, the literary picara may mention it but dismisses it as negligible. Never, for example, does she bemoan her lack of family or children; indeed, she abandons or avoids the family structure, instinctively asserting her autonomy over any entity which seeks to control her. The picara-saint exerted control over her society by her isolation in the desert, monastery, and hermitage. As disciplined as the picara is in her tricks, the picara-saint used physical discipline and self-denial to prove her autonomy until the church recognized her uniqueness by raising her to sainthood. In *Holy Anorexia*, Rudolph Bell claims that a woman saint who tried gain autonomy over her mother to please her father (and her church) often did so by starving herself into the condition we recognize as anorexia nervosa. For example, Catherine of Siena and Rose of Lima each thwarted her mother's desire for a profitable marriage by self-induced starvation. Margaret of Cortona, the fourteenth century mystic, fled a repressive stepmother to live with her noble lover for nine years, to bear his son, and to find finally his murdered body. As a repentant Magdalen, she sought refuge with the Franciscan tertiaries who were, quite understandably, leery of her reputation. Alienated by her society, she served the lowest forms of that society in good works for the poor, starving herself in the process. While the lack of primary texts cannot prove that the distinguishing mark of modern anorexics—that thinness is preferable to heaviness—is present in the stories of these saints, their lives were held up as examples to be emulated. While most religions have those enthusiasts who use physical purgation to achieve spiritual gain, thinness has long been the hallmark of the ascetic. The celibate brothers and sisters of the Ephrata Cloister, an eighteenth century Anabaptist community in eastern Pennsylvania, fasted themselves to an ascetic thinness, even making their doorways and stairways narrow to accommodate only thin people.

While autonomy can be seen in a woman's control over her body, it can also be seen in her dedication to the spirit of a larger entity like a fertility goddess; homage to such a being must engender a desire to be fruitful like her and sacred prostitutes became part of the urban culture. Millett claims that it is "little wonder that the origins of prostitution lie in temples converted from fertility rites to the cult of patriarchy" (Millett 56). Her profession was a sacred one, commanding respect and, even though Scriptures inveigh against goddess worship, the only prohibition that the Israelites had was that the daughters of priests could not become state prostitutes.

Scriptures hold the clearest image of the temple harlot in the story of Tamar and Judah. When Hebraic culture established the Levirate, which commanded a man's brother to beget a child upon the widow, the law was both a protection for the women, who could then claim tribal status, and an economic device to insure that "the widow of the deceased shall not marry anyone outside the family" (Deut. 25:5) lest any lands or inheritance escape control of the extended tribal family. Its statement in Deuteronomy also emphasizes the necessity to maintain the blood lines so that a man might not die without issue: "The first-born son she bears shall continue the line of the deceased brother, that his name may be not blotted out of Israel" (Deut. 25:6). If a brother-in-law refuses to marry the widow, she has the right to "strip his sandal from his foot and spit in his face" (Deut. 25:9), thereby impoverishing him and disgracing him in the eyes of his society. The thirty-eighth chapter of Genesis cites the confrontation of Judah, the son of Jacob, and his daughter-in-law Tamar. When Judah's oldest son Er dies without issue, Judah orders his second son Onan to beget a child upon Tamar so that Er's line and therefore his own line would not die out. When Onan frustrates any possible conception by withdrawing before completion, Tamar is again left childless. Because Judah's youngest son Shelah is too young for marriage, Tamar is sent back to her father's house where Judah advises her to "stay as a widow in your father's house until my son Shelah grows up'—for the he feared that Shelah also might die like his brothers" (Gen.38:11). Tamar's position is one lacking in power; as a childless widow, she could not claim autonomy as a wife or as the mother of a son.

As the years pass and no provision is made for Tamar, she takes off her widow's garments, veils her face with a shawl, and sits down on the roadway to await Judah, her father-in-law, who assumed she was a temple prostitute. According to one critic the "Hebrew word *qedesha* literally 'consecrated woman,' designated a woman who had ritual intercourse with men in pagan fertility rites...a word that refers to a higher social class than that designated by the term *zona*, common 'harlot' " (Gen. 38:21, fn.). Greenberg asserts that while the temple prostitutes of Sumeria were called "assinutum," the feminine form of *assinu*, because "though sexually active as hierodules, they were supposed to avoid pregnancy. They thus limited themselves to a method that avoided the risk of conception (anal intercourse)" (97). Because Tamar's urgency for a son thus drives her to pose as a woman who cannot conceive, Judah does not expect their sexual exchange to produce progeny. She is promised a kid from his flock but requires his seal, the cord on which it is suspended, and his staff, all identifying items, to insure her payment. (This may be an early form of the signet ring as identification or payment for a night of love, a literary convention which is used by Shakespeare in *The Merchant of Venice* and *All's Well That Ends Well*). When Judah's friend Adullamite takes the requisite kid as payment, he inquires after a temple prostitute, only to be told that no prostitute has ever occupied that space. Judah decide to "let her keep the things...otherwise we shall become a laughingstock. After all, I did send her the kid, even though you were unable to find her" (Gen. 38:23). The exchange of dialogue over payment for the harlot's favors and her insistence on immediate payment of his seal and staff as surety for his payment make a minor drama in itself. Rather like Shakespeare's lawyer-like heroines of Portia and Helena, Tamar's cleverness is proven in the way she defends herself against the charge of harlotry by producing the items at the right time and denouncing her father-in-law for his neglect. Rather than being reprimanded for her harlotry, she is praised for her cleverness when Judah acknowledges that "she is more in the right than I am" (Gen. 38:26).

Tamar is an excellent example of a picara. She acts as an autonomous entrepreneur, one who circumvents the social code of ethics when justice is denied her. In doing so, she uses deception in her adopting the guise of the "lone traveling harlot who plies her trade on the roadside and expects the wealthy nomads to be her customers" (Patai 147). She employs disguise by using the traditional veil to hide "her face by covering herself with a shawl [so that] when Judah saw her, he mistook her for a harlot, since she had covered her face" (Gen. 38: 14-15). But her deception extends beyond mere disguise into the picaresque survival mode since Tamar must dupe her father-in-law into doing his duty as the picara must manipulate and deceive in order to preserve her life.

Other women in the Bible are forced into being equally deceptive or manipulative in their sexuality. When Naomi accepts her daughter-in-law Ruth's allegiance to leave her own people to follow Naomi back in Israel, the bond of economic survival between them is similar to that of a bawd and her harlot. Although Scriptures assign a religious or spiritual reason, Naomi's actions are close to the stereotype of the yenta or matchmaker of recent dramatic fame, when she advises Ruth to lie down at the feet of the sleeping Boaz until he awakens. Ruth then asks him to "spread the corner of your cloak over me, for you are my next of kin" (Ruth 3:9) to force him to marry her according to the Levirate law. By Naomi's cleverness, Ruth circumvents the law as Tamar did for her own picaresque purpose of survival; Boaz gives her six measures of barley to return to Naomi while he arranges their marriage. Naomi's skill is so great that she becomes honored among her society and is praised for her daughter-in-law "who is worth more to you than seven sons!" (Ruth 4: 15).

Sexuality is also Esther's basic lure in her choice of clothing. In the first instance, it is her simplicity of dress which appears foreign and therefore attractive to the king; in the second instance, when she risks her life to enter the king's presence unbidden, she not only dresses herself splendidly but she also staggers and comes near fainting, which forces him to run to help her. Both times she deceives the king by concealing her heritage. Judith is another picara of sorts; as a widow, who controls her own destiny by managing her household, she prays that her "guileful speech brings wound and wale on those who have planned dire things against your covenant" (Judith 9:13). Refusing to reveal her plan to the besieged city leaders, she takes off "the garments of her widowhood...and put on the festive attire...Thus she made herself very beautiful, to captivate the eyes of all the men who should see her" (Judith 10:3-4). Refusing to reveal her ploy to the city leaders, she poses as a willing harlot and spy to gain entry to the Assyrian camp. This decision is furthered when she leaves the camp each day to pray: when she leaves after killing Holofernes, she is not hindered by the soldiers; when she insists on bringing her own food to the feast in a pouch, she deceives them by concealing Holofernes' head in the pouch. When she has Holofernes' bodyguard excluded from the festive tent, she furthers deceives them by rolling the body off the bed and disarranging the canopy and covers. Although Judith is probably a mythic compilation of Israelite sufferings and victories, she embodies the survival characteristic of the picara.

Rahab's story told in the book of Joshua may be that of a prostitute or of a tavern owner whose house was used as an inn. When she is ordered by the king of Jericho to "put out of the house the visitors who have entered your house" (Joshua 2:3) she denies that they are with her, hides them the next day, and lowers them from her window in the city wall the next evening. The payment she extracts is that the invading forces spare her family; the sign of her protection is the scarlet cord hung from her window. Notice that the woman who risks her life for the escaping Israelite soldiers is a city picara. Seldom is the picara in the country since her proclivity to deceit implies other beings and a society against which to rebel and a society large enough to contain her and disguise her.

If we can believe history, Greek society tended to divide women into those who could entertain by the intellect or entertainment (the *hetairai*) or those who could produce a family. That the two were antithetical is understood; love and marriage did not always cohabit. The duty of fathering the new generation did not prohibit a man from enjoying sexual favors outside the home or in seeking intellectual stimulation from a class of women who were set aside for that purpose, much as the scared prostitutes had been in earlier societies. If we can believe literature, Homer's *Odyssey* presents all possible types of women in his society from the *hetaira* to the faithful Penelope, each of whom is in sexuality for her own reason. The triple goddesses of Hera, Aphrodite, and Athena govern the theogony with the first two being the more sexually active while Athena, the goddess of wisdom and warfare, is Odysseus' mentor and travel guide. Because they are superior to mankind, what looks like prostitution in Aphrodite and pride and greed in Hera are morally acceptable because of the strong desire for fecundity imbedded in them as goddesses. Thus, the two aspects of the picara—sexuality and avarice—are part of both goddesses' repertoire: Aphrodite's avarice and pride for the golden prize as the most beautiful leads to her giving Helen to Paris; Hera's pride in wanting to be named the most beautiful forces her into helping the Greeks against the Trojans.

Even the lesser forms of the goddess such as Circe and Calypso favor human heroes, even reluctant ones, reinforcing the male belief that women's sexuality is so rampant that it cannot be satisfied by mere mortals. To disguise their feminine pleasure in intercourse, the lesser goddesses must resort to charms and spell to seduce him; if their sexuality or intellect do not seduce him; their goddesshood will force him. Odysseus flees Calypso's sexual gluttony; he carries the sacred *moly* to protect his virility from Circe's power. As Martin Seymour-Smith claims, Circe is a

whore rather than a prostitute; if she whores for gain, then it is for straight forward sexual, not financial gain...For the always sexually eager woman, besides being a ubiquitous male fantasy-figure, really can be found...If some women are drawn to prostitution for other than economic reasons...no one will deny that this is the case...then is Circe's predilection a frequent motive (39).

In many senses they are Homer's version of the sacred prostitute, the *hetairai* whose position in society was higher than that of a common prostitute. The goddesses exhibit their autonomy in their actions. However, as the emanations of these two sexual goddesses, lesser goddesses like Circe and Calypso place malevolently sexual lures in his path. Even as innocuous a goddess as Ino gives him a sexual symbol in the magic girdle which protects him from drowning as the caul protects the child in the amniotic fluid in the womb.

Athena alone of the major goddesses is not sexual; her temple has no sacred prostitutes. Rather, her appeal is partly warlike which fits the actions of the returning warrior; for example, she is forever sprinkling magic dust to endow him with muscles and heroic powers. Her intellect appeals to Odysseus because it is the base of the cleverness in the deceptions and disguises she encourages in Odysseus. Since Greek society valued intellect in a woman enough to give her a special status of *hetaira* rather than common prostitute, it seems natural that Homer should use Athena as the goddess aiding Odysseus to regain his homeland and recover his inheritance. She is the intellect, and, as such, she helps him where the other two goddesses, Hera and Aphrodite, are indifferent to his sufferings. His wanderings are beset by mortal love-starved women: Helen, the seductress, darning Menelaus' stocks; Altinoos' wife, the mother-queen whose knees offer protection from harm; Penelope, faithfully weaving her deceiving shroud; Nausicaa, desiring the handsome sea-born stranger. Although they are not goddesses, these women are motivated by the need to procreate and by sexuality. Each in her own way is autonomous in her actions.

This distinction between sacred prostitute and common one is maintain by other authors. Petronius' *Satyricon* both parodies and exemplifies the leaning of aristocratic women to degrade themselves in sexual excess with menials or inferior men. Juvenal's Messalina and Catullus' Lesbia are nymphomaniacs whose sexual excess carried their reputations down into the Renaissance where the honest courtesan was seen as an emanation of the mother goddess in her fruitful role. Lawner details the portraits in which the courtesan was used by showing mythological figures, like Flora, appearing as the embodiment of springtime and fertility or in her role as lactacting mother with the exposed breasts of the courtesan model.

One of the archetypal portraits for which the courtesan posed was as the Magdalen, the penitent prostitute. Christian tradition embroiders the scriptures to concoct the tale that Mary Magdalene was the prostitute who wiped Jesus' feet with her hair. That she was from Magdala only means that she is connected with the fish-figure of the goddess (for Magdala meant fish-towers) and fish— mermaids, sirens, lorelei—are continually associated with Aphrodite's birth from the sea.

In fantasy, the same name continues in Bradley's use of Magda or Magdalen for her heroine in *Thendara House* and *The City of Sorcery* where Magda "repents" of her rash claim to be a Free Amazon and enters a year of housebound seclusion to study the society until she is accepted in the final union with the mystical gray sisterhood. (For a detailed account of the religious sources Bradley uses, see my article on Bradley and the Beguines in *Heroines of Popular Culture*).

Fascination with the occult led literature to explain any rise in prostitution as attributable to the work of the devil. Many early literary works, such as the Middle English ballad of the "Daemon Lover," rely on the supernatural as motivation for prostitution, as if the picara-prostitute were a throwback to a Pre-Christian demonic influence. Shakespeare's use of the courtesan in *The Comedy of Errors* plays on the belief that pagan witches inhabited Ephesus and his Antipholus comments repeatedly on the bewitching atmosphere of the town. In the prose narrative of the fifteenth century Flemish play of Mary of Magdalen, entitled *Mary of Nimmeguen*, the heroine becomes the devil's mistress before repenting of her sins. It seems more than a coincidence that Defoe has Roxana living in Nimmeguen at the end of the novel even though Roxana acknowledges her connection with the devil in equivocal passages: "The ignorant Jade's Argument, That he had bought me out of the hands of the Devil, by which she meant the Devil of Poverty and Distress, shou'd have been a powerful Motive to me, not to plunge myself into the Jaws of Hell, and into the power of the real Devil" (38). Courage also speaks of Simplex as being "deceived by French whores like me and probably even by broomstick riders, thereby becoming the devil's own kinsman" (182). This taint of witchcraft appears as magic in fantasy literature. Even though picaras claims that the "Devil of Poverty" forced them into prostitution, they see the moral wrong but not the criminal wrong. Courage says that "there is nought else to be expected from loving whores than all manner of uncleanness, shame, ridicule, poverty and misery, and worst of all a bad conscience, too" (183). Roxana is keenly aware of her position in society: "The Whore skulks about in Lodgings; is visited in the dark; disown'd upon all Occasions, before God and Man; is maintain'd indeed, for a time; but is certainly condem'd to be abandoned at last, and left the the Miseries of Fate, and her own Just Disaster" (132).

The picara is always a city girl, especially when she is a prostitute. From Marseilles to Venice, the courtesan is an economic resource; even inland towns like Rome and Jerusalem attract prostitutes. But where the active prostitute is always a city person, because she needs a steady stream of clients, the reformed prostitute often becomes a hermit or abandons the city as a source of sin. The silence of Mary Magdalen's cave of repentance never enticed the picara; contemplation is not her scene anymore than inactivity is. The picara at the end of her career seldom leaves the city although she may seek repentance in other forms by living a quiet life. When Courage tries to retire to the country, she is pursued by billeting soldiers and returns to her immoral ways. However, a picaresque autonomy was achieved by the harlots of the desert by their fleeing the city and by their abandoning their ill-gotten gains. "Life in the desert, *anachoresisis*, was a practical demonstration of freedom from the limitations and responsibilities of society...By their successful careers [as prostitutes] they had achieved a freedom from the control of father or husband, and from the domesticity inevitable for a woman of good reputation" (Ward 63). Enjoined by the Scriptural admonition that spiritual matters are preferable to earthly ones ["Mary has chosen the better part and it shall not be taken from her" (Luke 10:42)], women faced the age-old dichotomy of choosing either the exalted purity of the Mary image or the immoral image of Eve and Mary Magdalen. The picara's autonomy forced her to opt for the latter. To add to the superfluity of Marys is the blending of the life of St. Mary of Egypt into that of the Magdalen. Well known in both Eastern and Western church from the sixth century, the story tells of a young harlot of Alexandria who paid for her passage to Jerusalem with her favors, was converted, and who fled to the desert to live a life of sacrifice for forty-seven years. Discovered by the monk Zossima, she relates her tale, dies, and is buried by the monk with the help of a lion. Variants of the tale repeated are in the lives of many desert saints.

While the character of the prostitute does occur long before picaresque fiction, it is in the drama that the stereotypes of the prostitute survive best because drama is so immediately reflective of its society. The ancient stock characters of the courtesan and her bawd can be traced from the earliest drama to the latest soap opera. In the Greco-Roman theatre, actresses and acrobats in the comedies were often courtesans on the side while the courtesans of the Greek comedy parallel the later picara-prostitute figures consistent in drama. Within the stock characters bequeathed by Greek and Roman theatre and the Italian *commedia dell'arte*, the character of the naughty young maidservant—Columbina, Franceschina, Fioretta, and the other soubrettes who assist in assignations with the *inamorati*— emerges as the second female lead in the drama because of her loose morals, her willingness to be bribed, her sympathy for sexual desires, her charm. She is a constant character, persisting down through opera and drama in Despina in Mozart's *Cosi Fan Tutte*, in Luce in Shakespeare's *The Comedy of Errors* and in Louka in Shaw's *Arms and the Man*.

While the hagiological legends of Mary of Magdalen appear in the miracle plays, it is the figure of the bawd who first substantiates the picara in drama. While early English stage had had its "Interludium Puella et Clerico" with the Dame Siriz [Ceres] acting the bawd with her tale of the weeping bitch, literature "before the creation of Celestina...had stereotypes for this part; the main character in the twelfth century French *fabliau* 'Richeut,' the psuedo-Ovidian Vetula, La Vielle in the *Roman de la Rose*, the female go between the Middle English poem *Dame Siriz*, and others" (Schlauch 126). For example, the Spanish and bawd Celestina, first encountered in the loose dramatic structure of the novel *La Celestina*, "may well have been intended as an interlude, complete in itself" and its first English translation is attributed to an "anonymous verse interlude, which appears to have emanated from the circle of Sir Thomas More" (Cohen 10, 17). Thus, the most important influence on many Continental picaras, the Celestina of Fernando de Rojas' proto-novel, is dramatically conceived and structured in dialogue as a tragedy for the young lovers, Calisto and Melibea, but as comedy of sorts because "its subject was not the loves of Calisto and Melibea...but the seduction of Parmeno, the faithful servant, by the wicked Celestina" (10): its ambivalent title, The Comedy and Tragi-Comedy of Calisto and Melibea, best indicates this. Rojas claimed that he rewrote the outline of an anonymous manuscript in the manner of the comedies of Plautus and Terence in 1500 and fleshed out the remaining twenty some chapters on his own. Whatever her source, the bawd, as Cohen describes her, "is a sempiternal figure of Spanish literature...a figure of Falstaffian proportions, infinitely guileful and in the end almost lovable if only for her abounding zest" (15).

Zest is the word which best describes the early bawd; she lives for survival and for herself. The final form of the prostitute is in the bawd character, who appears most vividly in the plays: the old woman—Celestina, Siriz, Ceres—who arranges assignations for profit. However, the bawd is not to be confused with the dowager-dragon stock character of the older woman who desires the young man for herself. In contrast, the bawd may speak longingly about her sexual desires and her past excesses but she never seems to desire them at present. As a bawd, the picara employs prostitutes as her means of production, uniting her picaresque avarice with her temporary profession. In the later picara, however, the literature neglects the picara as a bawd because the relation of the picara's story itself is of most importance while that of the bawd is vicarious and secondary. The picara will make use of her bawd as a confidante and a protectoress. The role of the mother as bawd is sometimes mixed in the prostitution. In Lucian's *Dialogues of the Courtesans* Corinna fears becoming a common prostitute until her mother convinces her that she will be a high-class courtesan, not a street walker.

The bawd is sometimes the courtesan's mother, reflecting the myth of Demeter searching for her daughter Kore. Later this mother-daughter myth merged into the St. Anne (or Elizabeth), Virgin Mary and Christ Child figure which Barr sees as triad formed by Karr's Frostflower, Thorn, and Starwind, the "new atypical nuclear family (swordswoman, sorceress, and their son) which stems from a new atypical definition of the natural and the spiritual" (89). In addition, the bawd often is linked with other beings who may or may not be bawds; she has a heritage which she passes onto her daughters and a confraternity to which she belongs. For example, another picara Justina in Francisco de Ubeda's *La Picara Justina* extends the boundaries of the picaresque in her marriage to her fellow picaro Guzman de Alfarache. While Juliet's nurse is married and Mistress Quickly is not, Grimmelshausen's Courage marries her Simplicimus for a while in between her bouts of prostitution.

From Celestina, Shakespeare formed Juliet's nurse. Nor should Shakespeare's familiarity with prostitution be a surprise when legal documents prove that the theater owners like Alleyn and Hemminge were brothel-owners who thriftily built both the theaters and the brothels outside the legal jurisdiction of the city of London. In *Measure for Measure*, Mistress Overdone and Pompey are both brothel-keepers, closed down by the officious and equally lecherous Angelo, while the lavicious scamp Lucio must marry the prostitute who has borne him a child. The courtesan in *The Comedy of Errors* is an independent entrepreneur insisting on the gold chain and gold ring due her for her favors at dinner while Cassio in *Othello* is said to be dammed in a "fair wife," an euphemism for his courtesan Bianca. While high class courtesans sat masked in the privileged seats and the orange girls sold their favors along with their fruit to the groundlings, Doll Tearsheet and Mistress Quickly in *Henry IV, Part II* played out the relationship of prostitute to bawd. Real-life heroines have always provided sources for other dramatists. From Cleopatra's alleged seductions, to Mary of Egypt's sexual servicing of armies as penance, to the Byzantine Empress Theodora's conversion from actress-courtesan to benefactress of convents for converted prostitutes, writers have found no difficulty in transferring real women into stage prostitutes. Aretino's 1525 *La cortigiana* portrays Camilla of Pisa; Webster's *The White Devil* uses the real life tale of Vittoria, implying her prostitute status in the euphemistic title; Marston's *The Roaring Girle* is based on the life of Mary Carleton Moders, a real-life picara; Marmion's *Holland's Leaguer* is based on the bawdy career of Elizabeth Holland.

John Marston's *The Dutch Courtesan* details the revenge of a courtesan Franceschina, one of the clever serving maid soubrettes of the *commedia dell'arte*, a "punk rampant" (II ii 83), the embodiment of all passions to which man is subject, and a foil to show off the bombastic piety of the comic Malherueux. "No Got [God] in me but passions" she exclaims in her broken English (IV iii 40-1). Much in the manner of Falstaff's defense of his "vocation" as "Diana's foresters, gentlemen of the shade, minions of the moon" (I i 26-7), Marston's male picaresque character of Cocledemoy upholds the rights of women to be prostitutes. "Every man must follow his trade and every woman her occupation" (I i 95), he reasons for if the "poor decayed mechanical man's wife, her husband is laid up; may she not lawfully be laid down when her husband's only rising is by his wife's falling" (I i 95-8). Marston's use of Dutch for the courtesan reinforces the picara's international appeal: he refers to her as "Tanikin" or diminutive of Anna in Dutch (I i 141). She is a "froe," mispronunciation for the Dutch "frow" and the Flemish "Vrouw." She is a "cockatrice" (II ii 95) or "short heels" (II i 92), a variant of the later cant phrase of "roundheels." Marston's picara wears the death's head ring on her third finger, typical of procuresses at this time when the medieval belief prevailed that, though a woman gave a heaven of pleasure, she was actually a pathway to hell. Death and his companion vice of the lustful bawd sit besides the gates of hell. With a long history on stage, the entire play was recast by Aphra Behn as *The Revenge; or, A Match in Newgate*, adding melodramatic effects of a "very stagy melodrama and vulgarity that is totally lacking in the original" (Marston xii). In it, the courtesan repents, is married off, forgives her lover and repudiates Marston's meaning of moral satire. As the main story was passed over the subplot of the deceived vintner rose, it further deteriorated into a low comedy form by Christopher Bullock in 1715, a ballad-opera *Love and Revenge; or, The Vintner Outwitted* and existed as farce for another two hundred years.

Thus, so strong is the Continental tradition of the picara that the particular English qualities of a picara, like Defoe's Roxana, for example, are merely incidental realistic detail while her basic picaresque character is almost identical with that of her Continental prototypes. While the bawd is a stock character in drama, the emergence of the picara in novel form took more time.

In literary prostitution, the two visible aspects of the prostitute character—the prostitute and the bawd—appear disguised in the picaresque genre as the courtesan and her confidante. For example, from her paid position as the wetnurse to the Bohemian child, Courage's unnamed nurse protects the girl by having her masquerade as a boy; she later is addressed as Mother by Courage, serving as her bank, her bawd, and her blind. After she leaves the protection of her English Lord, Roxana has Amy arrange "Company, and that of the greatest Quality, of Subjects I mean, who frequently visited me, and sometimes we had meetings for Mirth, and Play, at my Apartment, where I fail'd not to divert them in the most agreeable Manner possible" (183). Amber and Scarlett and Becky are all courtesans in that they are fairly faithful to one lover at one time;

they are not streetwalkers and would take umbrage at the suggestion. Defoe establishes a tight relationship between Moll and her governess until the relationship matures into that of a courtesan and a bawd. In an expanded segment, the young Moll expresses fears at being put into service as a maid for "they will Beat me, and the Maids will Beat me to make me do great Work" (11). In return, the governess assures her that she shall not go out to service until she is much older.

> "Ay, says I, but I then must go at last..."
> "What, would you be a Gentlewoman?"
> "Yes, *says I*," and cry'd heartily...
> "Pray, how will you come to be a Gentlewoman? what will you do it by your Fingers Ends?"
> "Yes," *Says I again*, very innocently.
> "Why, what can you Earn," *says she*, "what can you get at your Work?"
> "Three-Pence," *says I*, "when I spin and 4d when I Work plain Work."
> "Alas! poor Gentlewoman," *said she again*, "Laughing, what will that do for thee."
> "It will keep me," *Says I*, "if you will let me live with you..."
> "But," *says she*, "that will not keep you, and buy you Cloths too...it will hardly keep you in Victuals."
> "Then I will have no Victuals," *says I*, again very Innocently, "let me but live with you." (11-2)

The exchange is, of course, a foreshadowing of the monetary arrangements made between the courtesan and her bawd. Defoe makes full use of irony in Moll's protestation of innocence because the journal is written after she lived her life while he makes Roxana the prime example of the autonomous woman who allows her bawd Amy to arrange her life, as long as it harvest her money.

The novel heroines tend to lapse into a free-form prostitution or to become courtesans. They seldom become streetwalkers, forced to earn their bread by immediate exchange of monies for favors as lower prostitutes do. Indeed, the period in which a novel is written often dictates the extent to which the picara is sexually involved or described. Pamela's Mrs. Jewkes and her girls at the breakfast table discussing their uncles and Clarissa's procuress watching her rape at the keyhole have ancestresses in earlier novels. In *Vanity Fair*, Thackeray cannot come out and say that Becky is living by prostitution but he can suggest it in the illustrations; Becky's sly smirk convinces us. When Thackeray describes Becky's bedroom, its careless jumble is a sign of her profession: "One of her gowns hung over the bed, another depending from a hook of the door: her bonnet obscured half the looking glass, on which too, lay the prettiest little pair of bronze boots; a French novel was on the table by the bedside" (689). In Dutch paintings, shoes left awry are always signs of loose living; in Regency England, brown boots were worn only by demimondaines. Becky is careful to sit on the bed herself, lest Jos Sedley sit on the brandy bottle, rouge pot or plate of broken meat she has hidden beneath the covers. Her casual relationship with the Bohemian crowd in the boarding house, "as dirty a little refuge as ever beauty lay hid in" (688), condemns her more than Thackerary's preachings might.

Scarlett and Amber are little better. While Scarlett is bound by the *mores* of her society to make appearances substitute for reality, she never panders herself physically but does manoeuver her marriages into financial advantages. She is constantly warned by Mammy and Ellen her mother to avoid wrong-doing which she conveniently interprets as avoiding the appearance of wrong-doing. Not getting caught is the secret. Because Atlantan society would not tolerate a courtesan, Mitchell splits the picara traits, giving the ambition and avarice to Scarlett and the prostitution side to Belle, the town bawd. Again, appearance is all. The licentious Restoration culture molds Amber's character as a courtesan seeking the highest position as Lady Ravenspur or as a mistress to the king, as in the case of Barbara Palmer, Lady Castlemaine.

The fantasy picara does not consider sexual affairs as prostitution since no money changes hands. Unlike her early picara-sister, the fantasy picara reaps the benefits of society's swing toward sexual freedom. Prostitution as such is not an integral part of the fantasy picara's life; as a modern woman and the product of her society, she refuses to be seen as a sexual object. The best single example of prostitution used in fantasy is in Janet Morris' Silistra series: *High Couch of Silistra* (originally entitled *Returning Creation*), *The Golden Sword*, *Wind from the Abyss*, and *The Carnelian Throne*. Told in autobiographical form, the heroine introduces herself as the Well-Keepress of Astria on the planet Silistra, Estri Hadrath diet Estrazi, "sought and celebrated for my beauty and lineage...I was high-couch in the greatest house of pleasure in the civilized stars. I commanded a great price" (*Couch* 2).

Her name may be derived from "estrus" or "oestrus," the period of female sexual heat, or from any number of mythological goddesses. "Estri" and "Astria" are both variants of Astarte, the Ugaritic Ashtoreth mother of gods, Ishtar (the Mesopotamian form of Inanna), the Egyptian Isis, and the Celtic Oestre, from whose name we get Easter. "Estri" is a form of the Scriptural Esther, a variant of Hestia, the Olympian goddess of the hearth, and of Hester Prynne, the adultress of Hawthorne's *Scarlet Letter*. Estri's character is most like that of Ishtar who describes herself as " 'a prostitute compassionate am I' " because she "symbolizes the creative submission to the demands of instinct, to the chaos of nature...the free woman, as opposed to the domesticated woman" (Hall 11-2). Linking Estri with these lunar and water symbols is not difficult because of the moon's eternal virginity (the strength of integrity) links with her changeability (the prostitute's switching of lovers). The moon goddess Ishtar may take many lovers but she is never dominated by them. She retains her individuality while blending both her masculine and feminine strengths in reflecting the light of the masculine sun and in retaining her feminine distance and coolness in her changeability. Even the moon's familiar symbol, the *labrys*, that two-headed curved axe of the Minoan age, representing the two horns of the waxing and waning moon, appear in Lake of Horns, the site of her major battle and of her eventual capital city. In addition, Estri carries in her boots eight "razor-moon" knives.

Just as picaros are associated with moving waters (Monteser 113), so are picaras linked with still waters. Morris strengthens the moon imagery by having Estri as a well-keepress because wells, fountains, and the moon as the orb which controls water have long been associated with fertility. Hall calls woman's role as "the fundamental guardians and converters of elemental energy (tending hearthfires, drawing well water, bearing and feeding children)" (32). While the moon goddess's fertility may not be in bearing children, it is that of one who disrupts society to force changes, to sensitize the psyche to new forms of potentiality, to engender compassion and understanding of the self. From the naiads and the mermaids to the lorelei and the sirens, the water goddesses have been such seductresses whose symbols are those derived from the sea origin: the fishnet, the comb, the long hair, the mirror, the moon and water. Estri's hair is only one example: ankle length at the beginning of the novel, when she is only a seductress, she cuts it shorter, when she is searching for her identity, because the cutting of hair is universally the sign of a new commitment. In a sense, she is like the moon because she is apparently eternal, never waxing or waning except in her pursuit of the quest; she is the prototypical wanderer like the moon and Ishtar. She is the eternal night symbol of the moon in opposition to the Day-Keepers or *dharen*. By the fourth book (*Throne*), she becomes the dharenness when she became couch-mate of the dharen Khys, her sun-god-lover. Like the moon she reflects the light of her father's race and of her couch-mate Sereth so that, by the end of the tetrology, she is the couch-mate and co-ruler with Sereth of the planet. In essence, she has completed her journey toward self and has emerged into her full strength in that state that her lover Khys describes as "that transcendent sexual ritualization . . . that 'hermaphroditic match' " (*Wind* 357) of balanced powers of sexual opposites. If she is the moon, the men in her life—her father Estrazi, her god-lover Khys, her desert lover Chayin and her dharen-ruler Sereth, her torturing lover Eviduey, her savage lover Delicrit—are all forms and emanations of Inanna's sun-god of her son/husband/ lover.

As Estri is bound to the well of her grand-mother Astria, she imitates the water goddesses by having temple prostitutes. Yet, like the Babylonian Ishtar, whose temple prostitutes practiced sodomy to prevent conception, Estri is not easily made fertile; it takes a superior being of Khys, her father's equal, to impregnate her. This is in keeping with the practice of many tribes who arrange the sexual destinies of children through their aunts or uncles rather than mothers or fathers. "Foster parentage was a common institution among the Indo-European people, and in many instances the foster father was a mother's brother . . . Under these circumstances, it would be natural for the foster parent to supervise initiation, and perhaps to ritually sodomize his ward" (Greenberg 109). In the same manner, women are often deflorated by an aunt or midwife before marriage to prevent the bride's hostility toward her husband. Estri's early life is reluctantly arranged by her uncle, her mother's brother, who has himself some affection beyond the normal for her dead mother. Estri's parents wish her no harm but they do provide a quest for identity beyond that given to her by her mother's brother; it is her father who rescues her from the father's daughter's brother of her grandmother's prophecy. It is her half-sister's brother Raet who first forces her powers to emerge; it is Khys, another relative of her father's, who captures and impregnates her. In this device of the picara being governed by an uncle reappears in other picaras such as in Jo Clayton's Brann and Skeen who are victimized by their uncles. In part, the shifting of responsibility from the parents to the parents' sibling is an aspect that Bruno Bettleheim stresses in his work on myths—that the normal human cannot accept the fact that their parents might not love them and might want to harm them. Thus, it is the stepmother rather than the mother who seeks the death of Cinderella or Snow White.

Even so, Estri follows many of the picaresque traditions. Her mother dies at her birth, leaving her to be raised by an uncle, who urged her mother to abort her and who she admits "would rather have drowned me upon the day of my birth" (5). At her majority (her three hundredth birthday), she is given a silver-cubed hologram letter from her mother, containing a videotape of her conception by the savage bronzed barbarian god from another world. The language used is that of a temple prostitute to her client, expressed in the explicit sexual language which makes this type of fantasy border on acceptable soft-core pornography. If Estri's mother then acts as a bawd, willing her lineage as Well-Keepress to her daughter, then Estri's great-grandmother Astria as foundress of the Well becomes a further mother-bawd figure when she offers her prophetic advice in her letter: "Guard Astria for you may lose it, and more. Beware of one who is not as he seems. Stray not in the port city of Baniev...look well about you, for your father's daughter's brother seeks you" (14). Having no brother that she knows of does not stay Estri from undertaking the heroic quest of finding her father.

To do so, she is given a ring with a spiral of diamonds and rubies set in black stone as an identifying roadmap mark for her quest. Her mother advises her that "the ring is the key. Keep it on your person, even in sleep, until you rest within your father's house. It will identify you and keep you safe among his people, should your search take you so far" (9). Although the ring device harkens back to the exchange of Judah's identifying seal as payment to Tamar for her services as a temple prostitute, the ring is more akin to a fantasy device than a picaresque one. To insure the safety of the ring, Estri has it woven into the belt or *chaldra* which she wears low on her hips like the *celsus* of Aphrodite and like Ishtar's golden girdle of stars, which she must remove before she journeys to the land of the dead. While the knot in this *celsus* is traditionally untied only by the husband, the "husbands" of the temple prostitute toss coins into her lap. At one point Estri stresses that she is worth thirty gold coins in opposition to a coin girl who "couches for pay outside the Well system" (*Couch* 227). The *chaldra* or belt of interwoven chains represents the responsibilities of the Silistrian to his or her society. While there are over two hundred possible tasks a Silistrian may attempt, they are divided into high and low chaldra; for example, "the chaldra of reproduction, of begetting one child...is symbolized by the bronze chain before the chaldra is met, and the golden chain after the child has been produced" (*Couch* 2). At the beginning of the novel, Estri's chaldra belt contains eighteen chains; to go on the quest of her mother and father, she must have another chaldra constructed and blessed to include the red thread of the quest. The chaldra is wide enough for her to slip her father's ring through its chains and, instead of being welded about her hips, it fastens about her body with a hidden lock.

To be chaldless is to be outlaw or outcast in the manner of the Levirate law which allows the offended woman to strip her brother-in-law of his sandal for neglecting his duty to beget a child on her. When Estri is returned to Silistria, she is captured by a desert nomad Chayin who forces her to remove her chald to become his *crell* or low slave; she has become Inanna who has to remove her veils or Ishtar who must remove her golden girdle to enter Hades. Unlike her successful ancestress Esther, when she attempts to kill him for reducing her to the low status, she is thwarted and beaten for her efforts.

To be an outcast in Silistria means travel and Estri is a traveller between stars and planets as well as between time. As is typical of a *hetaira* or a courtesan, Estri travels from lover to lover, each one instructing her about herself and bringing her closer to her quest; this travelling becomes, then, her own version of the picaresque travel episodes. In the fantasy picaras, the quest often overrides the picara's urge for survival as she places herself in danger for something beyond her own comfort. For Estri the search for her father brings her into contact with various lovers; they, in their turn, aid her on her quest for self-identity. "Each maiden psyche in turn is then set upon a path of wandering—in desert, forest, sea—out of which it emerges open to love...all wanderings is (in this case) back to the Father" (Hall 160). Estri wanders the desert in *The Golden Sword*, the sea or lake in *Wind from the Abyss*, and the forest in *The Carnelian Throne*.

Throughout her ordeal, she exhibits other characteristics of the picaresque form. Her story is told in an autobiographical style, a challenge when you consider that her memory is taken away between books two and three. To overcome this, the third book is prefaced by an explanatory author's note in which she claims that she wrote the book without knowing her true self: "I was Estri because the girl Carth found wandering in the forest stripped of comprehension and identity chose that name" (xi). Each of the books exhibits a consciousness of its form as an historical autobiography; the author appends glossaries for each novel and includes prologues, epilogues, biographical sketches, and copious notes to guide the reader into a better grasp of the multi-levels of the work.

Often the picara adopts needlework as a cover for prostitution. Thus, immediately after she introduces herself, Estri identifies her planet as the source of the "scintillating, indestructible web-cloth woven by our domestic arachnids" and of the "intelligent builder-beatles [sic] who exude from their mouths that translucent superhard substance called gol" (*Couch* 1). These two items, spider webs and "gol" [golden honey or amber] are produced by spiders, the medieval models of feminine deceit, and by bees or ants, the medieval model of community life whose workers are all women. It is not surprising then that Estri links these items with the third product for which Silistra is famous: "And perhaps you have seen no web-cloth, no gol... and are not interested in sex (*Couch* 1). According to Hall, the temple women who nurtured the young Zeus on mead were called the "melissae" or "bee maidens" because they serviced the womb-like cave of Zeus-Trophonios where initiates could seek self-knowledge through amnesia, such as is imposed on Estri by Khys.

As the well Keepress, she is "High Couch," a designation for any woman who can demand thirty gold coins of the realm. However, in the second book *The Golden Sword*, while she values herself accordingly, she is made a low slave by the desert chieftain Chayin with no rights over her own body. In the third book, *Wind from the Abyss*, even her personality is stripped from her as her lover Khys imprisons her psychic abilities by a throat band and her memory by oblivion. She is made to bear his child, a monster, whom she abandons as soon as possible. Eventually in the fourth book, she helps a contender for the carnelian throne to achieve it and restores unity to the planet.

In summary, the prostitute nature of the picara which gleams through Estri's adventures is more noticeable because of her declared profession as courtesan. In the fantasy, however, the promised adventures of a courtesan become reduced to the quest theme with a female as the hero. There is little of the pugnaciousness and persistence expected of a picara; Estri is not an entrepreneurial agent in her own destiny; rather, she takes no overt direct action to change her status once she has left the Well. Despite her calling, she is dependent upon men for protection and for emotional support. In this she follows the general outline of the fantasy picara who is more the daughter of romance than of Roxana.

The true picara is more autonomous. If her yellow courtesan veil serves to obscure the grey dullness of her marriages, it makes her a more easily recognizable figure in the tapestry because her veil is highlighted by the white silk of her autonomy.

Chapter Seven
Wanderer and Warrior

Textural effects are also produced in tapestry by the use of slits. A slit is a turn-back in the weaving, either caused accidentally where two areas of different colour coincide along the line of the warp, or created intentionally by the weaver...They are used to suggest shadows and can also help to break up an uninteresting plain surface. When the human figure occurs in a design for tapestry, slits are of great importance in the modelling of flesh and in indicating the structure of bones and muscles. They are also useful where a slight, but definite line is needed in a place where a change of colour or an outline in colour might appear too hard or heavy. (Rhodes 54)

Imagine the silvery grey shadows of the elusive wanderer and the purple bruises of the warrior swirling around the picara's figure, highlighted by her white autonomy and defined by the intentional slits in the tapestry.

Wanderer

Because the common metaphor for life is that of the journey, the two aspects of travel and of war are closely related. Where the hero's quest results in his self-identity, the picara participates in a quest for survival. She may possess the masculine strength to adventure but lacks the masculine reason; she may be the feminine Chaos but lacks the nurturing aspect of motherhood. Where the hero's inwardly feminine quest results in spiritual reconciliation, the picara's inward quest never leads to any resolution because she never accepts her spiritual side. She is the eternal pilgrim, seeking peace over the next hill, never finding it in herself. She wants food—not the pallid bread of Lazarillo or the Eucharist— but the exotic food of new challenges, of new places. If one country or city cannot provide such nourishment, another will. Except in her memoirs, the picara seldom looks back or reflects on where she has been; she regrets little and would change little because change itself is an active element in her life. Changing scenes is as easy as changing aspects of her nature and travel becomes the *raison d'etre* of her existence. For the picara, the wanderer motif can be subdivided into her recognizable aspects as a nomad, gypsy, messenger, pilgrim, hunter, linguist, and finally as a soldier or warrior.

The nomadic life itself parallels the chaos of the picara's life and justifies her adventure-seeking. In her role as Chaos, the wanderer is one who chances change and growth by exposure to different cultures, always open to the new adventures of a "stranger in a strange land." In contrast, the agriculturalist is one rooted in the soil, one not open to change, one whose feminine pre-occupation with feeding her children puts her into opposition with the masculine nomadic or hunting traditions. The picara is no mother or agriculturalist, waiting for growth; she is an adventuress, seeking change, reaping harvest. The picaro wanders because he is cut off from the feudal system; the picara wanders because it is to her economic advantage.

Even within the nomadic life, which stresses interdependence of individuals within a tribal structure, the picara is made uneasy when she cannot exert her autonomy. Even in the utopian community of women, she fights to define herself as an eccentric individual. Often that fight forces her to disrupt the placid utopia: Sargent's *The Shore of Women* creates a city utopia where women assume both male and female roles in the city, save for conception of children; the men travel in nomadic groups and are kept ignorant of technology. The heroine Laissa tries to circumvent her city's restrictions by raising the daughter of her twin brother Avril and her outcast friend Birana in the city. So also in Sheri Tepper's *The Gate to Women's Country*, the younger heroine's escape back into her feminine utopia means that she must surrender her personal autonomy for the common good when she learns that the romantic love the male hunters offer is a farce. Joy Chant's heroine in *When Voiha Awakes* is a leader who questions the wisdom of her feminine utopia. While the fantasy picara challenges her utopia, she is content to try to reform the system from within. The role of the dissident is adopted by the villainess who disrupts the utopian life. The outcast brigand Thella in Anne McCaffrey's *Renegades of Pern* seeks only her own survival at the expense of the communal good; as such, she has strong picaresque qualities.

Because raising a child requires a commitment of time and energy that the picara is unwilling to invest, the fantasy picara often turns her child over to the community, in the manner of child abandonment. Charnas' Alldera, who wants no part of her child, is mildly pleased that the girl has four nomadic "share-mothers" to raise her in the wilderness. In contrast, Sargent's Birana does not really want to give up her daughter but realizes that nomadic life outside the city is not fit for humans so she allows her friend Laissa to adopt the child. McIntyre's Snake is reluctant to adopt Melissa because of her own nomadic life as a healer. Tepper's heroine must learn of the real genetic makeup of the children born in the women's country and must reject the false romanticism of the outcast male warriors before she can become a full participant in governance. In fantasy, the union of two or more women acting as one often become the agents of continuing a society by adopting a child to raise within a community such as Charnas' utopia or Green's Amazon warriors and Bradley's Free Amazon society. Often seen in iconography in the configuration of the Renaissance portraits of St. Anne, the Virgin Mary and the Christ Child, the two women and one child is a familiar theme. In contrast, the hero seeks a single father; the heroine finds many mothers. Karr replicates this triad in her Frostflower, Thorn, and Starwind triad.

In contrast, the picara has nothing to do with such configurations of women's communities or mother-models because they impinge on her autonomy. Sargent's Laissa rejects her society but brings her adopted daughter into it. Charnas preserves the autonomy of Alldera by having her reject all attempts to incorporate her in any society. When she escapes from the male-dominated Holdfast, she prefers to run wild with the Riding Women rather than stay with the free fems who are semi-nomadic and are tied to their wagons and their raising of grain. She eventually abandons them all to live by herself like a desert harlot for a good part of the novel. In part, Alldera's calling as a messenger has given her the skill in running which becomes a metaphor for her restlessness. While a picara may be a messenger, she is more likely to be a spy; in this, she is motivated more by her greed for money than by her patriotism. For the most part in fantasy, the messenger's life is a selfless one and not truly picaresque. Mercedes Lackey's heroine in her *Arrows of the King* trilogy is messenger of the king, retiring only when life in the saddle was too much for her advanced age. Bradley's Free Amazons are used as messengers and travel guides as are Lynn's Sorren and Norres. The latter pride themselves that they are incorruptible, a virtue with which the picara is not burdened.

Another aspect of the picara's life is found in the stories of the pilgrim saints whose journeys satisfied both a physical and spiritual restlessness to find the perfect saint's tomb or religious site. From the beginnings of Christianity with the travels of the apostles and disciples, the pilgrim has been a respected person whose wanderings justified his life. Chaucer's Wyf of Bath and Madame Eglantine provide literary analogues to the very real wanderings of Margery Kempe and Christina of Sweden. The wanderings of converted prostitutes like Mary of Egypt lose no validity in being compared with an historical figure like Helena, mother of the emperor Constantine, whose extensive journeys from her home in Colchester to the Holy Land led her to discover the True Cross. The picara's travel to a sacred site like St. James Compostella in Spain serves to strengthen her Spanish heritage; her tales ignore cultural boundaries to follow the road of the wandering troubadours and Goliardic scholars.

The wandering saint or mystic, thus, may have been an unnoted source for the picara. The women mystic, suspected of hysteria or deception, parallels the accusations of witchcraft attached to a picara like Celestina; also the healer or miracle worker whose touch brought physical and emotional relief is paralleled in the picara's sleight-of-hand cures and in the wandering witch of white magic, the sorceress, the wise woman. In addition, the trade of begging, typical of the wandering saints, parallels the picara's ability to obtain money under any pretense. While the journey of the pilgrim saints may have been undertaken to escape temptation, the journey of the picara provides the means to escape persecution as well as prosecution.

Tales of other groups became intertwined with those of the picara because of their peripetic life style. The gypsies, in particular, influenced the picara with their distinctive Romany language and nomadic customs. In their refusal to conform to city living, they imitated the picaresque wanderlust while their disregard for authority, the implications of theft and immoral life style, the suspicion of witchcraft in their fortune-telling all added up to the fear of the gypsy. Courage easily acclimates herself to the gypsy life because it suits all aspects of her personality while Moll leaves them because she is fastidious. While the novel picara seldom mentions gypsies, the fantasy picara is often the wandering space pilot or nomadic navigator who takes jobs on whim. In the same manner, the traveling troupe of actors or charlatans who followed the circuit of the feudal castles and towns were tarred with the same brush as the picara; anyone on stage must be immoral. The disfavor of the official church in declaring all actors excommunicated further separated her from her religion. Often the improvisational skits of the *commedia dell'arte* troupe, whose script adjusted to each new city, gave an outline of the picara's ruses and scams.

In contrast, when people had left the encastled strengths of the feudal holdings for the walled protection of towns, the picaro rebelled and satirized the new mercantile society that shut him out. At the same time, the picara, who loves the interaction and bustle of the towns, was born to travel from town to town, lover to lover, adventure to adventure. As society shifted from the enclosed feudal kingdom to the town structure to the exploration of new worlds, travel was rendered obsolete as a sufficient symbol for life's journey. In its place, "seafaring proved a rich field [because] preachers could now draw upon the vivid details of overseas exploration and trade...whose mundane details were most frequently spiritualized, just as seafaring tended to supplant overland pilgrimages in the imagery of labor" (Starr 23-5). This same seafaring image recurs in the fantasy picara's penchant for spacecraft as transportation and her involvement in science fiction.

The concept of the wanderer extends beyond the limits of the earth into the galaxies of the universe, bearing with it the same traits that the earthly picara took on her travels. Clayton's Aleytys follows this picaresque pattern. When her mother Shareem is stranded on a primitive planet by the crash of her spacecraft and forced into pregnancy by a barbarian, she names her daughter Aleytys or "wanderer" in her native tongue. When she abandons the child to return to her highly technological planet, she leaves a book of explanations and instructions for Aleytys' quest to find her true heritage with her mother. "We're wanderers, we Vrya, spacefarers...The stars are our sea marks, the universe our home" (*Diadem* 52). After nine books of wandering, Aleytys does come home to her mother or, more correctly, to her mother-substitute; like a heroine, she finds many mothers. Her work as a special agent for the galactic undercover agency of the Hunters allows her to find her son, her mother(s), and her series of lovers.

In her guise of the hunter, the picara is again a wanderer. While her aspect of Diana the huntress places her in the forest, her image is far removed from who one hunts to feed herself. In the novel picara, the image is more the romantic concept of the huntress of hearts, someone who uses her survival skills to marry well. Becky is netting a green silk purse to capture Jos Sedley; May Welland in Edith Wharton's *The Age of Innocence* defies her society to be an archer and marries Archer Newland. In the fantasy picara, the hunting image returns to its primal meaning; despite her initial resistance, no picara hesitates killing if it means she can eat. For example, the world of Green's Jalav and her warrior tribes predates even nomadic herding since they forage the forest for food daily with no preparation for the future; what they capture that day they eat. If the skill of foraging belongs to the primitive huntress, the art of scavenging is no less an attribute for the picara in a bombed-out future universe and the picara is no less adapt in finding food. Russ's Alyx forages on the hostile planet of Paradise; other picaras scavenge from the ruins of cities or deserted stockpiles. In future utopias or technologically superior worlds, the picara must still kill to eat, as Clayton's Brann does. When she must kill, the fantasy picara does so cleanly and with an apology so that she becomes part of the Great goddess tradition which holds all life as sacred.

One outstanding feature of picaresque travel is the autonomy that fluency in language gives the picara. The picara's retelling of her verbal disguises, deceptions, and escapes become as important as the scams themselves. Her fluency in her native language due to her city upbringing permits her a broader range of action than if she were limited by a regional accent or country twang. Accents, however, are used to connect the picara with the Greek *hetairai* and Renaissance courtesans whose intellectual discussions attracted as much attention as their promiscuity. For example, to stress the international flavor of the picara, Marston's Dutch Courtesan Franceschina is given an accent which is a "helter-skelter of Germanic, French, Italian, as well as pure English, pronunciation, added to conventional grammatical error [to set] his courtesan off from all his other characters with a ridiculous stage Dutch accent" (Wine xix). Courage speaks to her scribe "in a manner which showed her good intellect and also made it clear that she lived with gentlefolks" (193), even though she admits earlier that she "could speak German fairly well, but as all Bohemians, I did not let on that I did" (37). Courage's refusal to talk to her scribe "in gypsy dialect" (193) implies her facility with that language and the exoticism of the gypsy life. Amber convinces herself that she is worthy of the stage because "her voice was good [and] she had lost her country drawl" (174).

While Defoe's Crusoe has only a limited need for verbal fluency since he is isolated on one island, Defoe also suggests exoticism in the location of that island near the river Orinoco, the Amazon river in South America near Surinam which was the site of Aphra Behn's *Oronooko* some forty years earlier. Defoe's Colonel Jack acknowledges some familiarity with Spanish and French while his Moll is far too English to extend her facility with language beyond her native tongue. Roxana adopts a disguising accent when she "so us'd myself to THEE and THOU that I talk'd like a Quaker too, as readily and naturally as if I had been born among them" (213). English is not her native language, although she states that she "went to English schools [and] learnt the *English* tongue perfectly well...but spoke what we call Natural English" (6). Although she is French by descent, she brags that she retained none of the "Remains of the *French* language tagg'd to my Way of Speaking, *as most Foreigners do*" (6).

Likewise, Roxana's fluency in several languages suggests her as the foreign prostitute so feared in English literature. Her later acquisition of Italian serves merely to underscore her general education as an upper-class woman, although she avers that "I got pretty well Mistress of that, before I had been there a Year; and as I had Leisure enough, and loved the language, I read all the *Italian* Books I cou'd come at" (102). Her knowledge of Turkish contributes to her profession as a courtesan: "I learnt the *Turkish* language; their way of Dressing, and Dancing, and some *Turkish* or *Moorish* songs of which I made use, to my Advantage, on an Extraordinary Occasion some years after, as you shall hear in its Place" (102). It is the dance and the songs which propel her into the court life and secure her fortunes for a while. Even Amy comments on Roxana's skill with language when she speaks of her relief that her mistress will not have to learn "the Devil's language, call'd HIGH-DUTCH" (23). Her knowledge of Dutch nearly leads her into trouble on her drive to Pall Mall; when the Quakeress recognizes the language but not the content of the conversation, Roxana passes off the gentlemen's remarks with a casual "I know very well what they are talking of, but 'tis all about Ships and Trading affairs" (218).

Just as Roxana can claim French ancestry, Thackeray's Becky has her artistic ability from her father and her French heritage from her mother, an opera-girl "who had had some education somewhere" (10). Consequently, Becky who "spoke French with a purity and a Parisian accent" (10) becomes so good a linguist that she is able to "talk French" (11) at Miss Pinkerton's school. This ability in French enables her to tour the cities of Europe from Russia to Italy to Germany with impunity. Becky's descent into the bohemian boarding house at Baden Baden is characterized by her use of French to talk to young George Osbourne and by her use of German with the students when she mocks the ease with which she has again seduced Jos Sedley. On the other hand, while Scarlett shows no particular need for verbal skills beyond English, her French ancestry is traced through her grandmother Solange Robillard, "a dainty, cold, high-nose Frenchwoman," (31). Oftentimes the picara's language facility is hidden, appearing only in the social cliches needed to disguise the lower social origins of the picara. Thus, a modern picara like Capote's Holly Golightly sprinkles *bon mots* from French, colloqialisms from her Texan ancestry, Portuguese words for her Brazilian lover, and slang from her gangster dealings into her speech to enhance her cosmopolitan image.

In all cases, the verbal dexterity of the picara adds to her flexibility in her travels because she can enter any society by adopting a verbal camouflage which enables her to pull off her scams. Courage is "forced to quit the city" (166) when the magistrates realized the extent of her illicit activities; Becky leaves various cities one step ahead of the authorities and impatient creditors. Forced to scrounge out her living after Rawdon Crawley refuses to help her any more, she is banned from several of the cities for improper conduct which Thackeray details in his forty-fourth chapter tantalizingly entitled "A Vagabond Chapter." Hinting "at the existence of wickedness in a light, easy, and agreeable manner, so that nobody's fine feelings may be offended" (617-2), Thackeray satirically chronicles Becky's descent from the pension in Boulogne to the boarding house at the German watering spa, insisting that "she was, in fact, no better than a vagabond upon the earth" (681).

Fluidity in traveling from house to house is raised to a picaresque virtue when it saves the picara's reputation. When Roxana's Dutch husband suggests that they move, she hears him "with a great-deal of pleasure, *as well* as for his being willing to give me the Choice, as for that I resolv'd to live Abroad, for the Reason I have mention'd already, *namely*, lest I shou'd at any time be known in *England*, and that Story of *Roxana*, and the Balls, shou'd come out" (241-1). Oftentimes, when she cannot handle the matter herself, the picara surrenders her autonomy and delegates unpleasant duties to her confidante so that she can concentrate on picaresque livelihood. Courage's nurse and her lover Skipinthefield run her household; Moll's governess is her friend and her fence as she descends into theft. The rigors of such a peripetic life are eased by confidantes like Amy who act as a protective camouflage to offset the picara's doubtful reputation. Amy often tends to the chores of relocating, even to suggesting the lodging itself as she does with the Quakeress' home, and Amy arranges the abandonment of Roxana's five children while Roxana stays immured in her former house. But even as close a confidante as Amy cannot neutralize the picaresque restlessness which prevents the picara from settling down into a normal household. Roxana herself remarks that "I myself had not always a fix'd Abode" (240).

So also Amber, Moll's and Roxana's counterpart, is forever changing lodgings to escape detection in the early part of the novel. When she acquires her maid Nan Britton, she allows the capable confidante to arrange the particulars of each move; it is Nan who takes the household into the safety of the country when the plague hits London. Even when Amber hopes to deceive the court about following her married lover Bruce Carlton, she has Nan at her other home "packing and getting the children and their nurses ready to go" (745). When Nan takes Amber's place when she has an assignation, it always represents some form of travel from lover to lover or from source of wealth to source of wealth. Carried out in a laundry basket, Amber attempts to blackmail one of Charles' ministers while Nan, disguised as Amber, leads the spies on a dull chase. Knowing her alter ego Nan will follow, Amber's last action is to take a coach for flight to Americas, to her lover's Virginia plantation, just as her ancestress Moll finds her lover in Virginia. In contrast, Scarlett's travel is limited to a small geographic area around Atlanta and Tara and an even smaller social arena of the South's restrictive society which limits her movements to traveling from husband to husband; for her to take a lover would endanger her social strata, something inimicable to her continued possession of Tara. Her marriages are upwardly mobile ones, each husband richer and more prominent than the last. While she scorns her sister for marrying for love and beneath her station, Scarlett's rejection of love wraps around to haunt her when she cannot recapture Rhett's love. The novel is saved from a romantic ending by Scarlett's picaresque optimism.

Travel entails difficulties for the picara. To the early picara, packing up and moving was an adventure because wealth was portable; the picaro had none to speak of so that the next town might provide better luck; the picara's wealth is in portable gold jewelry to be sold as her body is sold. To the later picara, however, her autonomy is compromised by tangible possessions instead of immediate cash and her avarice demands retention of these goods. Where Roxana seems to worry excessively about the moving of her household goods, it is because those goods represent real money. Having had the humiliation of seeing her home stripped of its possessions, Roxana thereafter deals mostly in goods which are immediately convertible into cash: the plate service and gold and jewels of the Prince, the Holland bills of credit, and the handling of her monies by Sir Robert Clayton. Whenever she holds onto household goods, Roxana faces a tangible threat to her safety in deception. When she and her Dutch merchant husband offer the Quakeress an annuity, Roxana hedges about the amount of dinner service she possesses, explaining

My meaning was, about the Box of Plate, a good part of which I gave her, and some I gave to *Amy*, for I had so much Plate, and some so large, that I thought if I let my Husband see it, he might be apt to wonder what Occasion I cou'd ever have for so much, and for Plate of such a kind too; as particularly, a great Cistern for Bottles, which cost a hundred and twenty Pound, and some large Candlesticks, too big for any ordinary Use. (254)

In a similar manner, when Amber has to hide her ready money and jewels from the nurses, she hides them in the bed of the plague-stricken Bruce. Her household goods are equally well cared for: "the silver has been stored with Shadrac Newbold but there was pewter enough in the kitchen to make a handsome show" (366).

Scarlett differs slightly from the picaresque norm because she has substituted the estate of Tara for the immediacy of cash which the usual picara desires. This is in keeping with the changes in economic systems: whereas Roxana is a leading proponent of new mercantilism, Scarlett is shown as being foolish in her holding onto the land in opposition to the "newer" economy represented by Rhett and the bankers. While the tangible wealth of the family silver has been saved by putting it in the well to protect it from the invading Yankee armies, the three remaining bales of cotton do not suffice for the taxes and she is land poor. Her heritage of Tara is more the dream vision of her father than it is a viable reality of landownership for Scarlett herself; in contrast, her lumber mill, store, and saloon allow her entrepreneurial skills to emerge whereas the farm flourishes only when the Yankee overseer/farmer tills it. Scarlett is both romantic and picaresque in a way no other picara is; Moll, for example, sells her Virginia holdings to live more comfortably in England.

Flexibility in language and in travel implies that the picara adapts readily to a variety of national cultures without necessarily losing her own national personality: new countries and new cultures provide new contrasts and new fields for the picara to test her autonomy and for her author to satirize. Certainly the picara is aware of her nationality in contrast to others, but the nationalism dissipates as the picara grows older. While the early Courage refers to herself as a Bohemian in contrast to her German Captain, her nationalism fades as she becomes a mercenary soldier, a sutler, and finally a gypsy who has "visited every corner of *Europae* several times" (191). Even with this widening tolerance of nationalities, Courage still retains enough nationalism to make moral judgments of a prejudicial nature, such as her pejorative reference to "French whores" (182). In a similar burst of nationalism, Long Meg of Westminister goes to fight the French at Boulogne for Henry VIII, bests a boastful Frenchman by beheading him, and returns to England with a royal annuity for her bravery.

In like manner, Defoe uses Roxana to satirize certain foreign traits although her views toward a country are not necessarily those of Defoe. Even though she steadfastly considers herself "an *English-Woman*, tho' I was born in *France* (111), she does not mind living in foreign countries; in fact, when she is in France she "began to think we might take up our constant Residence there, which I was not very averse to it, being my Native Country, and I spoke the Language perfectly well: so we took a good House in *Paris*" (51). She enjoys several cities in Italy, with a limited and Puritan tolerance:

I began to be so in Love with *Italy*, especially with *Naples* and *Venice* that I cou'd have been very well satisfied to have sent for Amy and have taken up my Residence there for Life.

As to Rome, I did not like it at-all, the Swarms of Ecclesiasticks of all kinds, one side, and the scoundrel-Rabbles of the Common People, on the other, make *Rome* the unpleasantest Place in the world, to live in. (103)

Amy, however, dislikes foreign countries and warns Roxana that she would be better off in England than to "lay your Bones in another World" (238).

Roxana and the picaras regard the exchange of countries much the same way they regard forms of money: whatever brings the highest return is the best. Rather than lose the valuable service of Harry her ostler, Long Meg takes his place in order that her tavern be kept solvent. Mary Carleton Moders changes scenes along with her disguises; Moll Flanders moves about London with the skill of an escape artist. Becky follows the watering spa circuit because it brings in money; Scarlett flits between Tara and Atlanta to protect her investments; Amber willingly leaves England for the wilds of Virginia because her "investment" in Bruce Carlton is her major wealth. In her criminal aspect, the picara finds fluidity of change permits new fields to be cropped. Even so slight a picara as Capote's Holly is in imitation of a "travelin' man" of southern jargon, a restless wanderer. The only physical item she can afford from Tiffany's is her business cards which indicate her mood: "Miss Holiday Golightly, Traveling" (11). Even her songs, those "harsh-tender, wandering tunes that smacked of pineywoods or prairie" (16-7), are reminiscent of her earlier life in Tulip, Texas. While she does travel from lover to lover like all picaras do, she also skips out of the country to avoid the police. The narrator receives a postcard from Buenos Aires explaining why she left Brazil; the last she is heard from, she has had a portrait carved by a woodcarver in East Anglia, Africa.

With all her traveling, the early picara is surprisingly tolerant while the novel picara and fantasy picara show increasing tolerance as the global village grows smaller. Each new place presents a new page for the picara's memoirs and each new face presents a new possibility for a scam. If the picara dislikes anyone, it is the individual within a race, not the race itself. Science fiction presupposes galactic equality of the races or species; fantasy follows suit and the fantasy picara shows tolerance for all races and species. She may prefer one race over another; she may dislike some racial feature but she accepts all life in all its forms, harkening back to her roots as the Great Goddess. In turn, the picara's society does not much like her. In the early picara, her skill at her tricks and her prostitution are enough to make her an outcast. For the novel heroine, the educative novel or *bildungsroman* shows how alienated she was from her society. In the fantasy picara, her ability for sorcery or psychic powers separates her from her society. Often the fantasy picara dislikes her home culture because it restricts her abilities. In addition, fantasy forces a whole new vocabulary to develop: the picara is no longer an "outlander" or "foreigner" or "stranger" but an "off-worlder" or "offplanet" or "different" in her ways or looks.

For example, when Clayton's Aleytys learns of her mother's rape and her own superior abilities, she leaves her home planet where she had been made to feel as an outsider. What separates her first is her red hair: she is called a "red bitch" (20). Although roughly four percent of the world's people are redheads, literature uses red hair to symbolize the alienation of the hero or heroine from society. In romance and in fantasy, red hair is usually an acceptable and desirable attribute of the heroine in particular. While the red hair of Scarlett and Amber makes them admirable romantic heroines, Becky's sandy hair shows the Victorian prejudice against red hair. In Bradley's Darkover novels, red hair is the sign of the chosen ruling caste. Sometimes picara's racial features are foreign to her childhood culture. Jade Darcy is an outcast for three reasons: her "Oriental face which she'd inherited from her Japanese mother" (13), the scars on her back from her bionic surgeries, and her computer-enhanced abilities as a fighter. She is forced to work on the backward planet of Cablans (Calibans?) to avoid discovery as a CARC, a "computer-augmented-reflex-commando" (186), until another Terran, Megan Cafferty, becomes her mentor and business partner, much in the manner of a bawd and her prostitute.

Another type of prejudice exists in the society which kills or rejects anyone different. For example, Serroi in Clayton's Duel of Sorcery series is a "misborn," a child conceived at Winterdeep, the wintering place of the windrunners [horses] during a night of festivity before her tribe's departure for summer lands. For two years she is normal but "in Serroi's third year pale green splotches like old bruises darkened her small body...by the end of the third Wintering the splotches spread to her face and the eyespot began to take shape between her brows" (*Moonscatter* 61). Before her tribe can sacrifice her to the fire, Serroi is saved by the wizard Ser Norris, who uses her talents to deepen his own by making her in charge of a menagerie of his genetic experiments. Maxwell's Firedancer series has the golden-haired Rheba introduced against a similar galatic melting pot; she is a firedancer from the destroyed planet of Deva, whose light brown body is overlaid with "almost invisible...whorls and intricate patterns of a young Senyas fire dancer" (2), the *akhenet* energy patterns that deepen as she grows in strength. Her companion and mentor Kirtn is a Bre'n, "a tall humanoid with very short, fine coppery plush [and] a mask of metallic gold [around] his eyes, emphasizing their yellow clarity" (*Firedancer* 1-2). He is forbidden access to the nightclub, the Black Whole, because he is a "furry" and not a "smoothie" like Rheba. Similar prejudices follow them in their adventures.

Sometimes the picara's powers alienate her from her society. Frostflower must travel in both books about her to the city and away from her safe country-sorceress homeland. Both trips end in her imprisonment because she is a sorceress in a city of farmer-priests who fear her powers. Green's Terrilian is a Prime empath whose abilities segregate her from her family and her society; she continues to be an outsider on Rimilia because she is a non-conformist who refuses to accept the local customs of banding women as slaves. Her real alienation comes when no one, not even the man she loves, understands or sympathizes with her inner empathetic feelings. It is not until the final book that she realizes that her empathy has been doubled because her lover Tammad is a latent empath who has been reflecting her own emotions back into her mind.

Most fantasy authors deal with prejudice within their novels by using an artificial caste system. Bradley's is the most elaborate with the restrictive families of Darkover basing their prejudice on the possession of the psychic power of *laran* by certain members of the clans. Loosely based on Gaelic structure, the establishing families developed the power into an elaborate system of priestesses and towers. As the novels emerged, the power system was more defined and more individuals accepted or rebelled against the system. The Darkovans' resistance to off-world travel and ideas come to fruition in *Thendara House* and *City of Sorcery* where Magda and Jaelle exchange cultures. Magda tries to reconcile her Darkovan half with her Terran half in her entrance into the house of the Free Amazons or Renunciates while Jaelle, a Free-Amazon from the restrictive chain-bonding society, attempts to adopt the Terran life style for love of Magda's former husband. Both women experience prejudice in their new cultures; their solution is to chose a spiritual realm over a temporal or material one, when they become one of the gray Sisterhood, a semi-mystical order of *laran* believers. To do so, they travel to the City of Sorcery where they are once more outsiders but ones who are accepted into a community of people who have similar beliefs.

The travel of the fantasy picara depends on the world to which she is traveling. As the picaro became the satiric yardstick of his society, so also does the picara become the measuring stick of her society by the choice of the worlds she visits. Where the novel picaras could not escape their worlds except by fleeing from country to country, the fantasy picaras can choose new planets and new species. In summary, where the old world in destroyed and a civilization destroyed, the picara is bereft in the same way that the rejection of the family hurt her. She must reestablish herself in a new society, a challenge always. Some picaras leave their home worlds because of prejudice as in Clayton's Aleytys and Serroi. Some are stranded on or abducted to a foreign planet and happens to Aleytys' mother Shareem, Bradley's Zygedik, and Morris' Estri. Some choose exile on an inhospitable planet as in Goldin and Mason's Jade and Russ's Alyx. Some leave their home world because of an evil person as in Clayton's Serroi and Skeen. And some just leave because their home world is boring.

Oftentimes the picara's world, reminiscent of the war-beset world of the early picara, may be destroyed, providing the motivation of revenge or the intent to reestablish the world somewhere else. Clayton's Brann has her home world of Arth Slya destroyed by soldiers and by an earthquake; that, coupled with the enforced stripping of her womanhood to make her into a feeding machine for the Changer children, sends her on her errands to right the wrongs of the world. When Deva, the world of the firedancer Rheba and her Bre'n mentor Kirtn, is destroyed by a planetary accident, scattering the Senyas and Bren'n races, they try to find other survivors to insure that the race will continue; she finds one immature male Lheket and his nurse/mentor Ilfn so that she is assured of bearing children eventually but "first she has light-years to go and promises to keep. She had to deliver each one of the people on the ship to his, or her or *hir* home" (*Illusion* 6); the series ends with the third book when the characters are enroute to another planet. Some picaras go to a better world. Aleytys ends up on Vryh as the heiress of her mother. Bradley's Camilla, Jaelle, and Magda go into the mystical gray Sisterhood of the city of sorcery. Atwood's handmaid may or may not go to a better world since her ending is left nebulous. Some picaras find a sort of peace in a community of women. Clayton's Serroi joins the *meien* of women, her Deel seeks out and rejects the Sayoneh community in *Bait of Dreams*. Green's Jalav is quite happy with her home world's tribal structure of women warriors although she ends up with the promise of further adventures off-world.

The picara tries to reform her original world or make it better as a result of her increased powers and integrity. Sometimes this is in the nature of her profession: McIntyre's Snake is a healer who discovers the reproductive system of the dreamsnake and who gives that knowledge to her fellow scientists and healers. The picara who is a witch or sorceress does likewise; her professions profit from her adventures and increased knowledge. Morris' Estri is a more powerful and sorceress who brings peace and harmony to her land because she is a fully balanced person. Karr's Frostflower is a stronger and more convinced sorceress and her companion Thorn is a better warrior. When the profession is one of soldiering, the increased knowledge leads to better protection for the warrior's people. Abbey's Rifkind and other princesses gain strength from their adventures. Vinge's Arienrhod tries to remake her society to suit herself but her daughter is a better ruler for having experienced the pain of growth.

If she cannot control the world she inhabits, the picara can sometimes control the time and the morality. If Dickens' Oliver Twist can grow so morally straight and true in his Victorian slums, then the heroine from galatic slums can also grow morally true. Alienated or not, the fantasy character is morally sound even when those around her are not; she must ultimately be honorable enough for the reader to identify with her. Morality shifts as the time period shifts. The early picara considers her lies, thefts, and violences as equally sinful as her prostitution while the later picara considers her sexual pecadillos as her least serious offense. What each fantasy picara considers to be her worst crime depends on her created world: to the sorceress, the misuse of her power; to the political picara, the corruption of a government; to the wanderer, the imprisonment of other; to the sexual being, the dehumanization of the individual. No picara heeds the morality of her own times (her nature as an oppositional being forbids it) yet critics judge the picara's morality according to that of the critic's own times.

Attention to historical detail is not needed in the early picara's stories because it is the story itself that is of interest; the later novel picara, dependent on the author's recreation of history from records, is prized for accuracy. For example, Defoe used the life story of Moll King whose 1718 transportation for stealing a gold watch and recapture in 1721 illustrates the temper of the times toward stealing in a mercantile society. Even Moll Flanders, who wrote her story in 1683 as she claims, is very much a woman of Defoe's 1720s. The facts of her life are truer and clearer because they are illustrated in literature. Roxana also has a misapplication with time. If she is the mistress of Charles II, and he died in 1685, she was two years old at the time of their affair. This inaccuracy does not affect the impact of Defoe's moral lesson any more than the impact of the moral teaching of Scriptural picaras like Judith and Esther is lessened by the fact that they probably did not exist.

In the fantasy picaras, however, time travel, time suspension, or time distortion may force an "artificial" sense of time within the story through a created literature. In a pseudo-medieval world, ballads create a sense of distancing for the reader. Indeed, the original stories of the picara followed the song routes of the ballads and romances; it should not seem strange to have the fantasy picara accompanied by her music. In fact, many of the fantasies refer to or supply ballads to accompany the exploits of the heroes. Moon's Paksenarrion is framed with a ballad, never explicitly recited, but often referred to as true history. Karr's Frostflower and Thorn are the subject of a ballad in the second book. The modern picara may live in other worlds, post-nuclear or intergalactic, alternative universes or utopian earth universes, but she has her troubadours and her scribes with her.

Whenever the picara lives, she travels. If starships or magic carpets are acceptable means of transport to her, the same technology can give the picara instant language ability through a number of inventive methods. The easiest transfer of knowledge is through a translator, a natural object or being who interprets languages unfamiliar to the picara. Maxwell's Firedancer series introduces Fssa, a snake-like parasitic shape-changer who sops up energy to create different mouths to form different sounds he hears "to speak a multitude of languages simultaneously. The snakes had evolved on a hot, gigantic planet as sonic mimics, then had been genetically modified...The result was a resilient, nearly indestructible translator who needed only a few phrases to learn any new language" (*Illusion* 8). Grateful to Rheba and Kirtn because they tell him he is beautiful twice a day, Fssa provides much of the humor in the novels. While he is adept at direct translation, his often child-like comments irritate his listeners until Kirtn threatens him to bring him in line if he mistranslates. Rheba and Kirtn communicate in three ways: the precise and scientific Senyas language, the trilling whistles of the poetic Bre'n, and Universal. Other characters have equally diverse languages: the crystal construct nicknamed Rainbow who causes Rheba headaches by his crystalline exchanges, the guttural language of the J/ Taal bodyguards, the sign language they are all forced to use from time to time. Even the ghost in *Dancer's Illusion* communicates in a unique way: having entered Rheba when she sniffed a flower, the ghost guides her with a primitive binary code of itching—itch for no, lack of itch for yes.

Another form of language transference is the implant or enhanced language ability transferred by sleep tapes. It is a convention that knowledge enter through the senses and, since the perceiving senses are on the front of the head, the head is the logical place for language to be located. In part this convention is derived from Athena, the goddess of wisdom and of war, springing full grown from the head of Zeus. Hence Clayton's Aleytys' diadem goes around the head; Rheba's Fssa interpreter nestles in her hair and hisses in her ear; Snake's precious dreamsnake Grass circles her neck. A modern form of a hearing aid, the implant is usually in the head while the implant for contraception, say, may be anywhere on the trunk. Sleep tapes or ones used in cryogenic or suspended sleep serve the same purpose. Knowledge of language is not easily transmitted and the picaras have no special way of doing this.

Transference is not always voluntary. Although Clayton's Brann is raised in an idyllic valley of artisans, she wants to travel with her father to the fair the summer before she must choose her life work but must stay at home with her mother. Escaping to the mountain to daydream, she finds life "joyful when you felt like fitting in, but when you didn't, it was like a pair of new boots, blistering you as it forced you into shape" (*Drinker* 61). Her language and her life change abruptly when she is altered into a means to transfer life energies for the demon children who depend on her for food.

Style of language is also a distinguished characteristic of the picara. Aware of her presence in high heroic fantasy, the picara adopts an exalted prose style. The speech patterns of Green's Jalav resemble translated poetry; the normal speech of her Terrilian contrasts with the stilted phrases of the barbarian Rimilian warriors. Such a mixture adds to the texture of the novel but makes for heavy reading. Travel and language bring the picara into contact with other cultures, where some men may become lovers. The travel of the picaras has always been an euphemism for the switching of lover for lover so that in fantasy the master-to-master or lover-to-lover concept is replaced by a galaxy-to-galaxy progression. In the early picaras, this was especially true when travel was not as common for a woman. As the picara progressed, however, travel became synonymous with the status of the lovers and with the waxing and waning of fortunes.

For example, in the novel picaras the ultimate lover was the king or the ruling monarch of the locality. Amber beds Charles II, Roxana has her disguised royalty—both French and English, Becky reaches the heights of a lord in Lord Steyne, Scarlett must make do with the monetary "king" of Atlantan society, Rhett Butler. The fantasy picara's version of this ultimate lover is her (or her mother's) bedding of a divine person. Although such a divinity is only a lesser god, the coupling gives her a semi-divine status. If the birth of Arthur is hidden in mystery, why not the birth of the fantasy picara? Indeed, it is often this mysteriousness about her birth that leads to her rejections by her society. Being born of a higher race, the picara often dislikes the race in which she is brought up without knowing why. The revelation of her true parentage explains all to her. For example, Estri is captured, raped, and possessed by a being superior to her in kind; Khys is another species of being, more powerful than she, but of the same stock. Where she is only half divine, he and her father are full gods. Interestingly, in almost all the cases of divine/human picara couplings, the woman does not enjoy sex because she does not choose her lover. Often she loves a human who cannot compare with the god but who is preferable with his human weaknesses. Green's Jalav is raped by Sigurr, the male "god" of the male warriors; the experience is both humiliating and painful to her. Green's Terrilian is mistaken for a woman of the "superior" race by the monster in the cave; to punish her for her aberration, he rapes her in sight of her two lovers.

Sometimes the picara takes as lovers humans who are demigods in alternative worlds or counter-cultures. These men may be the best of their kind—a king or prince or warrior chief—but they are usually endowed with a musculature possible only with steroids. Despite this, their sexual stamina is equally prodigious and the heroine must use her wisdom to separate physical attraction from true love. The picara seldom bothers, taking muscles and devotion in stride. Green's heroines are so afflicted because her first books—the Jalav and Terrilian ones— are inversions of John Norman's male utopic fantasy or Gor, where all the women are slaves. The picaras sometimes take non-humans as lovers; for example, Aleytys has an affair with the ant-like creature in *Irsud*. Often the coupling is with a machine. Helva in McCaffrey's *The Ship That Sang* is a deformed woman whose brain and personality become the computer of the space ship; as such, she acquires a series of lovers, faithful and otherwise. Jade Darcy is a computer-enchanted woman who hesitates in revealing her scars to her lovers; Heinlein's

Friday in a similar position is renounced by her group family when they discover her android characteristics.

While she may wander for survival, for profit, for fun or for mischief, the picara is an isolated person whose professions as prostitute and warrior force her into social ostracism in her search for autonomy.

Warrior

In her chapter on "Heroic Fantastic Femininity," Marleen Barr claims that "female sword and sorcery writers create power fantasies for women" because the real problem is "how to balance career aspirations and a sense of independence with social expectations and familial loyalties" (*Alien* 87). The picara had that figured out long ago.

In not considering her role as wife of uppermost importance and in not conforming to "patriarchy's selfless, restricted definition of motherhood" (*Alien* 85), popular belief accords the picara the role of an Amazon, although she is seldom one. Amazons break into three categories: historical, legendary, and literary. Historical ones include those women who fought for their lives on the battlefields. Familiar to us are Boedicia and Joan of Arc, Molly Pitcher and the modern Chinese Li Chen; equally familiar are the legendary heroines of Penthesilia and Hippolyta; less familiar are the rogues like the pirate queens like Grace O'Malley, Anne Bonney, and Mary Reed. By far the literary Amazons outnumber these few women heroes because the Amazon as a sub-type of sword-and-sorcery hero has multiplied with the growth of fantasy literature. While an Amazon may be a soldier, a soldier need not be an Amazon and the picara falls into this latter category. She is an occasional soldier, using that profession as she does others. While she may be called a warrior for reasons of distinction, she is not truly a warrior. Readers do not identify with heroes or heroines who kill for the sake of killing and, while adventuring may lead to death of the enemy, death of the enemy is never the goal of the picara. His humiliation may be, his death is not. Against whom would she pit her intelligence if there no villains?

The concept that women left to themselves are dangerous because they would overturn patriarchy is an old one, stemming perhaps from the Lilith myth. The picaresque has more than a hint of revolution in it; while the trickster does upset society's laws for a period, the picara earns her survival by profiting by this upset.

War is the ultimate upset. War is the natural matrix for the picara since she is the feminine form of the Lord of Misrule in her trickster aspect and of Chaos in her feminine aspect of the Great Goddess. As such, war is her usual background and most picaras are connected with a war scene. Despite her shifting genres, the picara who is always a force in opposition to her society finds her natural habitat in the chaos of war which permits her autonomy to surface. Where drama imitates conflict in the mock war battles of love in Kyd's *The Spanish Tragedy* and Shakespeare's Beatrice and Benedict, the novel must construct oppositional forces from the moral conflicts of its characters; Celestina is framed as a drama while Defoe uses dramatic dialogue when he wants to impress the importance of Amy's threatening Roxana's daughter. However, the very nature of the literary genres of science fiction and of fantasy imply some sort of conflict and it is there that the picara finds her most modern emanation. Even modern romances are phasing out the jealousy factor as a viable reason for hostility in favor of career difficulties, single parenthood, and genuine affection.

Peace to the picara is an undesirable state of affairs. Peace is static and non-challenging. Utopias for that reason seldom work out for the picara. The picara is uneasy in a utopia; she might be expected to work to earn her bread. The feminist utopias are inimicable to her because she cares little for the common good. Dystopias are not her scene either. The narrator in Margaret Atwood's character in *The Handmaid's Tale* is uneasy because she cannot gain autonomy over her actions in the patriarchal society where everything is regimented. Her bed, her clothes, her food, her thinking, her sex life are all regularized by pseudo-religious training techniques which mock and imitate those used by order of pre-Vatican II nuns. (For further details, see my article in *Christianity and Literature*, September 1988.) Inwardly she rebels by telling her tale to the tape cassettes; outwardly, she conforms to survive. Whether she does survive or not is left ambiguous in Atwood's satiric inversion of light and dark: as she is mounting the steps into the dreaded black van, she comments, "Whether this is my end or a new beginning I have no way of knowing: I have given myself over into the hands of strangers...And so I step up, into the darkness within; or else the light" (378). The character of Moira, the narrator's friend, is closer to that of the picara; rebellious and foul-mouthed from the start, she escapes from the Rachel and Leah training center and is almost smuggled into safety in Canada. When she is recaptured and given a choice between the brothel or sure slow death in the Colonies as a garbage collector in radiation dumps, she willingly joins Jezebel's because the brothel ensures a moderately good life: "The food's not bad and there's drinks and drugs, if you want it, and we only work nights" (324). As a prostitute, she can outwit men, if only for a short time. Although the narrator desperately wants "gallantry from her, swashbuckling, heroism, single-handed combat" (324), Moira disappoints her with her resignation to her status. Within the interpolated tale, Atwood reveals another aspect of the picara in the stagnation that Moira accepts while the narrator/picara refuses to accept it.

The constant traveling associated with a soldier has always provided a reason for the picara to escape punishment for a crime or uncomfortable circumstances, to change lovers and vistas, and to deceive new societies. As a traveler, the picara wants to escape detection and the guise of a soldier sometimes provides this. Courage dresses as a soldier to escape rape. How much is she a soldier is detailed in the lists of her marches into Germany and Hungary with her captain lover. She profits from her booty since she is considered as a boy soldier and not a woman. Her pride, which forces her to fight the boy who insults her, leads to her revelation that she is a girl; her avarice leads to her becoming a sutler; and her lust leads to her prostitution.

But she is not an Amazon. Speier postulates that Grimmelshausen's own experiences with war and soldiering may have caused his formation of Courage yet he also claims that Grimmelshausen used earlier novel stereotypes for her. For example, her Amazon characteristics are found in similar seventeenth century German baroque novels of the virago, the ancient archetype of the warrior goddess

Athena. Speier claims that she is "as much a caricature and mockery of the amazon to be found in the conventional baroque novel as she is a picaresque character. Her relation to the ideal virago resembles that of Don Quixote to the knightly code...she is a counter-heroine" (35). In contrast, Long Meg of Westminster becomes a soldier, not for her picaresque sins but for lesser sins of patriotism and pride. When the king's constable tries to impress her ostler into the army, Meg beats him; when his captain comes to see what has happened, Meg informs him that "were it not that I reverence all soldiers and honor captains, I would strike thee too, if thou didst offer to press our man." She backs up her boast by wielding a weapon with such "nimbleness and activity that they all wondered at her" (103). Working as a laundress (perhaps a euphemism for a camp-follower), Meg defends the breached walls of Boulogne by calling up an army of "women soldiers to throw down stones and scalding water in such abundance that...she rebated them from the walls before the soldiers in the town were up in arms," pursuing the enemy as "one of the foremost with her halberd to follow the chase" (104). In the same conflict, she bests a braggart Frenchman in a David-Goliath exchange. Posing as a "common soldier, a young stripling," Meg meets him in a "long and dangerous combat" before she kills him: "When she had done, she pulled out her scimitar and cut off his head, and with that pulling off her burgonet, she let her hair fall about her ears, whereby the Frenchmen perceived she was woman" (104). Tinged with Biblical allusions to Judith and David, the story of Meg employs the picaresque elements of disguise and satirical humiliation for the enemy.

While Meg's adventures are more in the line of the jest book biographies rather than an organized picaresque life, her penchant is not toward violence but toward pranks. Like many fantasy heroines, she never willingly injures anyone, never kills recklessly, never abuses the strength or skill she has. What makes her popular is her non-threatening submission to her husband whom she refuses to fight. Although she marries a man equally big and strong, Meg refuses to battle with him even when he forces the issue:

...there he delivered one staff and took himself another, and told her that for that he had heard she was so mankind as to beat all she met, withall, he would try her manhood and therefore bade her take which cudgel she would. She replied nothing, but held down her head. And with that he laid on her three or four blows. And she in all submission fell down upon her knees... "Husband," quoth she, "whatsoever I have done toward others, it behooveth me to be obedient towards you, and never shall it be said, though I can swinge a knave that wrongs me, that Long Meg shall be her husband's master, and therefore use me as you please." At these words they grew friends, and never after fell they at such mortal jar. (105).

Meg's "manhood" consists in her strength, not in her aggression. Like a picara, she uses only enough force to preserve her life or to reduce inflated braggarts with her satiric way.

But the picara is not essentially a warrior for just any reasons. She seldom kills and when she does it is for self-defense rather than for aggression. Courage, however, confesses that if her captain had not "given me such good proof of his ardent love and continued to keep me hoping that he would surely marry

me in the end, sooner or later I would have shot him at some moment when
he least expected it" (103). When Scarlett kills the Yankee cavalryman who
threatens her family, she has only a particularly picaresque motive because she
reverts to defending her food as much as her virtue:

As he lounged up the walk, hand on holster, beady little eyes glancing to right and left,
a kaleidoscope of jumbled pictures spun in her mind...attacks on unprotected women,
throat cuttings, houses burned over the heads of dying women, children bayoneted because
they cried, all of the unspeakable horrors that lay bound up in the name of "Yankee."
...Now he was in the dining room and in a moment he would walk out into the kitchen.

At the thought of the kitchen, rage suddenly leaped up in Scarlett's breast, so sharply
that it jabbed at her heart like a knife thrust, and fear fell away before her overpowering
fury. The kitchen! There, over the open kitchen fire were two pots...dinner that must
serve for nine hungry people and hardly enough for two. Scarlett had been restraining
her appetite for hours, waiting for the return of the others and the thought of the Yankee
eating their meager meal made her shake with anger. (439)

When she kills him, her reaction is that she has committed murder rather than
an act of war or of self-defense. But when she sees his body "suddenly she was
vitally alive again, vitally glad with a cool tigerish joy...She had struck a blow
of revenge for Tara—and her Ellen [her dead mother]" (440-1). The same incident
provides one of the few times she feels close to Melanie, when Melanie appears
with a sword to defend the household; Scarlett sees that "beneath the gentle
voice and dove-like eyes of Melanie there was a thin flashing blade of unbreakable
steel, felt too that there were banners and bugles in her Melanie's quiet blood"
(441).

The picara does not worry about whether she is better than a man; she
knows she is even when she is a soldier, a common soldier, in opposition to
the fantasy picara who is often the leader. For example, princesses set on revenge
may disguise themselves as soldiers but someday they are going to rule countries.
Green's Sofaltis is the heir apparent to her realm but chooses to be a soldier,
one of a fighting fist, a select group of five soldiers acting as a unit. Thorn
in Karr's *Frostflower and Thorn* and *Frostflower and Windbourne* is a warrior
in a society which includes axewomen, spearwomen, watchgirls, swordswomen.
Although Thorn is the best of her profession, possessing even the swearing abilities
of a soldier's vocabulary, she is an outlaw in both books because of her compassion
and justice. High heroic fantasy almost demands that soldiering be used as a
disguise rather than as a profession. Mercedes Lackey's heroine never rises above
the ranks of messenger nor does Lynn's Sorren. Elizabeth Moon's Paks rises
in the ranks into being paladin but is still very much a soldier.

Most picaras who are involved with wars are not always combatants or victims.
Courage is a soldier and a sutler during the Hundred Years War; Meg is a laundress
and soldier. Scarlett is an entrepreneur during the Civil War and immediately
after it while Becky's major action takes place at the ball before Waterloo. Even
as humble a picara as Jo March in *Little Women* becomes the woman she does
because she is the breadwinner and father when her own father is off fighting
the Civil War. However, neither Roxana nor Moll have any connection with
the military. Since Defoe had no specific knowledge of that area, his novels
center on the battleground of business where neither heroic bravery nor honor

are victorious and only the neat categorizing of goods is valued. Neither of Defoe's heroines is particularly brave because soldiering can lead to death; the violence is always distanced from them. The murder of Roxana's daughter is done by Amy and is done in self-defense rather than in aggression.

Becky is less involved with direct "heroic" killing yet her story is set against the Napoleonic wars. The decisive scene with George Osbourne is set against the ball before Waterloo and she follows the fortunes of war at a safe distance. Had George survived, the story would have taken a different track, one perhaps involving the escapades of Becky and George in Europe. In the same manner, Amber's story is set against a war scene with the hostilities of the English Civil War separating her father and mother before their marriage. The war image continues in that of Restoration England where the monarchy had just been restored and the scars of the Civil War had not yet healed. The short Dutch-English war of 1666-7 provides plot complications and the machinations of Charles' court resemble the battle strategies with the plague and the great fires of London adding excitement for the story. Amber is never a soldier yet she willingly murders when she ignores the pleas of nurse Spong during the plague and leaves her to die of the plague. Bruce himself is forced to kill the other nurse, Mrs. Maggot, to save Amber and himself.

Another reason the picara avoids the military setting is that she is too lazy to exert herself in learning a profession, especially one which would endanger her survival. Again the themes of survival overrides all the advantages that war might have for the picara. She wants to stay in existence as long as possible; soldiering is dangerous and the picara is a survivor. In the game of war, since the picara refuses to play by the rules, honor means nothing, a fact which alienates her from the classification of Amazon. Where the Amazon is shown as one woman fighting among many women, the individual warrior who may or may not associate herself temporarily with some military operation is usually a loner. Often she is bent on revenge—Lynn Abbey's *Daughter of the Bright Moon* and Jade Darcy become daughter/avengers who are motivated into warriorhood by the slaughter of their families. Or she may be the sword-and-sorcery genre heroine who seeks her identity through her sword skills because she is at odds with her society, like Salmonson's Tomoe Gozen. However, the most frequent and the most picaresque is the occasional woman who must defend herself from time to time but who takes no pleasure in the act but rather in its result.

In some ways the picara is a warrior. She loves to adventure. Long Meg's stories show time and again that her spirit of adventure led her into her escapades, not her aggression. In fantasy the soldiering is a means of escape fiction. Charnas admits in her essay "A Woman Appeared" that when she was writing *Motherlines*, the science fiction field was limited to women who were pictures only "as victims (that is, compliant or conquerable objects) or monsters (insatiable or castrating subjects). I meant to write a book about women who were neither victims nor monsters" (Barr 105). The women soldier is neither. Women in the science fiction/fantasy genre tend to be warriors. Salmonson's Introduction to her *Amazons!* defends the premise that, while fantasy "more than any other form of storytelling, is mythological in scope," the women in heroic fantasy have been "either helpless, evil, absent, drawn funny, or at most inferior companions [while] men are heroic, if only in a roguish fashion; women are not" (13-5).

To find the heroic woman, fantasy writers go to the Amazon concept of the professional soldier rather than to the picara outright. The traditional source of the word "amazon" comes from the legend of the women's removal of the right breast, "*mazos,*" to facilitate drawing the bow; Nina Auerbach suggests it derived from the Greek for "without barleycake," an allusion which classifies the Amazons with savages like Homer's Cyclops who did not even have "good wheaten bread." Salmonson suggests that "the most plausible etymology of the word 'amazon' is that it is derived from the Circassion expression '*maza*' or 'moon' " (12). While she further postulates that the Eurasian tribe know as the Sarmations had women who sat astride horses and who went to war with their enemies the Scythians, she acknowledges that the archetype of the woman warrior probably predates written history. Auerbach concludes that most Amazon cultures were overrun and defeated by male armies and that, while a male "solitary adventurer will chisel his heroism" (4) from such an army, the same is not possible for the single Amazon. In modern literature, most Amazon stories resemble from Jorel of Joiry or the Red Sonya of Conan, women who tend to be as muscular as their overly developed heroes. (It is interesting to note that the word "hero" comes from Hera, the mother goddess in whose name great deeds were done. Hercules, the strongest of the strong, is the one whose deeds were dedicated to the glory of Hera. Why are female heroes not called *hera?*)

The picara does not usually participate in the Amazon society because it is a community and she is an individual. Yet the focus of the novel does not allow fantasy to deal with an entire community at once. This permits many picaresque elements to slip in. Sharon Green's series on Jalav is aptly subtitled "Amazon Warrior" because her heroine follows her Amazon heritage more than her picaresque. Brought up in female communities in the forests, Jalav steadily scorns the male concept of superiority throughout the five books even when her goddess Mida (Midol?) is proven to be all too human. Although she willingly does the bidding of her goddess Mida, Jalav wants only to be "Jalav's alone, to ride and do as she wished, to concern herself with neither gods nor warriors nor males" (*Battle* 12). As war leader of her tribe, Jalav identifies herself steadily as a warrior, although she often acts as an individual, albeit one who desires the general good.

One characteristic of her life as an Amazon is the primitive element which Auerbach stresses, "their inability to mold civilization from the land allied the Amazons to the barbaric and the savage" (4). Jalav cannot conceive of any life but that of her Midanna tribe, hunters and forest dwellers who live off the land without agriculture. She sleeps on "sleeping leathers," eschews any city softnesses, prefers raw meat to cooked, and can drink any male under the table. She admires most the warrior who can battle while pregnant, give birth to daughters, and whose stoicism against pain is as great as her pleasure with the captured men who are given the aphrodisiac drug "sthuvad" (stud?) to heighten their capacity.

Jalav's title as Amazon is the author's title; she prefers to be called the war leader of the tribes. Captured, beaten, enslaved, and raped by the sadistic offplanet "god" Sigurr, she cannot convince the men that she is an autonomous warrior until her father S'Heernoh brings them up sharply: "She is a warrior who would never even consider limiting your needs" (443). When the men agree to share her, Jalav questions as to what would be left to her life as a warrior if she no longer seek adventure. Her father contrives a solution to provide the continuing adventure of starting a new separate society to blend the women warriors with the men warriors. The final book is left open-ended enough to suggest the Jalav will do as she wants, even to acquiring a new male as a lover when "should the time prove uninteresting or too filled with annoyance [and] there would surely be other things to occupy a warrior, and even, perhaps, with the aid of Galiose's male Phanisar, as I no longer needed to stand as leader, a daughter...(446).

As the author responsible for creating the Free Amazons of Darkover, Bradley gives a fascinating history of her development of the amazon concept in the introduction to the first volume of *Free Amazons*:

> I had no notion, when I first created (out of a dream) the Free Amazons of Darkover, that they were to become the most attractive and controversial of my creations...
>
> The Free Amazons have undergone considerable changes since that dream (in 1962 or thereabout) created a Free Amazon, Kyla, as a mountain guide in *The Planet Savers*...
>
> I wrote *Darkover Landfall*, attacking the problems of survivalism, and not until *Shattered Chain* (1976) did I bring in Free Amazons as major characters in any book...
>
> *To Keep the Oath* (1979) dealt with the restrictions of Free Amazon recruitment in the society of Darkover—a restrictive society can remain so much longer if honorable escapes are allowed, and I regarded the amazons as one such honorable alternative. (7-11)

She followed the adventures of her major Free Amazons—Magda, Jaelle, Camilla, and Romilly—through *Thendara House, City of Sorcery*, and *Hawkmistress*. Camilla possesses skills as a soldier, as a fighter, as an autonomous woman in the three books about her (*Thendara House, City of Sorcery*, and *The Shattered Chain*) so much so that she has become a favorite character to Darkover feminists. She has her share of soldier stories and the physical training in self-defense she and Rafella give the novice amazons is thorough. When Magda tries to teach the martial arts she learned in her Terran Intelligence training, Camilla reassures her that she had to learn the centering technique for herself when she "studied swordplay among men; it may be one reason I am better with a sword than many men" (*House* 144). Yet, the Free Amazons can defend themselves more than adequately but discretion is always prized over violence. When an impetuous young Amazon responds to a lewd suggestion by slicing the offender open from his belly to his neck, Kindra reprimands her severely: "You could have freed yourself without bloodshed and made him look ridiculous, without ever drawing your knife. Your skills were taught you to guard against real danger of rape or wounding, Gwennis, not to protect your pride" (*Chain* 16).

Communities of women warriors abound in fantasy. Clayton's *Bait of Dreams* has the Sayoneh, a tribe of women merchants who trade in the compelling dangerous Ranga Eyes to sustain themselves. The leader of the Sayoneh is an old woman who justifies her actions in dealing with the stones by reciting her hatred of men: her father who had sold her into marital slavery for horses; her husband who killed her two daughters because they were not sons; her husband's men who had driven her out into the hills to rape. In contrast, the Sayoneh "found me and cared for me and loved me and gave me a haven, a home, a reason for living" (377). Her motive in selling the stones is revenge and survival of her adopted sisterhood. Other feminine communities exist. In *Motherlines* Charnas' Alldera meets several tribes of women who qualify as Amazons—the Riding Women of the Plains who create their daughters with the help of the semen of stallions in an orgy imitative of the Amazons' birth festivals. Joanna Russ's Whileaway community is threatened by the invasion of men in *The Female Man*. The direct opposite of this occurs in Pamela Sargent's *The Shore of Women* where the women control the city, breed with the outcast men to sustain children, and banish the boy children to the outcast men.

Interestingly while authors uphold the theory of gender-separate communities as valid in fiction, most women authors decry a segregated community as being unhealthy and unbalanced in reality. Charnas rejects such separatism as "not in my blueprint for Paradise and not the only answer to sexism that I hope to explore in fiction" (Barr 106). Bradley believes that, since an all female society would "self-destruct in one generation, I personally feel it's a cop-out to create a society where all the Y Chromosomes have all conveniently disappeared or died out." (*Free Amazons* 11).

If a distinction must be made between the warrior and the amazon, the latter conjures up a woman of immense strength, a female counterpart of the husky hero bulging with more muscle than brain while the woman warrior uses her brain to compensate for her lack of strength; for example, she learns where the center of her body is and uses the laws of physics to overcome size differences. Camilla admits that most men do not notice the difference in her stance, "thinking me a man, and it is true that I am very tall and thin, but my center is still lower than a man's of my height. I had to compensate for that and the constant practice to match myself against men gave me more skill than many of them" (144). Moon's Paksenarrion, as tall as her father and brothers but more slender, is described as going through extensive training to perfect her skills in swordplay to become a full-fledged soldier, living and adventuring within the ranks of a military company, involved in the good of the whole. So also Green's Sofaltis is part of a military unit.

Another heroine who uses trained skills to survive is Bradley's Zadieyek of Gyre in *Warrior Woman*. Captured and suffering from loss of memory, Zadieyek is saved from prostitution by her instinctive skill with a sword and is made a gladiator. She is befriended by Hassim, her mentor, Beizun, another woman gladiator who has sold herself into slavery to pay her debts, and Ifani, a rich woman who becomes her patron and lover. In her search for her identity, Zadieyek explores other cities, looking for other women gladiators to complete Ifani's dream of an all-female team of fighters. A pair of amber earrings jog her memory that her name is Amber but nothing else looks familiar until she is faced is the arena with a novice fighter whom she recognizes as Jade, her male sword-mate. Discarding their swords, they perform an intricate acrobatic routine to please the crowd. As one-third of a six-person martial arts group from an advanced planet, Amber and Jade buy her freedom and that of Beizun and fly off to their next assignment with Beryl, Emerald, Agate, and Ivory. Other than an emphasis on sexuality—heterosexual rape and homosexuality—the novel presents nothing new about the picaresque except that the heroine is able to fight with a gladiatorial sword but prefers the milder skills of acrobatics and of evasion rather than direct confrontation.

Such compensatory skills pervade the novels. Clayton's Gleia combines her early street fighting skills with acrobatic skills to dissuade her attacker: "Gleia danced back then dived under his arms, opened a cut on his leg, ran full out away from him, leaped over a watcher and stopped" (73). Some like Deel in Clayton's *Bait of Dreams* are professional dancers who evade attack. This is untypical of the picara who cares little for success or failure to countries, men, or ideals as long as her own safety and comfort is assured. Green's Terrillian tries her best to learn swordplay to defend herself but she is unable to lift the swords of the Rimilian males. Her only defense is her empathetic abilities. So also is Green's Inky proficient at the acrobatic arts in contrast to the multi-sword of her gladiator hero. Deceptively small, they wield powers she attributes to martial arts skills. Barbara Hambly also claims the use of martial arts to hone the edges of her heroines. Starhawk, the second in command to the male Sun Wolf, is as skilled as her commander and a lot more intuitive. In *The Ladies of Mandrigyn*, the pair teach reluctant women how to defend themselves against the wizard; Sun Wolf is tricked into the training when he is given a poison whose antidote is secret.

The warrior women in Jo Clayton's Duel of Sorcery series (*Moonscatter, Moongather,* and *Changer's Moon*) are the "meien" or pairs of "weaponwomen, sent out from Biserica (a training school for shrine for keepers, meien, healwomen) on three year wards...[they] generally serve as bodyguards, guards of women's' quarters, escorts for women traveling...duties that require integrity, intelligence, agility, skill with assorted weapons" (*Moonscatter* 12). The major character Serroi becomes a meie after a brutal childhood where she is the pawn of an evil wizard Ser Norris in his attempt to control the universe. Her powers are channeled into his genetic experiments until she grows strong enough to break free and join the women's group with mixed feelings for "the promise of the Biserica, whatever else it was, it meant hard work, accepting responsibility, and in the end a kind of freedom not found anywhere else in the world" (289). There in the training school are found all the occupations needed to maintain a community. Serroi and the younger Tuli become meie or messengers who travel to all parts of their world marked on the map by "all the black lines, the red dots that were cities, the silver peg that marked the wards of all the meien still out of the Valley...[she was] appalled by the sheer size of the world...so many lands, so many different people" (*Moonscatter* 286). The meie are primarily weaponwomen in opposition to the "sleykyn" (slay kin?) who are weaponmen who serve as "bodyguards, assassins, torturers, muscle for ambitious lordlings, raiders, spies" (13). While Serroi possesses powers, she also values her weapons: "her graceblade...the wooden hilt she'd shaped so carefully to her grip...the satin-smooth wood oiled by her hands till she and it were linked as close as mother and child. She slid her hand along her weaponbelt..." (*Moonscatter* 55).

If the scope of the Amazons and the warrior women exclude the picara, she can still be found in some of the fantasy characters in her martial aspect. Just as Athena is both military and wise, so also does a martial disguise serve the picara well. If she is a soldier it is because she is forced to it, not that she chooses it. Her character does not exemplify the desirable (and masculine) qualities of honor and courage and loyalty expected of a soldier. Barr claims that women warriors are science fiction's answer to the double standard, representing a "phallic femininity—which is heroic and often fantastic—[which] encompasses both masculine and feminine attributes and allows the swordswomen to function as androgynous wholes" (98). It would be repetitious to cite the outrage of the female critics who complain of the dearth of believable women in early science fiction and fantasy. The soldier's bravery exists in obeying the rules or codes, not in questioning them; the princess waiting to be rescued follows a code and she seldom rescues herself as a soldier; the Amazons also follow their code of loyalty.

But life is not that black and white. The picara is a soldier more in the image of the trickster, the conniver, the goldbricking sly servant, who evades real responsibility of real wars. She is the Parolles or Falstaff who slips out of moral responsibility, the Arlecchino who evades the draft, the Hawkeye or Klinger of M*A*S*H who so confuses the army that the enemy is also confused. Indeed, many of the actual women warriors, cited by Salmonson in her introductions, are known for evasive actions and deceptive maneuvers rather than for their brave deeds. The picara is in between the Amazon and the pacificist; she will not kill unless threatened and she will avoid violence when possible, much preferring the blood to remain inside the human body. Her skill is in her confidence games which offset the grim gore of the male war game. She never loses sight of the basic fact that the world is constructed in opposition— them against her.

She is never community-minded unless it is to her advantage.

Nina Auerbach claims:

As a recurrent literary image, a community of women is a rebuke to the conventional ideal of solitary woman living for and through men, attaining citizenship in the community of adulthood through masculine approval alone. The communities of women which have haunted our literary imagination from the beginning are emblems of female self-sufficiency which create their own corporate reality, evoking both wishes and fears. (5)

The picara has already done this—lived as a solitary woman feasting on men and women. The emblem of self-sufficiency is in the tale of the woman alone without traditional support of family, progeny, profession, or heritage; wealth alone suffices because it buffers her from the real world's pains and deprivations. As the picara learned long ago, alone is better. Throughout the entire span of the genre, the picara as a type existed, sometimes masquerading as a villainness, sometimes as an all consuming Great Goddess, sometimes as a housewife. But always she was her own woman-solitary by choice, symbiotic by nature, self-sufficient by accumulated wealth. She is still a fictional character and is no more real than the wimpy fainting heroines or many breasted warriors of the pulp covers.

The picara does no nurturing, no healing, to balance out the killing aspect of her nature. She is then far less heroic than the woman warrior, far less sacrifical than the mother, far less forgiving than the religious pilgrim. The purple bruises of her warrior motif fade into the light violet-gray of her deception and the silver gray of her wandering becomes the smoky-gray of the magician's disguise as she escapes punishment once again.

Chapter Eight
Disguise and Deception

When, however, the designer has acquired a full awareness of the limiting effect which the occurrence of slits in woven tapestry may have upon the work, he should not overlook the fact that they can also offer him great assistance in producing a pleasing design: they are most useful in suggesting relief and in creating the effect of light and shade without having recourse to changes of colour or to the weaving of areas of shadow...What should be aimed at, therefore, is not designs which seek to avoid the use of slits, but those which reveal a mastery of the correct and effective use of the slit technique. (Rhodes 34-5)

In her travels, the picara learns to blend into her surroundings. As a thief, this ability to fade into the crowd allows her escape. As a linguist, her accent supports her deception. As a courtesan, the picara adopts a dress suitable to her station—subdued for genteel society, seductive for less than genteel. Every garment she wears is a calculated move in her game plan; each setting she inhabits is a ploy; every color she chooses has meaning and symbolism. Although her autonomy is sometimes hampered by the necessary camouflage of her disguise, her need for survival overrides her individualism. Like the chameleon, the picara changes her exterior markings to mislead her public. To show this, this chapter will detail how clothing—its form, cut, color, and connotations—effect the disguise motif and how the subtle pink-grays of disguise blend into iridescent deception.

Disguise

While clothes have always indicated status, clothes in literature often become symbols of character as well. Lazarillo rejoices when he obtains "an old fustian jacket and a worn coat with braided sleeves and a vent. I also got a cloak which had had a fringe once" (76). To possess a cloak which once bore a fringe makes him a grand figure indeed. In societies where the making of cloth entails great labor, clothes follow a close third behind food and shelter as needed for survival; for the picara, clothes become both the expression of her avarice and a necessity of her profession as courtesan.

Where the tale uses a garment as a magical device like Fortunatus' cap or as a symbol like Cinderella's slipper, the early novel seldom includes details of clothing—its cut, color, or connotation. Even with its textural verisimilitude, a novel such as Aphra Behn's *Oroonoko* shies away from the specifics of color or cut; even Defoe's honing of verisimilitude neglects color for the most part. Later writers of the picaresque employed different levels of texturing, according to their times: Dickens and Thackeray depended heavily on the cut and mass of clothing to delineate character but not the color; as historical authors, Mitchell and Winsor used a wider palette of color and sensual detailing to clothe their picaras; the fantasy writers employ all these techniques to convince the reader of the reality of their created worlds.

Occasionally, one item of clothing will assume proportions beyond its expected role to become a literary convention whose implications and connotations extend far beyond its actual use. Such clothing Robert Alter calls "emblematic" (41), one characteristic of which is its exotic appeal. For example, Aphra Behn's description of her feathered dress in *Oroonoko* is extremely explicit for so early a novel and, even though it falls short of details like color and cut, the description retains its exotic appeal. Behn claims that the Indians in Surinam used feathers to make for themselves "short habits of 'em, and glorious Wreaths for their Heads, Necks, Arms and Legs, whose Tinctures are unconceivable. I had a Set of these presented to me, and I gave'em to the King's Theatre, and it was the Dress of the *Indian Queen*, infinitely admired by Persons of Quality; and was unimitable" (2). So "unimitable" is the dress that its exoticism linked it with dance to become both a disguise within the novel and a convention in later literature. Indeed, records show that Killigrew's 1663 production of John Dryden's and Robert Howard's *The Indian Queen* had heightened the exotic setting of the play by placing it in Mexico or Peru rather than in Surinam; its fifth act opened with the Temple of the Sun scene with Ann Marshall resplendent in Aphra's dress as Zempoalla, the villanous queen. To accompany Behn's feathered dress, Killigrew purchased "silks to the value of forty pounds 'for to cloathe the Musick for the play called the Indian Queene to be acted before their Majesties Jan. 25, 1663' " (Nicholl 50-1). In comparison, Defoe duplicates this literary convention by having Roxana revel in its use of her seduction of the King: she is equally thrilled that the mysterious masked "Person [who] spoke in *French* to me" might be the king and "that it was the finest Dress he had ever seen." Her disguise is enhanced by his comment that "I had a Christian's Face...adding that so much Beauty cou'd not be *Mahometan*" (174-4).

While Roxana's dress is not specifically Indian or feathered, it is exotic, having been obtained at "Leghorn, when my *Foreign Prince* brought me a *Turkish slave*...and with this *Turkish slave*, I brought the rich Cloaths, too...the habit of a Turkish Princess" (173). So also Defoe, no less a devotee of strange new worlds than Behn is, would not scruple in "borrowing" the tale of Behn's lending the dress to the players for Roxana, especially if the tale of the Indian Queen's dress were floating in the literary community. It is possible that his Roxana "borrowed" more than the Indian Queen's dress from Aphra Behn. Behn's mention of the dress appears in her 1688 novel, written twenty-five years after she obtained it and lent it to Killigrew's 1663 production; Defoe sets his story of Roxana in the Restoration, roughly contemporary with Behn's setting, but some forty to sixty years prior to his 1724 edition of Roxana. Such rearranging of times and cultures did not concern early writers. Where Defoe replaced Behn's Surinam with Roxana's Turkey, in his *Robinson Crusoe*, he reveals some knowledge of that area of South American near Surinam when he has Robinson shipwrecked near the Orinoco (Amazon) River. Nor did ethnic differences bother writers: Metzger in his introduction to *Oroonoko* comments that "like many of her contemporaries, Mrs. Behn does not distinguish between Negro and Moor, freely mixing African and Oriental habits" (xiii).

The dress is also expensive. Every picara values her clothes for their monetary worth as tools of seduction more than for their emotional worth. Courage judges the cost of her clothes as indication of the wealth of her lovers; rich clothes will attract more lovers and more gifts. While Roxana values the Turkish dress for its intrinsic worth (it cost "sixty Pistoles in Italy, but cost much more in the Country from whence it came"), she values it more for its erotic allure: "It is not a decent Dress in this Country, and wou'd not look modest; neither indeed, wou'd it, for it was but one Degree off, from appearing in One's Shift" (247). Once again the lack of specifics entices rather than satisfies the reader as the use of the word "shift" more fully suggests sensuality than any description could. In Roxana's case, whatever the worth of the dress means to her, it serves to unite the two picaresque traditions of disguise and deception: for example, the origin of the dress is hazy since Roxana claims she obtained it at Leghorn in one passage (173) and at Naples in another (246). The dress involves itself in *Roxana* as an external disguise but the dance that goes with it is used for both disguise and deception. Here Defoe expands upon his source for, as John Robert Moore points out, the dance is "an amplification of two contemptuous little passages in *Memoirs of Grammont* and it involves such a glorification of the facts that it reads almost like a travesty" (43).

The actual similarities between the two pieces of literature begin in the title where Roxana's pseudonym "Mlle. de Beleau" seems to be a combination of the names of the Mlles. Bardou and Bellenden, two ladies-in-waiting, at the court of Charles II. It is the same Mlle. Bardou who "was with Flamerens and sometimes toward the conclusion of the ball, possessed of castanets and effrontery, she would dance some figured saraband or other" (Moore 43). Defoe's alteration makes Roxana's dance

a Figure which I learnt in *France* when the Prince de____desir'd I wou'd dance for his Diversion; it was indeed a very fine Figure, invented by a famous Master at *Paris*, for a Lady or a Gentleman to dance single; but being perfectly new, it pleas'd the Company exceedingly and they all thought it had been *Turkish*; nay, one Gentlemen had the Folly to expose himself so much as to say, *and I think I swore, too* that he has seen it danced in Constantinople; which was ridiculous enough." (174-5)

Roxana's swearing, or thinking she swore, completes the disguise of the Turkish dress itself and completes the misconception about the dance. The gullibility of such a society to assume that a dance performed in Turkish garb is Turkish encourages picaresque tricks.

So potent is the convention of the exotic dance and dress that Thackeray uses the combination to characterize all women, who attend Vanity Fair. In chapter fifty-one, at the charade party, it is not Becky who is dressed as a Turkish enticer; rather another woman is in the "gorgeous Oriental costume; the black braided locks are twined with innumerable jewels; her dress is covered over with gold piastres" (536). Called the "Mahometan" and part of a Turkish harem, the woman provides a temporary rivalry for Becky who surpasses her in her disguise as Clytemnestra. More importantly, in her disguise of the "Old French costume...in powder and patches, the most *ravissante* little Marquise" (540), Becky enthralls the audience with her dancing and singing performance of the ballet-opera *Le Rossignol*. Terms used to describe her conquest are those of Oriental slavery: "Lord Steyne was her slave...she might have had pearls melted down into her champagne if she had liked" (542).

Similarly, Amber's connection with dance first occurs when she auditions for the company of actors: "Killigrew gave her a signal and Amber began to dance. It was a Spanish saraband which she had learned more than a year before and since performed many times" (176), the same saraband that Roxana used to seduce the king. In a later scene when Amber is about to meet her rival, she wants a dress "different from anything she has ever seen, a gown no one had ever dared to wear...'something they can't *help* staring at,' Amber told her, 'if I have to go in stark naked with my hair on fire' " (646). The dress she orders has to be sewn on her; its sheath skirt is "covered with black beads, that looked like something black and wet and shiny pouring over her hips and legs [with] sheer black tiffany...floated down over the train like a black mist" (647). However, the dress does not have the desired effect since her lover Bruce's attitude makes her feel like the "commonest kind of drab, displaying herself for any man to see and appraise and—worst of all—reject" (654).

The external habit of the picara has as its purpose the representation of a state of being other than what is actual, but sometimes the disguise backfires. Courage gloats over her "striking dress in Vienna in the latest style, as the noble ladies were wearing them in Italy" (46) despite the fact that she is not allowed to wear the dress because it might endanger her position. Like Amber's dress, Roxana's dress provides moral punishment when she tries to use it as a diversion for her honest Dutch merchant. The cautious Roxana, knowing that the dress itself is easily remembered, stipulates that "I wou'd dress me in it, if he wou'd promise me never to desire me to appear in it before Company" (246). Defoe does not let even such innocent conjugal play escape with impunity for the Quakeress is present at the wearing of the dress and she is also present when Susan, Roxana's daughter, describes in detail the famous Turkish dress that her famous mistress once wore as the Lady Roxana. The dress becomes the external symbol of the internal sense of insecurity which avarice causes in the picara.

The convincing details of cut, color, value, and exoticism in her disguises serve to strengthen the picara's place within the novel genre and to move her from the unspecified fabric of the tale to the specific texturing of a novel. Like a magician, the picara practices the art of misdirection in her choice of costume to disguise herself, just as she changes languages and settings to deceive others. Courage deceives her society by dressing as a gypsy despite the fact that she "did not even have pitch-black hair like the others, but rather it [was] somewhat yellowish." Her remedy is to smear herself "zealously with goosefat, louse salve, and other hair-dying tinctures so that in a short time I looked a hellish black as if I had been born in the middle of Egypt" (189). Her disguise is so successful that she becomes queen of the gypsies and her deceptive coloration extends to the story's lesser figures. Skipinthefield "disguised himself, putting on his head a wig and wrapping himself in a borrowed black cloak" (134) in order to steal the emerald from the rich young lady of Casale.

Roxana's use of exotic disguise to represent herself as someone else unites her strongly with the picaresque tradition. When she teases the Dutch Merchant that she has a dress in which "he wou'd not know his Wife when he saw her" (246), it serves as a disguise. Amy also "had dress'd herself in that Habit of a *Turkish* Slave" (247) so that the Merchant is fooled. Both women are skilled in picaresque complexity of disguise, deceit, and cleverness. For example, Amy's elaborate scheme to get Roxana cleanly away from the court and the "old wicked L_____" (208) lands them both in the Quakeress' household where Roxana finds that the Quaker dress provides the external habit necessary to maintain her isolation from the undesirable nobleman. Consequently, she "pretended...to be extremely in Love with the Dress of the QUAKERS, and this pleas'd her [the Quakeress] so much, that she wou'd needs dress me up one Day in a Suit of her own Cloaths; but my real Design was, to see whether it wou'd pass upon me for a Disguise" (211). Amy agrees that "it is a perfect Disguise to you; why you look quite another-body. I shou'd not have known you myself" (212). Defoe extends the disguise element within the same incident to Roxana's coach which is renovated into a "plain Coach, no gilding or painting, lin'd with a light-grey Cloathe, and my Coachman had a Coat of the same and no Lace on his hat" (213). In addition, when Roxana courts the friendship of the Quaker woman, she presents her with a "Piece of very fine new Holland" (212) cloth, despite the Quakeress' protests that the cloth is too rich for her station in life. Roxana cannot understand the Quakeress' reasoning: "I thought she had meant she must not wear it so fine, because she was a Quaker; so I return'd, Why do not you *Quakers* wear fine Linnen neither? Yes *says she*, we wear fine Linnen when we can afford it, but this is too good for me" (213). Earlier when she tries to buy the Quakeress' clothing as an effective disguise, Roxana pays her for the clothes in an untypical spurt of generosity, giving her three guineas more than they had actually cost, because "this good (tho' unhappy) Quaker has the Misfortune to have had a bad Husband" (212) as Roxana has had.

This concept of color as a disguise can leach over into a uniform style or color or type of clothing providing the desirable camouflage which also encourages Roxana's picaresque quest for eternal youth: "It makes you look ten Years younger than you did" (211), Amy says. The lack of noticeable color in the Quaker's dress of grey-brown homespun, highlighted with white linen bands and collars for cleanliness, appeals to Roxana as a disguise because it contrasts with her previous elaborate style. Where several centuries earlier, the European clothing industry began to employ alum to stabilize color, machine-made and brightly dyed stuffs replaced the simple homespun undyed wool and linen. Certain colors began to indicate society status: Margery Kempe was forbidden from wearing white clothing since white was reserved for the religious as a outward sight of their vow of celibacy. Religious orders later adopted black as a sign of their death and of their invisibility to the world. Since both black and white cloth (i.e. bleached as opposed to unbleached wool or linen) involved an additional step in preparation, such cloth cost more. Francis of Assisi sported bright finery in his early days as a living advertisement for his cloth merchant father's wealth; when he joined the penitential movement, he adopted the garb of the poor—a drab, grey-brown, undyed homespun, cross-shaped habit girdled with a rope. Until the adoption of brown as their official color in 1895, Franciscans wore gray unbleached wool which often had a bluish tinge; today, some Franciscans retain black as their major color because it was the color that set the religious apart from the world. During the twelfth century, the beguines adopted the ubiquitous gray-brown wool homespun ("bege" in French) which gave rise to their name. When the thirteenth century Augustinian bishop Jacques de Vitry, supported the Beguine Mary of Oignes, the beguines were wearing a "uniform grey dress to distinguish them from others" (Beck-Fink 245). Later illustrated plates and painting show that the beguine's gray was replaced by blue and white or black.

In literature, the growth of the dyed cloth industry appears in Chaucer's Prologue which includes a weaver, a dyer, a haberdasher, an upholsterer as well as his Wyf of Bath who, despite her penchant for red stockings and gaudy clothes, was such a good linen-weaver that "she passed hem of Ypres and of Gaunt" (1. 448). Color became the hallmark of one's station in life as sumptuary laws restricted the wearing of certain fabrics and colors to certain social classes. Courage is dressed in "scarlet" and "green velvet, of expensive English cloth [high quality wool]...trimmed with silver lace" or in "black silk [with a] purse of snow white Urach Linen" (189). In the development of the novel form, color becomes a vital part of the picara's personality. While red would seem to designate prostitution, yellow was the color of moral disgrace and uncleanliness as in the courtesan's veil, black the color for concubines, and green used for the fertility elements of witchcraft. Color is also a later factor in verisimilitude. Aphra Behn uses no color in describing her Indian feathered dress; Jane Austen's descriptions of dresses in *Northanger Abbey* center on the durability of sprigged muslin, not on its color. Defoe uses a minimal amount of color to stress the cost of the apparel rather than its emotional appeal: Roxana's dress in "fine *Persian,* or *India* damask; the Ground white, and the Flowers blue and gold." (174). Just as the Renaissance painters limited blue to Mary because blue was the most expensive pigment, blue in clothing is on a par with the "gold" threads, the product of the Cologne beguines who were gold-spinners. The dress is valued for the expense of its dyes, not for the symbolism of its hues.

Some authors use diamonds as their central "color." Defoe has Roxana adorn her Turkish costume with the "large Breast-Jewel which he [her Dutch husband] had given me, of a thousand Pistoles, upon the Front of the *Tybaia,* or Head-Dress" (247). She adds her own diamond necklace and other jewels when she "frequently put it on, and upon two or three Occasions danc'd in it, but always at his Request" (248). In the same manner, Thackeray employs the prismic qualities of diamonds as part of Becky's adamantine picaresque selfishness when she refuses to ransom her husband Rawdon from debtor's prison: "The wretched woman was in a brilliant full toilette, her arms and all her fingers sparkling with bracelets and rings; and the brilliants on her breast" (569).

Later authors find it needful to flesh out their historical narratives with description until color sometimes becomes identified with the heroine on a symbolic level. Amber is presented as having "honey-coloured hair" (4) because she traps men with her sticky sweetness and her "clear, speckled amber [eyes], brows black and swept up in arc" (4) represent the capturing of an insect in amber which looks like solidified honey. Thus, her name and her coloring are symbolically the same. Dressed in a "rust wool skirt over a green petticoat, white blouse and yellow apron and tight-laced stomacher'' (4), she combines all the colors representative of the picara—red, green, yellow, white. Yet, throughout the novel, the clothes she and the other characters wear are described in intimate detail, usually being shades of gold or black because "the stark black against her rich cream-and-honey colouring...gave her the look of a diabolical angel— at once pure, beautiful, corrupt and sinister" (647). Her fair coloring contrasts with Bruce's wife's darker hair and pale skin.

Besides the obvious color polarity of Scarlett's name and her complexion, Mitchell uses green to designate Scarlett's chief virtue—hope. In this she differs somewhat from the earlier picaras who possess no theological virtues because they are moral juveniles. As the color of witchcraft, green has always represented fertility and growth and magic. Seymour Smith quotes a character in Ben Jonson's 1614 *Bartholomew Fair* ordering the prostitute Ursula to "take them [a whore and a putative whore] in, open thy wardrobe, and fit them to their calling. Green gowns, crimson petticoats, green women, my Lord Mayor's green women!" (75). Green is also the greensickness or jaundice which some young girls get before and during puberty, a disease now thought to be a sign of anorexia nervosa. To an expert, a greenie or greenhorn is an unskilled person. When Brecht's twentieth century version of Mother Courage appears on stage, she seldom has anything green on the set, signifying her lack of hope for all colors are dulled when hope is absent.

Not so in Scarlett's philosophy. Her green eyes and red hair parallel the red earth and green spring field of Georgia early in the novel; even her dress is sprigged or flowered muslin, reminiscent of the Great Goddess' Primavera aspect. Mitchell returns to the same color symbolism in the latter part of the book where "white house gleaming welcome to her through the reddening autumn leaves [and] the dews falling on acres of green bushes starred with fleecy white, see the raw color of the red earth and the dismal dark beauty of the pines" (1037). All these colors—green, red, white, and black—are in Scarlett's blazon. She is the south, Georgia in particular, the surviving mother earth goddess who rises from the ashes of war with her green shoots and white flowers to revive life from the earth reddened by the blood of her sons and daughters.

Scarlett O'Hara is conscious of her feminine power over men caused by the three dresses around which her autonomy pivots. In each of these, the color is chosen to enhance her ethnicity, her exoticism, and her scheming ways. While the description of the first dress serves to set the scene as antebellum Georgia, it also characterizes her in its design, color, and purpose.

Her new green flowered-muslin dress spread its twelve yards of billowing material over her hoops and exactly matched the flat-heeled green morocco slippers her father had recently brought her from Atlanta. The dress set off to perfection the seventeen-inch waist, the smallest in three countries, and the tightly fitting basque showed breasts well matured for her sixteen years. (3)

The corset-tightening scene in the movie contrasts Scarlett's apparent fragility with the steel strength of her will. Green is Scarlett's color to offset her "magnolia-white skin" and her eyes of "pale green without a touch of hazel, starred with bristly black lashes and slightly tilted at the ends" (3). Throughout the book she wears green as a dominant color and not surprisingly so considering her ebullient hope at what fate gives her. The green of those eyes, however, "in the carefully sweet face were turbulent, willful, lusty with life, distinctly at variance with her decorous demeanor...her eyes were her own" (3). Such undercutting immediately following the description of the major character serves to warn the reader of her picaresque propensities. As "her own," her green eyes complement the dress and vice versa; the dress is her own as are her own eyes and ideas and plans. Her autonomy surfaces early when she fights Mammy about which dress to wear because she recognizes the effect of the dress on the men in her life. She rejects the "rose organdie with long pink sash [and] the black bombazine with its puffed sleeves and princess lace collar [and] the lavender barred muslin [and] the green plaid taffeta, frothing with flounces and each flounce edged in green velvet ribbon" (75) in favor of wearing the "green sprigged muslin" again because it shows her arms and neck to advantage.

The second dress is her widow's weeds in which she "sat like a crow with hot black taffeta to her wrists and buttoned up to her chin, with not even a hint of lace or braid, not a jewel except Ellen's onyx mourning brooch" (174). Her society demands proper demeanor but her rebellion is expressed in her hatred of the "tacky old grays and tans and lilacs" (175) that she will be forced to wear when she is out of mourning. She envies the other "frocks floating by, butter-yellow watered silks with garlands of rosebuds, pink satins with eighteen flounces edged with tiny black velvet ribbons, baby blue taffeta...foamy with cascading lace; exposed bosoms, seductive flowers" (175). She especially envies the other girl's wearing the shade of green, claiming that it makes her skin look as green "an an old cheese" (175). Ironically, it is at this ball that she perceives Rhett as the possible smuggler who provided the "cream-colored Chantilly lace that had come from Charleston on the last blockader" (175). He deplores the "system of mourning, of immuring women in crepe for the rest of their lives" (182) and suggests that only convention keeps Scarlett from appearing "in a red dress and lead[ing] a reel" (183). Once again the dress suggests dance and sexuality.

The third dress is the one in which Scarlett attempts to deceive Rhett into believing that Tara and she are successful when she wants his money for taxes to ransom Tara. Here, the story shifts. Because Rhett is a rogue scoundrel and a bit of a picaro himself, he is not as gullible as the unsuspecting victims of other picaras. Scavenged from her mother's moss-green velvet curtains, the new dress serves as a disguise as well as a symbol of the conditions of the south during the Reconstruction period: "there wasn't a nice dress in Tara or a dress which hadn't been turned twice and mended" (544). Mitchell's constant references to the lack of proper clothing since the war emphasizes Scarlett's concentration of her picaresque energy in not ever being hungry again and the extension of her avarice in its corollary about needing proper clothes to defend against deprivation.

The picara uses specific guises, such as color, to effect her aims until the disguises become literary conventions in themselves. Because the fantasy picara exists in a created world of magic, she uses color as symbols even more so perhaps than does the novel picara. For example, while Amber may have a penchant for amber colors, Bradley's Zadieyek/Amber uses the amber earrings as a memory-jogging device. The six members of her intergalatic sword group are colored semi-precious gems of Agate, Ivory, and Jade for the men and Amber, Emerald, and Beryl for the women. Primary colors are important. Lynn's *cheari* society of dancers are identified with red from their inception. Tarr's Lady of Han-Gilen series pits the red of the sun king Mirain's scarlet and the red-headed Elain's green. The various Amazon clans of Green's Jalav adopt separate colors to distinguish themselves: "all colors of our clans appeared upon her covering, against the black of all Midanna, the green, the red, the blue, the yellow, white and brown, orange and violet, gold and rose" (25). Here the sheer number of the clans forces the author to use secondary and tertiary colors for her warrior clans. The obligatory male warriors are distinguishable only by their own muted color-coded loincloths. Although Karr's sorceress Frostflower can wear brightly embroidered clothes at home, while traveling she must wear the brown or black enforced by the hostile world; her traveling companion Thorn wears the dark shades necessary for a mercenary warrior.

Colors which carry over their symbolism from earlier mythology have negative and positive qualities, sometimes in the same person. The gold of Maxwell's Rheba can be harnessed to heal or to kill. Abbey's Rifkind retains for her mother's ruby to help her as a healer. The black of Green's Inky is the invisibility she needs as a thief but also indicates her death to emotional life. The white of Tanith Lee's Anackire can be her innocence or her death color of leprosy or black to her sons and lovers. Vinge's snow queen is white in her "ancient feather cloak melting into the whiteness of the furs...white, the color of Winter, and of mourning" (505) contrasting with "glistening fish-net cocoon of silky green mesh" (511) of the sea image of her cloned daughter, Moon Dawntreader.

The rainbow of iridescent or opalescent colors sometimes provokes plots where not only the colors shift but the shape or density of cloth changes as well. Magical clothes serve as protective devices as when Ino's veil protects Odysseus himself from drowning or as sources of invisibility. Sometimes pouches or bags provide wealth or food or supplies; sometimes caps or hats, like that of Fortunatus, provide escape. Morris' Shebat wears a thin film suit which protects her from all harm and fantasy writers invent clever fabrics faster than technology can. For example, Anne McCaffrey's *The Coelura* features fabric spun by the rare coelura-creatures, a fabric which molds to the wearer's body, has a life of its own, and is constantly changing shape and color. While the heroine of this pleasant tale is far more of a romantic heroine, she still bears some characteristics of the picara in her resistance to marriage, her insistence on autonomy, and her avarice for the coelura and their products.

Often to the fantasy picara, while the color of the metal may become significant beyond its monetary worth, it does not mean that money is any less valuable to the picara as a business woman. Gold is always the sun's metal hoarded by dragons and valued by kings; silver is the moon's glow connected inevitably to women. Lesser metallic colors like copper appear in Patricia Keneally's Copper Crown trilogy. Iron is traditionally the metal which the world of magic abhors. Wherever futuristic metals abound and spaceships hover, traces of the picara can still be seen in the avarice of the heroine in adapting to new technology. While the picara's coinage may not be metallic, she does maintain an invisible credit line into which she deposits her earnings. Jade Darcy, for example, never handles money; her earnings are deposited into a computerized account which adds or subtracts from the balance as needed. The credit line of Heinlein's Friday is cut short when she leaves her governmental agency.

Features other than her dress may symbolize the picara; the length of her hair may indicate her status. Unbound hair is the sign of the uncommitted woman, one too young to be married or too sensual to stay faithful to one man, i.e. a prostitute. Jacobus de Voragine's *Legenda Aurea* cites many maiden saints like Agatha whose hair miraculously grew to cover them when they were stripped naked by their persecutors; so also are penitents like Mary of Magdalen and Mary of Egypt pictured with the profuse hair of the prostitute even after their repentance. The tales of Lady Godiva and Rapunzel reflect culture's association of women's hair and sexuality especially in the art of books covers where even the most feminist of fantasy picaras has abundant locks more suitable to Hollywood starlets than to practical women. All these images have their origins in the sensuality of the prostitute's flowing hair.

Where picara/prostitute rebels against her culture, her head covering or lack of it assumes importance. Where classical literature uses an armband or slave bracelet to show prostitution, the headpiece of the goddesses was often a diadem of gold or a nimbus of golden hair, rather like the image of the leonine sun king shaking his locks. Transformed into the halo on the saints, golden hair became the yellow veil of the prostitute in the paintings of Renaissance artists. For example, a saint like Catherine of Alexandria is a Christianization of these classical sun goddesses; her iconography shows her with the sun-wheel, which was to be the instrument of her torture until it was shattered by an angel. Her legend has her wearing a diadem as a princess of Cyprus although her cult actually began in Alexandria, famous for its beautiful courtesans and its library. There the rich young maiden Catherine was so learned that she converted her persecutors and jailors to Christianity, an imitation of the Greek *hetaira* who held intellectual salons. By defending both her virginity, which we now read as integrity, and her religious beliefs, Catherine retained her autonomy. In such martyrdom, a woman saint could become a model for autonomy in her defying the male authority figures of the persecutors. Like the desert harlot, the saint's life blended together to make one image—the consecrated virgin who saves her soul at the sacrifice of her body, and whose crown in heaven will be of finer gold than any earthly one.

The diadem often has supernormal powers and represents the crown of queenship such as in the crowns of Egypt which combine the bull's horns of the crescent moons and the full sun and the crown of Isis with its cobra-headed third eye. Clayton's Diadem series features the diadem as "a focus for psi-forces, a prison for the self-aware part of the wearer...gold-wire lilies with jewel hearts set on a chain of flat gold links" (*Endgame* vi). Her heroine Aleytys is possessed by the stolen diadem which in its turn has been possessed by three other distinct personalities, a Jungian quaternity of the three other selves within her. Harskari is the wise woman, Shadith, the younger anima or creative self, and Swartheld Quale is the masculine shadow or stronger part of herself. Together, they avoid the pursuers to keep Aleytys alive until, one by one, she can let them go into other bodies. Literally she bodies forth or externalizes the parts of her nature until she can incorporate their teachings into her own psyche. Because the diadem is invisible, it serves as disguise and as deception which enables her to survive the pursuit of the Rmoahl who want their diadem back. For example, in *Irsud* when she is host to a parasitic queen egg which will consume her in its birth process, she calls upon the three personalities, Swartheld Quale is particular, to break the grip of her attacker. She achieves her end through deceptive, almost trickster means.

But the diadem usually combines the wisdom of physic powers with the sexual energy of the *celsus* to increase femininity, the golden girdle of Aphrodite being the chief example. William Lederer points out that the Indian and Buddhist goddess figures often have a "type of ornamented girdle that does not conceal, but frames and accents their sex" (*Kiss* 141), that downward triangle which represents the pubic area, that seat of new life. Aphrodite's *celsus* with its husband's knot indicates that the unleashing of creative energy is not always visible. The girdle was transformed into the keys of the chatelaine, the lowered waistlines of medieval women, the pomander balls Queen Elizabeth is pictured with, the rope around the waist of the religious who used it as a reminder to curb sexuality, the cincture, the girding of the loins for action in Scriptures. For a picara like Morris's Estri to wear a hipbelt woven with quest strands serves as an identifying mark of the picara.

Deception

As the slits in the tapestry cause shadows, so does disguise blend into deception in the picara's figure without a seam. No where is that more apparent than in the confusion over her sexual status. The myth of the hermaphrodite, the myth of Teresias who lived as a woman for seven years at Juno's command, and the myth of Herakles who dressed as a woman to serve Omphale gives the picara a basis for her transvestitism. Where the myths may have their basis in psychological and physical abnormalities, the literary picara extends her disguise as a man to escape harm, to deceive others, and to entice clients for her lust.

While the tales of the saints do not contain hermaphrodism as such, the legends of women saints who masqueraded as men were popular sources for the medieval romance. The Bollandist Hippolyte Delahaye persists in looking beyond even these legends to the possibility of

an unambiguous trace of the Aphrodite cult [because] emphasis is put on the contrasts found in the Pelagia legends between pleasure and penance, sensuality and chastity, and on the recurrent theme of 'change' of sex. This is to draw attention to the goddess of Amathus in Cyprus, who could be regarded at will as Aphrodite or Aphroditos and was represented in women's clothes but bearded like a man. At the sacrifices offered to this deity men dressed as women and women as men. It is the cultus of the hermaphrodite. (154)

The female saint who poses as a man does so for two reasons: it disguises her from unwanted male attention and it is a practical style for someone intending to live alone in the desert. The desert saint flees to mountaintops for solitude or enters monasteries in order to preserve her virginity from a father who wants her to marry. Sts. Marina, Margaret of Antioch, Eugenia, Pelagia, and Euphrosyne of Alexandria are all variants of the same legend where they disguised themselves as men to escape persecution. The legendary saint is often accused of being the father of the child of a local woman but only after her death is the truth revealed that she was a woman all long.

Take, for example, the complicated legend of St. Pelagia as detailed by Delahaye. The four different saints who bear the name have some resemblance to each other, differing only in their deaths. One St. Pelagia in the fourth century, immortalized by St. John Chrysostom and St. Ambrose for her escape from violation by soldiers, asked to be allowed to change clothes and plunged to her death from the housetop, rather like Rebecca in *Ivanhoe*. Another is honored for being martyred in a heated bronze bull, an inversion of the myth of the minotaur's conception when Minos's wife was placed in her bronze cow. Another Pelagia of Tarsus has a similar story while St. John Chrysostom also related another story of penitent who retired from the world. All these stories merge into one legend known as "Pelagia's Repentance" which is attributed to a deacon James of Edessa and retold by historian Helen Waddell. The first St. Pelagia was honored by the church at Antioch for her renunciation of her licentious life as a courtesan. While she is out riding one day with her fellow actors and dancers, so the story goes, Pelagia is seen by a group of bishops when one of them, Nonnus, expresses his delight at her beauty to his deacon. When Pelagia later hears Nonnus preach, she repents her life, is baptized, flees the city in men's clothes, and lives undiscovered as a monk named Pelagius on the mount of Olives. Only after her death is it discovered that she was a woman and, as one of the penititent prostitutes, she became popular wonder worker. Notice how many of the picaresque traits recur—the theatrical connection, her profession as courtesan, her penititence, her flight of the world, her assuming male attire, her story being told by a churchman or scribe as a moral lesson.

The picara does not usually suffer from transsexuality or Eonism, a pathological and psychological condition in which a person identifies with the outward sexual attributes of the opposite sex. The latter term comes from the life of the Chevalier d'Eon de Beaumont, the eighteenth century diplomat who occasionally masqueraded as a woman to spy for Louis XV and who so confused the French court with his transdressing that he was ordered to dress as a woman to receive his pension. Thought at one time to be a bearded woman, d'Eon exemplified the archetype of the hermaphrodite of ancient times and gave credence to the mistaken perception of the bearded women saints.

The Pelagia legend bears its mark and it continues formally in the Church; there are bearded women among the saints: at Rome it is St. Galla, in Spain it is St. Paula, elsewhere it is St. Liberata, Wilgefortis, Kummernis, Livrade, Ontkommer and the rest...Aphrodite was the goddess of the sea, and was known under a number of appropriate titles...*Pelagia*, of which Marina is a translation. (Delahaye, 154-5)

For example, St. Wilgefortis, whose legend has her sprouting a beard and moustache to discourage a suitor, was crucified by her father. The legend is no more than a misperception of the crucifix of Lucca where the delicate features of the robed figure of the Christ appears to be that of a bearded woman, a *"vierge-forte."* The same crucifix which gave rise to the medieval oath "by the Holy Face" also contributes another source of the same saint's name in its German translation of "Holy Face" or *"Hilge Vartz"* or Wilgefortis (Butler II 151). The robe itself figures heavily in these misperceptions. The robed Christ of the medieval crucifix is in imitation of Eastern dress; the monk's robe is a fascimile of the same attire. The fact that the women who live as men do so in religion by wearing a masculine form—the cassock or alb and chasuble—of women's predominant fashion—the dress—does not negate their masculine appearance. Scriptural precedent has long inveighed against the wearing of female attire by men but, the prohibition of the woman's wearing of male attire has never been as harshly judged. As the early critic C.J.S. Thompson states such women were "victims of circumstances [whose] causes of their action among women, apart from the physiological, appear to have been a spirit of adventure, ambition, a psychological desire for domination...or a criminal desire to obtain money or property" (18).

Like the early saints, when the early picara wears male attire, she does so to preserve her virginity and to escape the ravages of war. The later picara uses breeches to further her picaresque tricks or scams; the fantasy picara does so to be comfortable. Often the need for male attire arises when a state of war exists. Joan of Arc wore armor on the battlefield and refused to wear women's attire in prison because she knew any relaxation of her male attire would make her susceptible to rape. What she saw as a necessity to preserve her virginity was perceived by her accusers as perversity and stubbornness. Courage's nurse warns her: "Maid Libushka, if you wish to keep your maidenhead, you must let me shear your head and put you in men's clothes; if not, I would not give the buckle off a chastity belt for your honor" (36). In a later chapter, she confesses that, while she rides a horse sidesaddle, she always kept a "stirrup hanging on the other side at all times and kept pistols and a Turkish saber under my thigh. Underneath my little skirt of thin taffeta I wore breeches so that I could sit up like a man at any moment and conduct myself like a young soldier on horseback" (114). When Courage finds that the amulet she bought keeps reappearing on her body even when she puts it in her pack, she mentions that she "found my treasured purchase [*spiritus fam*ilarius] in the pocket of my pants (for you should know that I always wore pants as well as a skirt" (114). She uses the breeches disguise only to protect herself, never for seduction. It is only when "the astonished soldier whisked his hand inside my trousers to seize me by that equipment which I, after all, did not possess," Courage is forced to reveal to her captain that she is a woman. Her transition from male back to female is effected quickly and humorously:

He consoled me most kindly and promised with high flown words to protect my honor like his own life; but with his deeds he too showed that he would be the first to rob me of my maidenhead, and I myself liked his unchaste groping better than his honorable promises; however, I defended myself valiantly; not, of course, to escape him or to flee his lustful advances but to really excite him and to make him even more lustful. (43-5)

Dressing like a man means acting like one: her nurse dresses her in "hose and a jerkin and taught me to take bigger steps and use other manly gestures [until] I was careful to suppress my girlish habits and to adopt manly ones instead. At thirteen, Courage learns to "swear like a trooper and to drink like a tinker." Later, wishing she "were a man, so I could take to war all my life" (97), she participates in the physical joy of plunder and the avarice of a soldier, earning the loyalty among the men with her prowess as a soldier and her skill as a sutler.

In real-life heroines, the picara often takes on the disguise of a man to avoid the dress of a woman. Moll Cutpurse, for example, claimed to be a hermaphrodite who developed an attire which combined both; she wore a doublet on top and a skirt on the bottom. Although she once was sentenced to do penance for wearing men's clothes, she rode astride a horse from Charing Cross to Shoreditch dressed like a man to win a wager. Some used dress to emulate soldiers. Catalina de Erauso was a Spanish nun who fled her convent to join the conquistadores; Mary Anne Talbot posed as a cabin boy and soldier. The life of Christian Davies, the seventeenth century Irish woman who sought her soldier husband as a soldier in the British army, resembles Courage's tale because she resumes her marriage when she finds her husband, becomes a sutler, and is an impoverished tavern-keeper telling stories at the end of her life.

In general, the picara may wear clothes as a disguise to deceive her society or her lovers but never to deceive herself. Yet, once in breeches, the picara refuses to give them up, even when she returns to her female identity. While the disguise of breeches may act as a deterrent to sexual abuse, the picara once again incorporates the masculine aspects into the feminine aspects of total identity by retaining the outward sign of the male. Her autonomy may be compromised by her need for disguise but her common sense overrides her need to show off. While wearing breeches is part of the picara's role as a soldier, it also indicates her dual role as an androgynous mythological figure who incorporates both sexual identities at once. Such play heightens the individual sexual identity of the partners and leads to a calculating erotic provocation to sexual excess. Essentially, the use of male disguise heightens the femininity of the picara, just as romance uses oversized masculine clothing to enhance a diminutive heroine. Since prostitution and promiscuity are her usual trades, this element of maleness is not only a characteristic of the literary picara but also a characteristic of the picara as a prostitute. The Renaissance courtesans took to posing as boys to attract bisexual clients, as Lawner's illustration of a courtesan wearing breeches beneath her skirt shows. Dr. Harry Benjamin notes that "a transient trend in clothing, attributable to Renaissance prostitutes, has a curious origin. They adopted a boyish garb designed to better compete with homosexual youths for the bisexual trade" (96). Certainly Shakespeare's hastening his boy-actors out of women's attire and into the more reasonable boy's attire in his comedies attests to this trend. The picara is not adverse to using disguise to attract males and the wearing of breeches is intrinsic for picaras from Courage to Long Meg to Moll, no matter how much they might protest.

The Biblical injunction against transvestitism has a significant bearing on Defoe's writings, because, while he may condone or permit disguise for deception, he shows no approval of women wearing men's clothes. At the base of his argument is the tacit understanding that, while such attire will entice men, the picara adopts it for other reasons. For example, Moll Flanders is forced into it by her need to avoid Newgate and by her governess who

laid a new Contrivance for my going Aboard, and this was to dress me up in Men's Cloaths, and so put me into a new kind of Practise.

I Was Tall and Personable, but a little too smooth Fac'd for a Man; however as I seldom went Abroad but in the Night, it did well enough: but it was a long time before I could behave in my new Cloaths: I mean, as to my Craft; it was impossible to be so Nimble, so Ready, so Dexterous as these things, in a Dress so contrary to Nature (214-5).

Despite her Puritan aversion to her male disguise, Moll uses it to become "Gabriel Spencer," perhaps an echo on the existence of a Barbara Spencer, who was burnt at the stake at Tyburn in 1721 for falsifying coinage (Starr 396). Starr adds that, although the name Gabriel Spencer was the name of the actor killed by Ben Jonson, "the echo may be a mere coincidence" (396) but Defoe may have connected the uncommon name of Gabriel with the acting profession. Moll flirts with bisexuality without ever committing it. She works so closely with her fellow thief that although "we grew so very intimate, yet he never knew that I was not a Man: nay, tho' I several times went home with him to his Lodgings...and four or five times lay with him all Night" (215).

In this expanded episode of the thief who got caught, Moll pulls off her clever deceit of the authorities in the best manner of a picara. Chased from the scene of the theft, she parts from her accomplice who is caught and ducks into the house of her governess. There she gets "time to throw off my Disguise, and dress me in my own Cloths," switches from male clothes to female clothes, gathers up her governess' granddaughter, and sits "at work with a great litter of things about me, as if I had been at Work all Day, being my self quite undress'd, with only Night-cloaths on my head, and a loose Morning Gown wrapt about me" (216-7). Her governess protests her innocence with all the conviction she can because, of course, she "had not receiv'd or admitted any Man into her House to conceal him, or protect or hide him from Justice" (218). Fearing that her accomplice might betray her by having "bought his own Life at the Expence of mine" (219), Moll worries until she receives the "joyful News that he was hang'd, which was the best News to me that I had heard in a great while" (220).

Whereas picaras like Moll or Courage are not unduly concerned with a charge of bisexuality, Celestina and Roxana never have to descend to this form of disguise because their strength is in their feminine appeal. Roxana never tries to imitate a man *per se* physically, but she does so emotionally and financially as when she refers to herself as a *"Man-Woman"* (171) to her financial mentor, Sir Robert Clayton. Yet Roxana does not escape the stigma of breeches. An interesting verbal similarity links Nell Gwynne, who was known for her breeches roles, with Roxana. Will Durant relates that, while Nell was riding with Charles, she was mistaken for Louise de Keromillac, his French mistress. To assure the crowd that she was not Louise, Nell called out: "Nay, good people, I am the Protestant Whore" (249). Like a journalist sensitive to popular tales, when Defoe has Roxana feel a need to confess her sins to one of the "romish clergy" while she is the mistress of the Prince, she protests that she "could never bring myself to like having to do with those Priests...but, In short, tho' I was a Whore, yet I was a Protestant Whore" (69). Amber has a similar exchange in her meeting in a coach with Barbara Palmer, Charles' mistress. As a re-creation of the Restoration depravity, Amber gladly steps into boy's clothes to please her lover but the disguise fools no one. Becky and Scarlett conceal their masculine traits under proper skirts because they are so involved in financial survival that bisexuality or transvestitism never appeals to them as feasible.

When the fantasy warrior adopts less cumbersome male clothing as a necessary disguise, she does it for practical purposes and not as a sign of bisexuality or androgyny. Although Karr's Thorn wears trousers because they are practical attire for a working warrior, she has to adopt female attire but never without a grumble about the skirt's restricting her movements. Some times she dresses as a man, once as a charcoal burner, once as a land worker; both times she changes clothes completely, conceals her swords, and lowers her voice. Even the sorceress Frostflower, whose moral code does not permit lying, is forced to disguise herself as a peasant woman. In particular, she has to wear an eye patch to hide her mismatched eyes which would reveal her as a sorceress. Morris' Estri wears a "tan-skin jerkin, cream-colored and sueded, and matching knee boots to protect my legs on the trail...a full coin pouch and double-bladed hunting knife" (18). In all these cases, the male attire is donned as protective coloration.

Bradley's characters are clothed with attire which proclaims their rank, their profession, their comfort, and their common sense which sometimes includes disguise. In Bradley's later works on Lythande, she introduces an androgynous character who dresses like a man because it is safer and more comfortable as she travels in a male-dominated society. On the other hand, Bradley's other character of Zadieyek/Amber in *Warrior Woman* dresses as a gladiator in her few "fighting-tunics" in a traditional society and wishes "she had courage to wear...a man's functional breeches and boots" (128). She participates in warrior games in the arena, has a female sponsor, and a female lover. Only when she is raped by a man does she feel violated because in her society of intergalatic sword-dancers, "women of my caste...were sworn while they still pursued the warrior's life, to remain untouched by any man" (195). Also in the Darkover novels, the character of Camilla, the *emmasca*, dresses as a warrior because she is a soldier for the major part of her life and her clothing matches her occupation. In Bradley's *Thendara House*, Magda abandons her confining Terran clothing for the anonymity in the concealing unisex Darkovan clothing while her counterpart Jaelle objects to the tight and revealing uniform she must wear in the Terran society. While Bradley seldom mentions specific colors except for fancy clothes and given the fact that Darkover is a cold planet, the typical Amazon dress of "low boots of undyed leather, fur-lined trousers, a fur smock...with heavily embroidered leather jackets and hoods" (*Free Amazons* 10) is a sensible choice for working women who are exposed to the elements. One important part of their outfit is the hood. From medieval days where the hood was a necessary part of dress to keep warm, the hood and scapular, that long loose length of cloth covering the front and back of a person but leaving the arms free for work, became associated with monastic life but only for men; women still wore the veiled headdresses rather than the simpler hood.

Clothing other than breeches can act as a disguise; masks are a favorite way to conceal the real features. A carryover from the morality play where the climax is when Vice strips away his mask of Virtue, the fantasy picaras revel in using masks to satirize their society and to deceive. The cover for Vinge's *The Snow Queen* shows Arienrhod placing the mask over the head of her daughter, an artistic rendering of the triune moon goddess replicating in her changing aspects. As the Winter Queen, Arienrhod wears clothing significant of the picara. Like Clayton's Aleytys, she wears a "snow-starred diadem" (20), her hair "free down her back like a veil, netted with diamonds and sapphires (443); like Aphra Behn, she wears an "ancient feather cloak...on all ceremonial occasions [and a simple white gown...white, the color of Winter, and of mourning" (443). Like the picara who supposedly reveals her true nature in her journaling, Arienrhod at her death "wore no mask— so that all the world could be certain that she was really the Snow Queen" (443). The entire society is based on the ritual of Change which involves the "revelers [who] hid their faces, cast off their own identities, becoming their fantasies" (409). The element of disguise is there also in the contributing character of Fate Ravenglass, the blind mask maker who is herself a secret sibyl like Dawn. The mask of the new queen becomes Arienrhod's most successful disguise, representing the *persona* she shows the world as well as acting as a specific disguise she hopes to use to deceive people about her death.

Arienrhod is fully a picara; she is selfish, interested only in preserving her own life ever at the expense of the death of the innocent mers: she plots the death of a third of the planet's population so that she can continue her reign; she abandons her daughter-clone to almost certain death on the Wind bridge and at the hands of an enraged mob. Her daughter sees that her "egotism saw only the thing she longed to see...only Arienrhod" (373). Survival is all and, strangely, she gets her wish in the end when the daughter she had fought is victorious; she will live on in the face and genes that her daughter bears. At the very end, she refuses to "look back at Moon once more or at Sparks. *Never look back* (453)." Her motto is the same as that of Scarlett or Becky or Amber or Roxana; she most resembles the latter because both were undone by daughters. Here is not a Demeter/Kore or Ceres/Peresophone figure who willingly allows the natural cycle of winter and summer to circle. Here is an autonomous picara out for her own good, a woman who can take solace in the fact that " 'we will live while someone remembers us. And they'll never forget me now—' Because her reincarnation already stood in her place" (453).

Moon is a picara in several different ways. Raised in love with her cousin, Sparks Dawntreader, also a "merrybegot" from the festival, she loses him when she is taken off planet to escape imprisonment by her mother. Lacking the need for survival of self that her mother possesses, she nonetheless is adamant in her pursuit of Sparks as her lover to complete herself. In the process, she learns her training as a sibyl, is captured by northern illiterates, meets and treats an injured policeman, escapes, outmaneuvers Arienrhod, gets Sparks in the end. She discovers that even being queen in not the sole answer for she must reform the society by including the Winter and offworld technology to prevent Tiamet from lapsing back into summer primitiveness. In doing so, she alienates some subjects; in being a sibyl, she alienates others. When she finally understands that "becoming Queen did not mean absolute freedom, but the end of it," she unconsciously reverts to the picaresque philosophy her mother had mentioned. "Tomorrow everything will start to fit into place, tomorrow we'll be free of today, and then on the day after..." (463-4).

Disguise appears in the thief character of Tor Starhiker who adopts the persona of Persipone, the "Hostess, the titular owner, of Persipone's Hell, the unquestionably the finest gambling hell in Carbuncle" (199). In her "midnight wig [and] golden crocheted cap" (199), like the recurrent yellow veil, and elaborate makeup and clothing, she is "window dressing to the obsession" (203) of the owner for continuity of hostesses who resemble his lost love; she allows a robot friend to pick her clothes because he chose the "styles that made the most of her flawed body [to] disguise her unrelenting plains" (202). She abandons her disguise only when she is rescued from being brainwiped into a zombie. Even the men adopt disguises. Starbuck is a titular position held by a series of offworld men as consort to Winter queen and who die with her at the Change. As such they wear a distinctive black outfit and cape with an exaggerated hunter's mask on their faces. While the first of these, Herne, is defeated by the later one, Sparks Dawntreader, Herne is so crippled by his fall in the Cave of Winds that he must assume an exoskeleton to encase his atrophied legs. The symbols of the impotent Fisher King, the King of the Woods, and the Red Horned Hunter are all suggested by this costume as well as by his name his true name, Herne, and his adopted name, Starbuck. The crippled Herne becomes a bartender in Persipone's nightclub to spy to offset Arienrhod's evil machinations. In the final scene with Arienrhod, Herne rightfully takes the place of Sparks, the current Starbuck, to be bound to her and submerged in the sea.

Another deceptive characteristic of the picara is her name change. The classical epithet sometimes became the nickname of the hero, especially in comedic literature: thus, Odysseus' epithets match his "odious" or deceiving quality and his wily ways. In tales, picaresque or otherwise, the nickname of the hero was a descriptive sign of the person's chief moral or physical characteristic. In the autobiographical picaresque tales, the names became a means of disguise and protection from governmental or church censorship. Just as the drama replaced typifying names, such as Vice and Virtue, with the name of the central character, such as Marlowe's Faustus or Shakespeare's Hamlet, so also did the early novel change from using a name to designate a type to using a name as a particularizing feature of a character as an individual: Fielding's Tom Jones is both a type (the common man) and an individual. This step toward the development of the novel genre is explained by Ian Watt's criticism:

The kinds of names actually used showed that the author was not trying to establish his characters as completely individualized entities. The precepts of the classical and renaissance criticism agreed with the practice of their literature in preferring either historical names or type names. (18)

The importance of changing names is traditional to most literature as well as to the picaresque. The picaro receives a name at some stage of his maturity that is significant of his character: Simplicius is indeed a "simple" or fool; Skipinthefield or Hopalong (Courage's husband) is flighty; Lazarillo is a *ladrone*, a Spanish beggar, or a *lazaro*. Seldom does the picara retain her original name since it would uncover her disguise. Further isolation of the picara occurs when she is forced to reject her original identity by adopting a new name.

In the case of the picara, such flexibility of names serves her well for both disguise and deception. Nicknames indicate the profession, physical characteristic, or notoriety which the picara achieves. For example, Celestina's name is an ironic commentary on her "heavenly" delights: Dame Siriz of the *Interludium* is Ceres, the Roman goddess of grain. Long Meg of Westminster is so named for her unusual height, Moll Cutpurse for her pickpocket abilities, the German Princess for the accents Mary Moders Carlton adopted. The point in the picara's life when she achieves a new name usually marks a degree of proficiency in one or more of her professions. Courage abandons her name of Libushka when she poses as Janco, the Bohemian boy; she receives her name "Courage" when she demonstrates that she has "courage" (bravery) while lacking "courage," the German slang for male genitals.

In her profession as prostitute, tradition dictates that the picara never use her given name. Burford claims that "from Roman times and probably earlier, all Brothel-keeping Ordinances contained a clause which required that the Whore, once registered, must choose a professional name by which she would always afterwards be known" (83). Whether this is to protect her family from shame or to add to her allure is not clear. In the Scriptures, Tamar never mentions her name to her father-in-law Judah when she pretends to be a temple prostitute; to do so would counteract her deception. Thus Elizabeth Holland became Madame Britannica Hollandia, a name which has survived even into the *Playboy* era in the columnist Xandria Holland. When modern striptease artists adopt seductive names like Gypsy Rose Lee and Tempest Storm, it is done to add to their drawing power. Oftentimes the prostitutes' names are derived from continental sources, Dutch and Flemish, Italian and French, a carry-over from the picara's tradition of travel. For example, while Marston's Dutch courtesan is named Franceschina after the Columbina character in the *commedia dell'arte*, her bawd Mary Faugh derives her Anglicized name from the expression "Marry, faugh," an indication of disgust. Wine suggest that it might also be from the Old English *faugh* or fallow ground, for the bawd is no longer fertile (4).

Of particular interest is the name Roxana. Perhaps influenced by the Spanish "Lozana" of the *Retrato de la Lozana Andaluzana*, the name has a long and worthy heritage even before Defoe used it for his heroine. The earliest use of the name "Roxana" or one of its variants is cited by Plutarch in his story of Alexander the Great. There Roxana, a Bactrian princess whom Alexander married to consolidate his conquests, evolved in legend into the paramour who arranged the death of Alexander's wife Statira. Perhaps the most accessible tradition for the name was from La Calprenede's *Cassandre* (1642-7), a poetic epic drama showing the rival queens, Roxana and Statira, vying for Alexander's favor. This French setting may account for the persistence of pejorative flavor to the name in England since the Restoration theatre was the first English theatre to admit women as actresses. And the first roles they played were that of "Roxana." In defiance of the Interregnum's prohibition of stage plays, William D'Avenant produced in 1656 a musical diversion of *The Siege of Rhodes* whose sole female character was Ianthe, played by Hester Davenport, the first recorded time that women appeared on the English stage. D'Avenant's 1662 production of the same play introduced a villainous woman named Roxalana as an Oriental or Persian princess, played by the same Hester Davenport who also initiated the role of Roxana in Nathaniel Lee's *The Rival Queens.*

What is importance is that the name "Roxana" or its variants had become so established as a name connected with the theatre and with villainy that the very name "Roxana" became a stereotype as a villainess. It is used as such in Montesquieu's *Persian Letters* and in Racine's *Bajazet.* This latter work may have been the play referred to by Defoe's Roxana when she mentions having seen a play of Tamerlane in Paris; since Bajazet is the Persian prince captured by Tamerlane, Defoe might easily have reversed the names of the heroes. A more immediate source for the name was in Roger Boyle's *Mustapha* where the evil queen was named Roxana; Boyle's source for this was Richard Knolles' prose history of the *The Lives of the Othoman Kings and Emperors*, where the character of Roxolana is the evil wife of Solyman (Nicholl 316).

As if the tendency to mistake the role with the person were not enough, the reputation of any French or foreign actress was besmirched by association with the theatre and its alleged immorality. Thus, any actress who played villainous or immoral women like Roxolana must have some stain of immorality about her. While Hester Davenport herself was not a mistress of Charles, the legend of her life was inextricable linked with the monarch. Tricked into an invalid marriage with Aubrey De Vere, the Earl of Oxford, she successfully appealed her case to Charles for a financial settlement for herself and for her infant son. Even though she retired from the stage at an early age, she was remembered by the name of her most famous role: Macqueen-Pope notes that "Pepys who missed so little, reports that being at the play he saw 'the old Roxolana in the chief box in a velvet gown, as the fashion is' " (59).

The connection between Charles, the name "Roxana," and the theatre was strengthened by the coincidence that Ann Marshall, a friend of Nell Gwynne, was often confused by Restoration audiences with Hester Davenport. This same Ann (or Anne) Marshall is used by Winsor as background for Amber's theatrical experience. While her closest friend is Beck Marshall, Anne Marshall is referred to when Amber claims that she herself "was ill suited to play the Egyptian queen—the part might much better have gone to Anne Marshall" (191). Although there is no evidence that Defoe knew the theatre intimately, it is more than likely that the vestiges of Restoration theatre and its legends contributed to his formation of his heroine. "Roxana," then, was a gift from these earlier associations with the theatre and the name Roxana is not given to the heroine until halfway through the novel when she becomes famous for her theatrical skills of singing and dancing. At the party at which the King is present,

one of the Gentlemen cry'd out, *Roxana! Roxana!* by——, with an Oath; upon which foolish Accident I had the Name of *Roxana* presently fix'd upon me...as if I had been

Christen'd *Roxana*...and so the name *Roxana* was the Toast at, and about the Court. (176)

Roxana's real name is revealed toward the end of the novel when she lets slip the fact that her daughter is named Susan, "for she was my own Name" (205). It is this same daughter who claims such a tenacious hold on her mother's affections, and possibly on her wealth, that she must be murdered for Roxana and Amy to have any peace. As the cautious reporter that he is, Defoe hedges on his heroine's name in the preface to *Roxana*. In this history of this

Beautiful Lady...it is necessary to conceal Names and Persons...[because] if we shou'd be always oblig'd to name the Persons, or not to relate the Story, the Consequence might only be this, That many a pleasant and delightful History wou'd be buried in the Dark".

The demands of autobiographical literature help to disguise the identity of the picara and to protect the reputation of the reputed writer who "dressing up the Story in worse Cloaths than the Lady, whose Words he speaks, prepar'd it for the World" (preface).

Moll Flanders is also a pseudonym for her "True Name is so well known in the Records, or Registers at Newgate...that it is not to be expected I should set my Name, or the Account of my Family to this Work" (7). Moll Flanders, as she calls herself, is a derivative of Mary and suggests Mary Magdalen; it is the cant name for a woman connected with the underworld. Flanders suggest her prostitute origin in the Netherlands as well as the Belgian or Holland cloth which she filches. While Winsor borrows more heavily from *Moll Flanders*, she uses a variant of the same name Susan in the Susanna, the daughter of Amber and Bruce Carlton. After her mother rejects the more common names of Judith (her own), Anne, and Sarah, Amber's name is accounted for by the color of her father's eyes. As a historical novelist, Winsor understandably mixes real and fictional people in her novel, borrowing from history and legend to achieve her end. If Amber as a mistress of Charles did not exist, Barbara Palmer and Nell Gwynne did. If Moll, Roxana, and Scarlett exist only in the dim light of literary history, Amber can claim them as ancestresses.

Fantasy heroines also carry type names, nicknames, or pseudonyms. In Bradley's Darkover novels, the names carry such weight that the characters are not allowed to name the city of sorcery nor the leader of the wicked sisterhood. Such power implied in names continues in the choice of character names. As the central character, Magda has three names: her Amazon name of Magda, her Terran name of Magdalen Lorne, which uses her father's name as a surname; and her Darkovan name Margali n'ha Ysabet, which uses her mother's name Elizabeth or Ysabet as a surname, combined with the name of a Darkovan heroine, Margali. This Margali was the "freemate" wife of the Regent Lady Bruna who entered into the "freemate" or marriage of females to protect her unborn son's inheritance. Magda herself forms a freemate marriage with Jaelle to protect both of their daughters from being absorbed into the male-dominated Darkovan society. With the Terran form of her name, Magdalen Lorne establishing the "lonely" or "forlorn" aspect of her character, Magda's name is most reminiscent of the Biblical echoes of the name: Magdalen is a form of Magdala, the Hebrew word for "fish towers" or "dried fishes" and Magda, like Mary of Magdala, is released from her seven demons of sexual and religious passions by the intervention of a higher love in her life. Also, like Mary of Magdala who supposedly retired to a cave to leave the world of men for the mystical pursuit of the otherworld, Bradley's heroine ends her purgative journey in a cave, that most feminine of symbols and a fitting entrance symbol to the Dark Sisterhood.

In contrast against the water image of Magda stands the desert or dry image of Jaelle, who comes from the "Dry Towns" of Darkover and who is a tent-provisioner. Bradley's use of the name Jaelle neatly weaves the "tent-dwelling" woman of Deborah's canticle, the Israelite heroine, Jael, the wife of Heber the Kenite in Judges 5:17-22, who pounds the tent peg through the temple of her people's enemy Sisera, with the Darkovan Jaelle. Even when Sisera's mother longs for the "spoils of dyed stuffs, embroidered, two pieces of dyed work embroidered for my neck (Judges 5:26-30), the love of finely embroidered clothing of Bradley's Amazons serves to connect them as weavers and embroiders, both conventual and beguinal occupations.

The third person in the inevitable feminine Jungian triad is the warrior Camilla, the *emmasca*, whose name carries several connotative echoes from earlier literature. The name Camilla is the Latin for a freeborn girl, one who is an attendant at a sacrifice; it is also the name of the virgin warrior queen of the Volscians whose death in the Trojan War is detailed in Virgil's *Aeneid*. Since Bradley borrows from religious sources, her Camilla may also have been derived from St. Camillus, a sixteenth century soldier and gambler who tended the wounded on the battlefield and who founded an order of medieval hospitalers. Camilla adopts the name of the Earth-born specialist Camilla in *Darkover Landfall* who must bear children she does not want for the community good because the spaceship survivors need to reproduce. Camilla the warrior also suffers from an unwanted pregnancy when she is kidnapped by pirates and raped and her unwanted child ripped from her womb by her ravishers, a mutilation which forces her clan to reject her as unfit for her hereditary office as tower priestess. Changing her name to Camilla to preserve her integrity and sanity, she sacrifices her femininity by the *emmasca* operation and denies her *laran* ability. Her subsequent masculine appearance and attitude make appropriate her choice of the name of Camilla, the woman lover of the blessed Cassilda, a tower priestess. Her real name, Elorie Lindir, contains one of the Hebrew words for God "Eloi," the Aramaic form which Christ used in his final cry from the cross.

Even in minor references, Bradley uses echoing names. Her priestess-healers of the dark mother of birth and death Avarra merge with the mercenary warriors of the Sisterhood of the Sword in the 1962 *The Planet Savers*. When Magda, for example, dreams of the goddess Avarra drifting "before her eyes again, her compassionate face, her hands outstretched as if to touch Magda's face...Magda suddenly felt a great peace and contentment" (*Thendara House* 93). "Avarra" may be a variant of the "Ave Maria" or the "Hail Mary," the common prayer to the Mary, the mother of Jesus, which bears out the dual role of the woman as birth-giver and death-dealer: the first part praises the life-giving nature of Mary, ending with the phrase "blessed is the fruit of your womb, Jesus"; the second part beginning "Holy Mother of God," describes the death-dealing aspect of asking her to "pray for us sinners, now and at the hour of our death." If the name of Avarra combines these two polarities of life and death, Bradley's choice of Evanda as the goddess of light and of growing things is a blend of Eve and Adam.

Vonda McIntyre's *Dreamsnake* also uses names as deception. As a prized student of healing, her heroine is given the honorific title of Snake, for her attempts to breed the rare dreamsnakes in captivity. Her triad of snakes serve as a disguise or protection for her personality and as such bear significant names. Mist, the albino cobra and the largest snake, is female, nervous, grumpy, but strong enough to belie her deceptively fragile name. Sand, the male rattlesnake, has tannish diamond markings and a nicer disposition. Grass, the alien off-world dreamsnake of the title, is a small green dream-producing snake used as anesthesia; his name may also connote the soporific effect of marijuana. The snakes wrap around Snake's body in imitation of their Jungian duties: wrapped around her waist, Mist is the life-sustaining gut-level shadow whose primal force injects energy into Snake; Sand coils around her arms as the practical male force of her *animus*; Grass, the Athena figure who sprang full-grown into Snake's life without earthly parents, circles Snake's neck as the *anima* or reasoning force. Like the Mediterranean mother-goddesses and the Cretan snake goddess show her with serpents twisted around her arms and with a skirt of seven flounces, Snake echoes woman's association with serpents. Coatlicue, the mother of Aztec gods, had the word serpent or Coatl as part of her title as the "Lady of the Serpent Skirt" and commanded serpent servants. In *Taliesien*, the Druids called themselves the "adders" and the Gaelic goddess Cerridwen's cart was drawn by dragons, a later form of the serpent. Even Athena, that most masculine of goddesses, used a sacred serpent to guard her temple of the Acropolis.

Sometimes the picara does not know her real name. Vonda McIntyre's heroine in *The Exile Waiting*, Mischa, links her loss of name with loss of social advantage, claiming that Mischa is the only name she has since "only people in the Families have a last name and only people in the Families have a school" (75). Sometimes the picara is given a name by someone else, usually to humiliate her. When Morris' Estri is renamed as a slave, she sometimes prefers her nicknames. Green's Dalisse Imbro shortens her name to Inky because of her black hair and her abilities as a sneak thief in the mists of the book's title, *Mists of the Ages*. Goldin and Mason's Jade Darcy possesses the bearlike strength of her D'Orsai family. Green's Terrilian's name is derived from her origins on the terrestrial sphere of the earth. Clayton's Brann's real name is replaced by the nicknames of Bramble, Bramblet-all-thorns, and Thornlet because of her thorny nature with her lovers and her tendency to roam like a bramble bush or a rambling rose. Karr's Frostflower and Thorn series reverts to the use of topical or descriptive names for the characters: Thorn, formerly Rosethorn, is the fierce warrior while Clodmule, Silverstroke, and Wasp are lesser warriors; Yarn, Brightweave and Small Spider are weavers; Spendwell is the merchant and Burningloaf is the baker (*Thorn*). Windbourne is the wandering sorcerer, Crinkpetal is the florist, and the messenger Turtlefoot changes his name to Swiftcurrent (*Windbourne*). Sometimes the heroine must discover her own name. Gleia in Clayton's *A Bait of Dreams* is really the treasured daughter Egleia in the dreams the Ranga eyes give her; her true heritage is lost in her early memories of "pain and fear. Dim images of adult faces...then a string of faces that came and went like beads from a cheap necklace" (11). Clayton's Aleytys is named that by her picara mother "with the hope in my heart that you were born true to the blood I gave you" (52), true to the wandering and proud Vrya blood. And sometimes there are just too many names: Tanith Lee's Vazkor and White Witch series involve names complicated enough for a Russian novel.

Whether it is a change of name or a change of clothes, the picara is skilled in disguising herself to deceive others to achieve her goals. In the early tales, the picara deceives to obtain goods to survive; her joy resides in a successful deception, a job well done, a society fooled. No where does the picara confess her crimes to satisfy her need for self-glorification or aggrandizing pride, as do the villains of Renaissance theatre who brag about their skills as deceivers. Oftentimes such deceptions are the expanded versions of the episodic tales of the early picara, transformed into the adventures of the hero or heroine.

Thus, Courage's adventures involve her ability as a trickster; she must disguise herself as a pious woman to win the confidence of the girl from whom she steals the emerald, as a gypsy to deceive irate peasants, and as a mother to deceive Simplicius. Each time she willingly disguises herself to deceive. Her most successful deceptions come in the marriage arena where she allows people to believe she is married or not to suit her purpose. She maneuvers Skipinthefield into a premarital agreement which effectively diminishes him. So also Lee's narrator in *Heroine of the World*, based on Courage's life, outmaneuvers her enemies by her use of the disguise of quietude; Silver Snow, the heroine of *Imperial Lady* by Norton and Shwartz, outfoxes her enemies with the deception of Confucian principles of harmony and quietude.

Roxana fully participates in the two aspects of deception: the need to be someone else and the inherent risk of discovery. When her jeweler husband is murdered in Paris, she assumes the role of the widow, deceiving the authorities and the Dutch merchant, protesting that "the greatest Difficulty would be to prove our Marriage, for that it was done in *England*, and in a remote part of *England*, too, and which was worse, it would be hard to produce authentick Vouchers of it because we were married in Private" (117). Roxana's refusal of his offer is based on the unusual deception which hides her real fear of the marriage. Since the Dutch merchant has already proposed to leave her estate intact and she has established that she had no living husband, Roxana's only recourse is to a moral standard: "After a Man has lain with me *as a Mistress*, he ought never to lye with me *as a Wife*" (152). Even when the Merchant admits that "if he had not expected to have made it an Earnest for marrying me, he would never have attempted me the other way" (145). Roxana, in a strange reversal of her opportunistic wish, refuses to marry him when she is confronted by his innate honesty and morality.

While this moral scrupulousity seldom appears in the picaro, it is not without precedent. Lazarillo is genuinely concerned with his hidalgo master: Moll berates careless parents for allowing their child to wear a gold necklace outdoors: Colonel Jacque refuses to oppress his black slave or to revenge himself on his first wife. However, when the picaro uses deception, he often succeeds in obtaining the object of his desires only at the expense of his bodily injury: Lazarillo steals the food but is beaten; Courage succeeds in stealing the jewels but is beaten. One major difference between the early and the novel picara is that the closeness of the picaresque tradition to criminal autobiography and jest biography allows the heroine to escape without serious harm. The early picara pulls off her deceptions better; the novel heroine is worried and harassed by conscience; the fantasy picara enjoys the challenge.

Fantasy picaras also deceive. As thieves they avoid detection; as prostitutes, they avoid arrest; as sorceresses, they invoke spells. One common spell is the disguise and the deception of invisibility which may be summoned by magic, by physical manipulation of psychic powers, or by technology. Often the powers to help in a deception do not come from the picara herself but are lodged in her extended family of friends. Like Odysseus, picaras can be covered with magical mists or spells as Rheba is in Maxwell's Firedancer series: again, the skill is extended to her by her friends, the illusionists. Green's Inky becomes invisible with the help of her electronics genius friend Lidra, although Inky's skills of a master thief allow her to sneak around undetected. Another spell is that of shape-shifting, where in a fantasy based on a medieval world, the power to shape-shift can help the heroine to escape her predators. Clayton's Skeen encounters Timka, the shape-shifter and Maxwell's Rheba contends with the planet of illusionists but seldom is the fantasy picara a shape-shifter herself. Rather she is a feinter, using acrobatic, psychic, or magician's skills to evade unpleasantness. In one sense, deflection can be both a disguise and a deception. A picara like Green's Terrilian can deflect one emotion and replace it with another to avoid detection. She can also project an unintended emotion onto an unsuspecting person to make them do or not do what she wants. While most of this deception is done for self-preservation, Green uses it as a humorous device. When two warriors insist on fighting over the reluctant Terrilian, she projects effeminacy on both of them, rendering them ineffective. At another time, she projects impotence on a warrior when she is lent as a "gift" to him by her lover Tammad. Her ability to project makes her lover Tammad resent and restrict it until he is made to realize that he is doing the same thing in a lesser way.

Thus, the misty shadows of the tapestry slits both disguise and mislead the viewer about the picara. If she seems to shift as the viewer watches, it is because she is basically insecure in her position within the tapestry, an insecurity which shows itself in the stark black of her isolation and the pale white of her sense of inferiority.

Chapter Nine
Isolation and Inferiority

When making corrections to avoid passing two weft threads through the same shed, it is necessary to watch carefully that no unwanted floating threads appear upon the front surface of the work. These floating threads...are sometimes introduced purposely in order to produce an unusual textural effect... (Rhodes 87)

Like floating threads whose purpose is color but not stability, the picara is never securely woven into the fabric of society. This chapter blends the gray-black of the picara's isolation from society with the pale yellow of her sense of inferiority.

Any successful hero must undergo annihilation of his deepest child-like self to be born to a new self, an adult or matured self; the testing implicit in the quest and the return of the hero are proofs of this reconciliation. For instance, the tragic hero accepts and reconciles with his fate because he sees his own rightness in it; the epic hero counts his sacrifice as nothing for the sake of his society. But the picaresque hero is an anti-hero, a social pariah, who never finds a satisfying answer to his quest for self-identity. He is, in the words of Robert Alter, "a man who does not belong, a man on the move" (107). Alter attributes the rebellion of the picaro to a reaction against social pressures to conform; the picaro's protest, he says,

reaffirms the primacy of individual experience—to begin with the most basic aspects of individual experience is a kind of existence where any larger order must be very much in question. It is a literary form characteristic of a period of disintegration, both social disintegration and disintegration of belief. Like Descartes, the picaresque writer finds any existing system to be of the shakiest kind, and he, too, tried to effect a basic reconstruction by beginning again with the one, self-evident fact of the experiencing 'I' (84).

The picara with her birth from journals and diaries, autobiographies and memoirs, emerges as the prototypal "experiencing 'I' ". In seeking her autonomy at society's expense, the picara's autonomy becomes her self-identity as she creates a world when she is the "the unanchored self (or Non-self)...the only possible self in such a world" (Miller 78). Thief, courtesan, deceiver, outcast, outsider— the picara is always at war with her society which is forever outside of her, her enemy, her scapegoat, her opposite, her gull, her field of action; she never seeks to reconcile with society.

Ironically, in seeking her autonomy, the picara obliterates her initial personality by her incessant disguises. Courage obliterates the delicately bred Libuschka to become the boy Janco, the soldier/courtesan Courage, and finally the gypsy queen who stains her golden hair with black dye. The "Susan" who was the unmarried daughter of the wealthy French emigre was annihilated by the artificial person "Roxana" who must disguise and dissemble constantly. Becky faces the same problems. As an early dissembler, she finds no difficulty in deceiving Jos at the end of the novel the same as she did at the beginning. To her, identity equals survival; she fights to retain her prestigious name and rank; when it is removed, she simply replaces it with a series of counterfeit names and titles. Who she is depends on who she is with or in whose company she is. In contrast, Amber never needs to seek herself; she is always Amber St. Clare and her own woman. Scarlett is the same; it is Rhett who correctly classifies her as he castigates her: "I think you'll always be more attracted by glister than by gold" (1035).

In opposition to the hero's quest for self-identity, the picara's search branches out into two elements: isolation and inferiority. Since the picara is out of sympathy with her own society and her own time, her non-conformity to society is simultaneously the cause and the effect of her isolation and her inferiority. Both are essentially negative to the picara's personality and both result in the picara's withdrawal from society. The process of withdrawal can be marked by levels of isolation and inferiority which the picara meets on her quest for self-identity. As novels progress, the emphasis on isolation and inferiority shifts but both qualities are always present in the picara.

Isolation

Within a feudal society, isolation was voluntary. Within the Renaissance utopias of Bacon and More, communal living isolated only the serious criminals. Not until Defoe created the isolated individualistic *homo economicus* in *Robinson Crusoe* did the value of individualism surface in literature. In many ways, the development of the picaro provides the transitional step from the community of the common good to the community of the individual good. As a self-sufficient being in a world of dependent beings absorbed by the elastic feudal system, he asserts his individuality by refusing to work in the mercantile society. As the earlier picaro was used as a satiric commentator on the values of his society, Defoe's picaros and picaras were used for less satiric intent and more as teaching devices for the emerging entrepreneurs. The novel picara bridges the gap by using social customs as the causes for her isolation and inferiority. The fantasy picara incorporates isolation and inferiority as part of her technological or medieval created world.

Where the outcast of the feudal society is the wanderer or pilgrim, the outcast of the mercantile Puritan society is the non-productive person. To a society where material output is valued, labor becomes a demi-god, and a society which denies one of its members the opportunity to work is a society which considers a non-productive person a useless burden, an isolate. For an unmarried woman, the task of survival is a hostile environment is made more difficult by the lack of a trade. When the picara must battle a society unresponsive to her needs, she becomes the isolated amorphorous island which she must reshape outside of the laws of civilization. While the picara is not topographically isolated, as Crusoe is, she is cut off from society by her inability to earn a legitimate living.

The traditional education of women encompassed the housewifely duties of maintaining a household—textile crafts, food preparation, childcare—to which later were added the finer arts of music, dancing and fancy needlework. As the industrial revolution progressed to the spinning jenny and the cotton gin, sewing became less of a cottage industry (where an entire family could be involved in the production of a single piece of yardgoods) and more of a capitalistic venture (where the means of production were located outside of the home). When the family's work was removed from the cottage as the center of activity, the value of that work was lessened and the value of the woman as a worker was reduced. Because the higher class women had the leisure to do fancier needlework like embroidery or tapestry rather than more mundane needlework, the connection between luxuries and prostitution arose.

Tradition also tells us that women like to group together to complete a task, that the aristocratic women sewing together had romances sung, that these romances became the forerunners of the novels which started themselves as literature for a feminine audience. Since many of these romances were based on courtly love, the suggestion of immorality lingered in any woman who did fancy work as opposed to honest sewing. The nursery rhyme "she shall sit on a cushion and sew a fine seam/ and she shall be fed on strawberries and cream" sums up the life of a courtesan as one who uses needlecraft as a euphemism and cover for her nighttime activities; she is "fed" on the sexually suggestive fruit of strawberries (such as are embroidered on Desdemona's handkerchief) and on the rich diet of cream. The assumption grew that women who did fancy needlework were courtesans and the literature seems to bear it out. For example, Celestina lists her occupations as a "seamstress, a perfumer, a master hand at making up cosmetics and patching maidenheads, a procuress, and a bit of a witch. Her first trade was a cover for the rest...As for maidenheads, some she repaired with bladders and others with a few stitches" (37-9).

Moll becomes the prostitute who "sews a fine seam" in opposition to a plain seam when, as a child, she protests that she can spin and work plain work enough to support herself. Starr quotes statistics from the eighteenth century economics that children were able to earn more than adults in spinning and that Colchester was the center of spinning with nearly 10,000 spinners in its immediate neighborhood (*Moll Flanders* fn. 161-2). Unfortunately, even the best of such needlecraft was not a marketable skill. In wanting to be a "Gentlewoman...to be able to get my own Bread by my own Work" (13), the child Moll does not realize that the woman "that mended Lace, and wash'd the Ladies Lac'd-heads" is no gentlewoman but a prostitute, despite, the child's perception that she "is a Gentlewoman, and they call her Madam" (14). Roxana complains that as "a single Woman not bred to Work, and at a Loss where to get employment," she is unable to feed her five children but that "if I had but one Child or two Children, I would have done my Endeavor to have work'd for them with my needle" (15). In addition, Roxana ferociously resents her economic liability as a sexual ornament who "had nothing to do, but to eat the Fat and drink the Sweet, to sit still and look around her; be waited on, and made much of; be serv'd and lov'd and made easie, *especially if the Husband acted as became him*...the Labour of the Man was appointed to make the Woman lie quiet and unconcern'd in the World" (148).

The novel picara dabbles at needlework. Becky is "netting a green silk purse" (31) when she tries to seduce Jos. Given the symbolism of green and of fishnets as signs of the ocean goddesses, it is no surprise that he ends with "his arms stretched out before her in an imploring attitude, and his hands bound in a web of green silk" (37). Amber uses "a piece of embroidery borrowed from Nan's work-basket" (279) to pose as the perfect housewife to seduce the City Merchant Samuel Dangerfield. Scarlett has less to do with sewing; in her typical picaresque way, it is she who finds the curtains to transform into a dress, and she who spreads out the pattern for it, but she does not sew it. Occasional references to her sewing usually involved her dislike of it: when she and the other women are gathered at Melanie's, waiting for the men to revenge her attack, she is too nervous to sew properly and throws her mending in anger and frustration at her inability to do anything more practical.

In the fantasy picaras, sewing is not a primary occupation. Even when the setting is pseudo-medieval, the woman is more likely to be a warrior or messenger than a seamstress. In fact, the entire fantasy genre (like that of women's writings in general) disavows any of the household duties as being worthy of the title of work. Any cooking that is done is usually done in the open in the primitive, medieval, or post-nuclear societies; in the futuristic societies, cooking is done by automation, a spaceship "automat" in the wall. So also with keeping clothes clean. Depending on the level of her fantasy civilization, the fantasy picara either washes the clothes by hand or throws them into a clothes-cleaner or clothes-provider in a self-contained unit in the wall. In addition, if one is to believe the cover art depicting the wearing of clothes in futuristic societies, the picara has little to worry about.

On a more practical level, when Madga in Bradley's *Thendara House* is asked what her skills are, she admits she cannot sew or embroider, weave or dye, much less cook or garden. This lack of skills isolates her from her new Darkovan community of women: she has to have someone show her how "to slice vegetables without cutting herself...resenting the waiting on table, and dishwashing afterward" (78). What isolates her even more is that she chooses not to tell the Darkovan women that she is half-Terran. Elain of Tarr's *The Lady of Han-Gilen* isolates herself in the falconry when her mother insists she practice her embroidery; Bradley's Romily does the same in *Hawkmistress*. Occasionally, the picara will sew for her own benefit but seldom for profit or sustenance. The heroine of Joy Chant's *When Voiha Wakes*, is a "weaver, not a spinner. Her delight was to see the pattern and the proper place of every thread in it, in planning how it might grow, in making something strong and harmonious out of diversity" (30). Some picaras are weavers of patterns, as Maxwell's Rheba who braids energy sources into weapons. Some weave minds into patterns as in Octavia Butler's Mindpattern series and Pamela Sargent's mind Net in Daiya in *Watchstar* while some picaras join psychic forces to increase their strength: Bradley's *laran* wielders meld minds together. Clayton's Terrilian and her Gleia use their empathetic powers to defeat enemies.

One positive use of sewing is in Clayton's *The Bait of Dreams* where Gleia supports herself by her fancy sewing. Even here the designs of the sewing are more important than the sewing itself: she wins her freedom from her bond by presenting the designs of future work, as much as by the actual stitches she has accomplished. In itself, this is a masculine aspect of the picara, the artist who can envision the pattern rather than the executor of the pattern. Gleia's occupation, however, is used only as a back-up for her primary profession as a thief. When she finds a Ranga Eye, a precious jewel which lures its possessor into a complacent ecstasy before draining him of his soul and life, she buys back her bond with the help of her sea-born friends. Living with them for a few years, she grows restless and seeks adventure, is captured and rescued, meets up with an offworlder juggler and a dancer Deel who help her find and destroy the source of the Ranga Eyes just after they have given her a glimpse of her true heritage as a descendant of Vajd, the blind dreamsinger, of the Diadem series. Throughout the novel in moments of stress, her sewing isolates her and comforts her but, whenever she sews on a shawl, she intends to sell it later.

The picara's economic individualism is hampered by the absence of parental guidance as her isolation is affected. Simplicimus is educated by the hermit; Courage is "guarded from common folk as a beautiful painting is protected from dust; my nurse kept constant watch over me, and...I was not allowed to play with the other girls my age" (35-6). Here Courage's isolation serves to set her above her society as befits the illegitimate daughter of the nobility, even though they disown her. Lee's *Heroine of the World* narrator is also protected from the world by her aunt is who is a courtesan. Roxana also experiences a sense of isolation as a child when her parents emigrate from France to England where she must learn a new language and new customs.

The absence of one or more parents is a given in tales where the hero is an orphan who must carve his niche in a hostile society; he resembles the mythic hero himself whose birth is masked in mystery and whose parentage is always clouded until he achieves his goal of self-identity and recognition of his father. The heroine, on the other hand, must be guided into marriage by a wise father and mother who provided for her welfare. Yet fathers in the fairy tales are nebulous or naive; Beauty's father gives her to the Beast to save his own neck; Cinderella's father lets his new wife rule the household; both parents reject Hansel and Gretel. If mothers do not appear as villains (because of the inherent belief that no one is so unlovable that one's own mother would wish him or her harm), step-mothers assume the mother's position. Sometimes in folklore, the heroine may have a fairy godmother but she has no effective mother figure. And the reason is simple. An effective mother would guide the child, either male or female, into the safe haven of marriage or reconciliation with society. Sleeping Beauty would have been kissed awake much earlier to insure the land's fertility; Cinderella would have not lost her glass slipper.

The isolating lack of parental control and guidance characterizes the picaresque figures; their parents are dead or ineffective. The picaro has no effective father usually because war has removed him from the scene before he can influence the child. Lazarillo's father goes off to the wars; Simplicimus is deprived of his parents before he is eleven. For the picara, the same situation occurs. Courage is raised by her nurse since neither her Bohemian nobleman father nor her impoverished noblewoman mother will acknowledge her. Amber's father is missing in the English Civil War; Scarlett's father Gerald is a casualty of the American Civil War's aftermath. Moll, the daughter of a transported Newgate criminal, is abandoned to the gypsies and her father never appears. Roxana, on the other hand, deviates slightly because she has a concerned and effective father who marries her off to an apparently prosperous husband. Indeed, this business acumen of her father asserts itself in Roxana's head for business. Her mother died before Roxana was nineteen, surely an age at which most maternal wisdom has been imparted.

The absence of the mother figure can possibly be explained by the significance of a child's being abandoned before he or she is weaned. Since hunger motivates the picaro, the deprivation of mother's milk might have influenced the moral character of the child. According to the old superstition that the milk on which a baby is fed somehow forms his moral character, it follows that a morally good wetnurse will produce a morally sound child. Many of the picaras call their confidante/bawd their nurses or mothers or governesses to show the complexity of their relationships. Early indications of this belief appear in Moll's concern with providing a good nurse and in Amber's insistence on seeing the home in which she farms out her son.

Certainly, the absence of a guiding mother or another protective female intensifies the picara's isolation from most feminine support groups; because of her threatening sexuality, the picara never associates well with other women as equals. The same is true of her reluctance to join a community of women; even in utopian literature, the picara is an outsider. So when the picara is deprived of actual parental guidance, she instinctively seeks another, older woman as her mother-figure or confidante: Moll has her governess, Courage has her nurse, Roxana has her Amy. Scarlett is brought up to seek the approval of her three mothers—Tara, her mother Ellen, and Mammy. When all three fail her, she is able to forge her own morality from the ashes of their teachings. Ellen fails her because she lived a lie as the faithful wife to a man she did not love; Mammy fails when she cannot adjust to the change in lifestyle: and Tara almost fails her by draining her financial resources.

Such a reason for the picara's lack of a mother may provide some clue to her formation as in the case of child abuse: a non-nurturing mother may beget a non-nurturing child; if the early picara is deprived of her mother's milk, she may grow up to abandon her child also. Even if the mother is present, she seldom gives good example. Lazarillo's mother undertakes an illegitimate liaison with a stable hand and turns Lazarillo out to protect her younger child. When this happens, the picaro never finds anyone with whom he can share his exploits and adventures. This is one reason why the picaro turns to the journal form to record his story as a substitute for the picara's confidante character.

In mythology, reconciliation with the mother advances the hero toward his integrity. Not until this happens can he be considered whole since the male and female parts of his personality are isolated and not integrated. In literature, where the mother often stands for the Great Goddess configuration, the hero must fight his way back to Nature herself to be fully actualized; the absence of the mother strands the hero in his journey and he must find her again in the sacred marriage. In addition, the picaro must search for the mother-figure by rejecting his motherland in his wanderings; the picara, as warrior, is sometimes asked to defend it as well. Such polarity is not resolved and the picara is often left stunted in emotional growth because she cannot reconcile with the mother-figure. The same is true in the picara's journey, although it is easier to see in the novels. Scarlett is so dependent upon her saintly mother as the guiding force in her life that she nearly despairs when she hears Ellen is dead; her devastation is complete when she learns that Ellen's true lover is not Gerald O'Hara. Amber is raised by relatives whose primary care is not centered on her. Becky's mother is long dead and her artistic father died early in her life, leaving her nothing but his temperament. None of the women fully recover from the loss of their mothers.

Fantasy picaras experience a different isolation but one no less severe. Because the fantasy picara has a delayed rather than a stunted emotional growth, her autonomy allows her to act as an independent agent much earlier. Her mother's death or absence is lessened by the picara's ability to be her own person. If the picara's mother is not dead, she is ineffective because of distance, or handicap, or disposition. Clayton's Aleytys' mother, captured and enslaved, is impregnated by the chief of the land before she escapes back to her advanced life on another planet, abandoning her daughter with a coded letter. If the child is clever enough to discover her mother Shareem in her homeland, the mother promises to acknowledge her then and only then. After nine books of wandering, Aleytys discovers that Shareem is weakened by her dependence upon Kell, another Vryhh who wants to destroy the half-breed Aleytys. Clayton neatly resolves the problem by having Harskari, the wise third personality imprisoned in the diadem, assume Shareem's body. Thus, Aleytys has her mother's body with her spiritual mother's mind inhabiting it. Essentially, this is the emergence of the real Aleytys who in a Jungian sense has become integrated because she is freed of the three beings who control her through the diadem, when each has found a body to suit himself or herself; Swartheld the masculine warrior part is lodged in a man's body; Shadith, the singer or creative aspect of Aleytys's mind is now a fourteen-year-old girl; and Harskari, the wisest oldest figure of the diadem triad, is now in her mother's body. The diadem thus freed can return to its rightful owners and Aleytys' search is over.

Self-identity is hard won by the fantasy picara. Because she did not emerge from the economic pressures of the dissolution of the feudal age and the emergence of the industrial age, she is often representative of the natural versus the technological. Her powers which isolate her are those of the inward journey— the psychic powers or those of witchcraft. Often she is valued for her intuitive knowledge rather than her training or technological skills. In the novel picaras, the very structure of the novel with its *bildungsroman* aspect encourages development toward psychic wholeness. Within the picaresque novels discussed, however, the character of the picara mitigates against wholeness. Because she is unstable to begin with, because she never learns from her experiences, because she is stymied at an adolescent level of development, the picara is damned. She is clever in a society that does not value a woman's intelligence; she is a good businesswoman in a society where her business skills are forbidden to women; she is sexual in a society where sexual equality is forbidden.

Measured against the Jungian concept of the integration of the entire person, the early picara has little *animus* or masculine reasoning force, little *anima* or feminine force and lots of shadow or negative energy. The shadow is the deep-seated survival instinct which drives her toward fulfilling her basic needs without regard to her other psychological needs or integrity. She never integrates her personality and therefore can never come to her community with valued skills nor enter into a committed relationship with anyone. If the picara is often isolated from her community, like Courage and Roxana, the community was limited to the European continent and England with an occasional reference to America as in *Moll Flanders*. The novel picaras have a bit more freedom. They are always city women: Becky is familiar with the Continental cities as is Roxana; Amber is reluctant to leave London. Scarlett who seldom ventures outside of her societies of Tara and Atlanta is associated with the south, never with the harsher Puritan north of America or the west because it is too primitive. Her evolution as an American picara continues in her role as the western saloon girl or the Barbary coast dancer.

The fantasy picara participates in the extension of the genre into the galaxy itself. Intergalatic travel enables her to escape from the limitations of her community and to seek adventure in others. The wanderer as galactic hobo is made easier by the technological advances where strength as such is not needed while cleverness is. The technology equalizes strength, except in the sword-and-sorcery stories, and the picara is as able as her literary sisters of the romance and "bodice-rippers" to handle a horse. Like her brother picaro who evolved into the space-tramp scoundrel, the picara is able to wander at will as a pilot, trader, smuggler, a woman completely conversant with modern space technology and fiercely independent in planning her own destiny and navigation charts.

Yet, the fantasy picara is only a partial picara. As an adventurer seeking self-identity along with societal approval, what isolates her usually is the prejudice of her community toward her differences. In this way, the fantasy novels follow the general trend of the modern novel to see the hero or heroine as victim, an alienated being unappreciated by the philistine village (albeit global) life. Often the picara must leave because she is more talented than her peers; she possesses a skill they do not—her magic or psychic abilities. In direct conflict with the original picara who left because her talents lay in avoiding work, the fantasy picara is willing to work in her own field but not in the traditional female roles like housework or child-rearing. Oftentimes she isolates herself from the community because she has broken the law by her theft, her powers, or her actions. One step ahead of the law, she never agrees with authority since she is a free spirit in her thinking and in her actions. For example, when Jaelle is about to be married in her primitive chain-binding society, she rebels and leaves. When Roxana is deprived of social standing, she leaves that society. Because the authority is often masculine, it looks as if the picara avoids men. Rather she avoids all restrictions on her development.

Isolation is linked in Roxana's case with self-preservation: she must preserve her status, her personal reputation, and her integrity. Consequently, after her near scrape with poverty, Roxana hoards money. In a sense, she isolates the money in order to preserve it, realizing all the time how unsatisfactory hoarding is. For example, when she is about to leave Paris for Italy, she fears most leaving her money, although the Prince provides an iron strong box and an entire household headed by Amy to protect that box. Still, she worries about Amy: "To leave all I had in the World with her, and if she miscarried, be ruin'd at once, was still a frightful Thought; for *Amy* might die, and whose Hands things might fall into I knew not" (100). While Roxana is demonstrating the avarice of picara, she is also carrying Defoe's capitalistic message that hidden money is unprofitable; when Roxana resumes life in London after returning from Holland, she commits her estate-managing to financier Sir Robert Clayton. Amber and Scarlett have the same problem. Amber feels safe in letting her money rest with Shadrac Newbold, the goldsmith. Scarlett finally agrees to invest in real estates and in banks. Her lumber mill is first run close to the cuff and her husband's store receipts find their way home to her pocket. Becky is more circumspect. She values the brilliants or diamonds that Lord Steyne has given her and the most vital scene between her and Rawdon occurs when he rips them from her. Interestingly, none of the novel heroines allows the absence of money to dissuade her from her enterprises. Money begets money and their scams often depend on the appearance, if not the reality, of money.

However, while her money is taken from its isolation to be safely invested, Roxana invites disaster by not isolating herself from fortune hunters. She admits her error in adopting the guise of a wealthy widow for "as I have said, I found that my Measures were all wrong, the Posture I set up in, expos'd me to innumerable Visiters [sic] of the Kind I have mention'd above" (169). Instead of continuing her isolation from undesirable wooers who only want a profitable marriage, Roxana, who wants a more profitable liaison, sets out to secure her maintenance at someone else's expense. Only when Roxana sees a profitable affair, which does not entail marriage, does she willingly emerge from her self-imposed isolation. For example, she wastes no time after her unsuccessful affair with the Dutch merchant: "And now I began to act in a new Sphere; the Court was exceeding gay and find, tho' fuller of Man than of Women, the Queen not affecting to be very much in publick" (172). Although she comments on the ironic reversal when the wife must hide and the mistress be seen in public, Roxana uses her personal isolation as a means to prevent scandal. She willingly isolates from dangerous societies to retain better the favors of her lovers; for the king, she retired for "three Years and about a Month" (181); for her Lord, she "began to consider, whether it where not more suitable to the Manner of Life I now led, to be a little less publick" (185); for her Dutch husband, she willingly accepts a quieter pace because he "knew that I had chosen a retir'd Life" (240).

Most picaras suffer ostracism by the various societies they enter. Courage speaks several times of being unwanted by the society; the good townspeople isolate her as a bad woman; the army rabble isolate her as a profiteering sutler; the gypsies, themselves already banished to the fringes of society, further isolate Courage as their queen. In Roxana's case, even her relatives ostracize her; her uncharitable sister-in-law and other relatives refuse to help her or her five children when she is abandoned by her husband. The incident actually works in two ways; as a picara, who must be unburdened in order to pursue her lovers, Roxana must be rid of her children. Secondly, within her profession of prostitute, the picara is ostracized by her society as a malignant influence. Although her removal from society is more for the sake of the lover rather than for the sake of Roxana (discretion is necessary for the Prince's reputation), the fear of discovery is never far from Roxana's mind and her isolation is partially based on a real fear of detection. With her jeweler husband, she had little to fear until he dies and she is left without any legal rights. However, a picaresque trick avoids any serious doubt of her rights to inherit his wealth; by staying in France, she is able to deny her knowledge of his English wife. In fact, she adds verisimilitude to her tale by the addition of some compliant, though imaginary, friends at Poictou, who witnessed the equally imaginary wedding of Roxana to the jeweler; the ruse succeeds and she obtains the dower rights of a widow.

Since the world accepts her as a widow, she abandons her isolation and resumes it only when the Prince requests it since that isolation prevents another danger: gossip.

If he thought fit, I would be wholly within doors...For, you are to note, that the People of Paris especially the Women, are the most busie and impertinent Enquirers into the Conduct of their Neighbours, especially that of a Single woman, that are in the World: tho' there are not greater Intriguers in the Universe than themselves. (67)

Roxana fears the French midwife and engages an English one. Furthermore, she has reason to fear retaliation from the jealous mistresses whom she supplanted. However, the strangest form of isolation is in Roxana's refusal to marry the Dutch merchant because he endangers her wealth. She leaves him and goes back to England to bear his child, but this obstinacy of Roxana in refusing a sensible and sensitive marriage is essential to her picaresque avarice which starts in the simple need for survival and extends into the Puritan commentary on money.

Since she sees material wealth rather than children as a source of wealth, children can complicate a woman's life so, in order to survive, the picara distances herself from her children. With this final estrangement from her children, Roxana's isolation is complete but, because she is a picara, she does not exhibit any loneliness or regret about her isolation. The progress of her withdrawal from society is marked by the loss of husbands, lovers, children, and friends. Even when the process is finished, Roxana still never reaches an answer about herself; she still is alone at the end of the novel, enjoying "outwardly happy Circumstances" (329). The same trend can be seen in Scarlett's final return to Tara, alone and pining for Rhett. Amber temporarily deserts her entourage of children, servants, and friends to flee to Virginia in pursuit of her lover.

The early picaras never seem to suffer from this sentimental sense of isolation. They care only that they are likely to be poor and therefore uncared for. Celestina does not mind being isolated; her children are adopted sons and daughters, those unfortunates whose lives she controls. Courage does not feel the isolation. Long Meg fits into her society because she is more of a cartoon character than a picara. The difference between isolation and alienation is most prevalent in the older and newer picaras. Where Courage and Celestina are alienated, it is by choice of life style. Where the novel picaras are isolated, they are victims more or less of their society's preferences. The newer picaras often choose a temporary isolation to perfect themselves or their powers. For example, Callista in Bradley's Darkover series isolates herself from her lover because her body's charges would kill any man who touches her, making her a form of the poison princess myth. Rheba the firedancer is dangerous for anyone to touch, save for her Bre'n mentor and the heat-loving snake Fssa. Somewhat the same reason exists for the android or computer-enhanced women who fear discovery; their strength might kill normal beings and they willingly isolate themselves from possible trouble. Just as the early picaras could contaminate men with the pollution of their sexual excess, so also the fantasy picaras have to exercise caution in their love-making. Clayton's Brann has to restrain herself from using excessive strength with her lovers. Megan in Stirling and Meier's *The Cage* has to be careful not to claw her lover with her steel-tipped cat's fingers. Karr's Frostflower must be careful not to touch a non-sorcerer because her society fears that even her touch can contaminate. Sometimes the picara isolates herself to improve herself. Callista must remain celibate to retain her powers, she thinks, and she spends most of her life denying her sexuality. Morris' Estri must isolate herself from the common man by setting her couch-price out of reach. Charnas' Alldera must isolate herself from the other woman, as desirable as those female communities are, because she has to test herself against herself.

Meditation or time to improve powers appears as a reason for the picara's isolation. Often this is a fairly short time, for example, the time enough to conjure up a spell. Since the nature of the fantasy genre involved a good deal of action, such meditative powers are usually told in retrospect or alluded to briefly. Clayton's Brann is one who uses the artistic side of her nature in throwing pots as a therapeutic device. Bradley's Darkover characters use their *laran* or psychic abilities as an energy force, even though those abilities sometimes harm them and certainly isolate them from the rest of their society. Magda uses her meditative isolation as a means of perceiving the future of the gray Sisterhood and the land of the mists.

Isolation as a test is part of the picara also. Moontreader, Arienrhod's cloned daughter, must undergo the suffering of the winter people to meet up with BZ Gundhalinu and profit from his learning. She must also undergo the love test of separation from Sparks. McIntyre's Snake must isolate herself from her healing college to find the dreamsnakes; she must leave her lover Arevin to pursue her quest. Green's Jalav must isolate herself from her beloved tribal structure to achieve her quest to unite her warrior tribes. While fantasy picaras are not misogynists, they do need a certain amount of isolation, leading to self-reflection. Like the hero of the western, the fantasy picara often wants to be left alone to live her own life in quiet. When outside forces interfere, she is upset. For example, Arienrhod alienates her society and isolates herself from it to increase the mystery surrounding her. Her final isolation occurs when her society demands her death in the ocean in contradiction to her elaborate plans to substitute her daughter.

Alienation is something which happens to the picara, not like isolation which she chooses. It is more typical of the modern novel with its connotations of fragmentation of the essential spirit of man as a result of the specialization of work. Is the picara alienated? In a feudal society, she was an accepted part of the whole fabric of life; in a mercantile society, she is more visible and less desirable; a flaw in Becky's makeup, her French father, perhaps, causes her visibility. When she wants to, she can blend into a society without any slub in the weave. In a fantasy world, the picara is more accepted because aliens are accepted. Part of the satire is in the fact that the fantasy world duplicates the prejudices of this world in alienating those who are different; the picara is alienated oftentimes because she is different for reasons beyond her control— she is the wrong color, or species, or sex. The grayish black shadows of her isolation blurs her outline only a bit.

Inferiority

Isolation can lead to a sense of inferiority in the picaro, stemming from the misalignment of his character with his society. Often the misalignment is most noticeable when the picaro tries to enter his society, only to find that he is deficient; the recognition that he is deficient provokes the picaro to trickery and deception. In fact, his inferiority often stems from his deficiencies, some of which he can turn to his credit and others of which he must accent as liabilities.

The picara suffers the picaresque disease of inferiority in a slightly different way from her brother picaro. As a woman, her reputation is immediately affected by her society's old prejudice against women without men, *"mulier non homo"*. The feminine nature of the picara increases her sense on inferiority in three ways. Physically, she is less aggressive; economically, she is less able to support herself, psychologically, she suffers from the concept that a woman is somehow flighty and less stable than a man.

In the early picaresque tales, the actual physical inferiority provides the basic conflict of the unfeminine picara: her physical differences separate her from men, whose strength she admires, and alienates her from women, whose weakness she scorns. The blurring of the sexual differences leads to two characteristics typical of the picara: aggressiveness and transvestitism. Though housed in a woman's body, the masculine aggressiveness and competitiveness of the picara often leads her to assume the role of a man, especially that of a soldier. The picara is often aggressive enough to defeat men on their own grounds and in masculine occupations. Courage, for example, is a superior soldier. Moll Flanders is a good thief; Roxana proves the best "She-Merchant" (131) of them all.

In adopting the masculine disguise of a soldier, the picara participates in a long line of transvestite heroines from the warrior queens to the wandering Elizabethan heroines of Viola, Imogen, and Helena. Transvestitism does allow the picara a mobility previously restricted to the male picaro; in fact, to preserve this ease of mobility, the picara often retains the transvestitism long after the need for it is gone. Courage persists in wearing breeches after she is acknowledged as a woman; Long Meg adopts breeches to perform her duelling pranks; Moll tries and rejects breeches as a disguise. Roxana is never tempted to wear anything but women's clothes; however, what may appear as a form of transvestitism in the earlier picara appears in Roxana as sexual ambivalence which borders on homosexuality in Roxana's unusual attachment to Amy. Although there is no overt action on Roxana's part, she freely expresses her discontent as a woman: "It was my Misfortune to be a Woman, but I was resolv'd it should not be made the worse by the Sex" (171). Further proof of her anti-feminine attitude appears in her revolutionary views which are radical enough to shock even the tolerant Dutch Merchant: "It was my opinion, a Woman was as fit to govern and enjoy her own Estate, without a Man, as Man was, without a Woman; and, that if she had a mind to gratifie herself as to Sexes, she might entertain a Man, as a Man does a Mistress'' (149).

Roxana's protests against the double standard of morality stress her consciousness of her inferiority in a male society. So also does her physical body hamper her individuality and her vocation when the frequent bearing of children endangers her vocation as a courtesan. An illegitimate child may prove an embarrassment, a burden, or a curse. Roxana is given sufficient reason to fear losing each lover—the expense of raising an illegitimate child could hinder his economic enthusiasm. She is adamant about ridding herself of the actual raising of the child since she knows she cannot fulfill the necessary responsibility that society demands of a mother. "Children are a Restraint to them [parents] in their worst Courses" (205). The full measure of this "restraint" appears when Roxana's latent sense of motherhood prevents her from disowning Susan, her inquisitive daughter, even though Susan represents an avenging spectre for her.

A further aspect of the picara's physical inferiority is her acute awareness of time. Since the main resource of the picara-prostitute is her body, the aging process of that body must provide a measure of loss for itself: the deterioration of sexual attractiveness aggravates the picara's inferiority. Courage realizes that fact when she undercuts her lament that "alas, the first bloom of my incomparable beauty had passed, wilted like a spring flower" with an ironic "I also had lost my wealth, which often helps old women to catch a husband" (167). Roxana also notes that age has diminished her charms but, unlike the earlier picaras, she has compensations. "However, I preserv'd the Youth of my Temper; was always bright, pleasant in Company, and agreeable to every-body, or else everybody flatter'd me...and tho' I was not so popular as before...yet I was far from being without Company, and that of the greatest Quality" (182-3).

The loss of sexual prowess aggravated by physical deterioration heightens the picara's psychological inferiority; as a prostitute, she never defines her role as an acceptable woman in a mature society. The development of the picara-prostitute is stunted at some point before her maturation. Harold Greenwald, in describing Cleland's *Fanny Hill*, remarks that

he recognizes that many of these women prostitutes, being arrested at a very early stage of development, are indifferent as to the sex of their partner. This coincides with their fixation at an early stage of development, when the individual is not yet differentiated into full maleness or femaleness as far as the emotional attitudes are concerned" (17).

This emotional retardation gives the picaro the charm of a rogue, a harmless, childish, child-like trickster; this same emotional retardation alienates the picara from normal human relationships which might mature her. Often the prostitute suffers from a hatred and distrust of men; since the picara is an occasional courtesan, she does not necessarily dislike men, though she seldom trusts them. Her autonomy forbids relationships and the development of family life, children, and social life which non-picaresque women seek.

Roxana, for example, possesses childish, not child-like, qualities of instability and obstinacy in her relationships. For example, she gives no valid reason for refusing the marriage proposal of the Dutch Merchant, except that it would endanger her autonomy. She does not even fully trust Amy; she leaves Amy to guard her treasures in Paris only when her avarice overcomes her emotional need for Amy's presence. In doing so, she exhibits the general psychological deficiency of the picara who substitutes avarice for every other emotion and the specific avarice of the literary prostitute who often "transforms this need for material possessions, some time reaching the level of insatiable greed" (Greenwald 6). But the voracious avarice of the picara is more than just greed for money. It is, according to Novak, "a state of desperation, usually associated with starvation and destitution, in which the victim is forced to choose between certain death and a life prolonged only by violating the laws of society, religion or personal honor" (Problem 513). The picara's need for self-preservation overrides moral law and personal integrity and she flees into prostitution as a livelihood which, in its turn, alienates her further from society and makes her feel inferior.

The picara's economic inferiority is attributable not only to her lack of livelihood but also to financial traditions of her society. For example, a woman's traditional sources of money were the dowry and her earnings. Defoe uses the statement of Roxana's marriage settlement to contrast with her economic woes after her inefficient husband mismanages her dowry: "At about Fifteen Years of Age, my father gave me *as he called it in French*, 25000 Livres, *That is to Say*, two Thousand Portion" (7). At the rate of exchange of fifty dollars per pound, the dowry of one hundred thousand dollars seems more than generous. Furthermore, at the father's death Roxana received five thousand livres more (twelve thousand dollars) which her brother loses. That Roxana is able to recoup her fortune through her own efforts makes the novel one of economic instruction more than moral satire. Both Defoe's heroines have this fall from comfortable circumstances through no fault of their own. He implies that any blame for their subsequent lives must be borne by the faulty economic system; any shame attached to their prostitution should be borne by the society which does not shelter them. From such conflicts, the plot of the novel emerges.

In contrast, the novel picaras, lodged as they are in the customs of their times, allow social inferiority to affect them. All Becky's conniving efforts are aimed at closing the gap between herself and her society, not to reconcile with it but to enjoy its benefits. While she manipulates appearances with an unerring eye to suit her station, she has the enviable ability to cut across classes; she would, her author assures us, "if a lord was not by...talk to his courier with the greatest pleasure" (688). Remarkably, she survives in whatever environment she finds herself, landing on her feet like the tabbycat she resembles. She adapts so well that her author is forced to defend her survival wiles against charges of impropriety. "If Miss Rebecca Sharp had determined in her heart upon making the conquest of this big beau, [Jos] I don't think, ladies, we have any right to blame her" (19). Any inferiority she possesses is in social power, social autonomy, if you will. That she rises above such power into her own form of autonomy makes her a picara.

Amber never feels inferior; although she recognizes that differences exist between herself and her society, she takes measures to eliminate anything that would make her different. She assesses herself periodically. When she realizes that actresses cannot be arrested because they have the protection of the Crown, she determines to avoid a repeat appearance at Newgate by becoming an actress.

"She had looked them [actresses] over and was convinced that she was better looking than any of them. Her voice was good, she had lost her country drawl, and her figure was lovely...What other qualifications did an actress need? Few of them had so many" (173-4). Similarly, any inferiority Scarlett feels is envy toward Melanie's strange sense of honor to which even hardened men like Rhett respond; when Rhett returns Melanie's gold wedding ring but not Scarlett's, she is peeved not at the loss of the ring but at her inability to see anything of worth in Melanie. Only at Melanie's death does she acknowledge Melanie as a "legend—the gentle, self-effacing but steel-spined woman on whom the South had built its house in war and to whose proud and loving arms it had returned in defeat" (1026). She has no reason to feel inferior because she has proven herself superior to most of the other women and men of the South. Her disdain for her sister Suellen for marrying beneath her, her hatred of the "poor white trash" for their slatternly ways, her protest at the bawd Belle, her obstinacy in hating the *nouveau rich*, the carpetbaggers, the Yankees, all make her feel superior. Her inferiority is in her moral standards which do not change until the last chapter as Rhett rejects her love.

If a picara does feel inferior, it is momentary. Most of all, she is realistic in admitting that men or monsters may possess greater strength than she does; she never admits that they are better. Because she is an outsider, the picara never gets close enough to any society to care whether they think she is inferior. Her pride, along with that of the hero, lies in her ability to outmaneuver the society so that she ends up in a superior position, having deceived them. To the fantasy picara, the self-knowledge she gains as a result of her quest outweighs any and all sacrifices she might make. Since knowledge of the self is self-aggrandizing, the picara never suffers from real inferiority.

Inferiority is not a prevalent characteristic of the fantasy picaras for two reasons: the nature of the heroic fantasy does not encourage "inferior" heroes and the modern stress on equality of the sexes softens blatant discrimination. Yet inferiority does exist in realms peculiar to fantasy—physical strength, knowledge, unequal opponents. But each inferiority is balanced by the fantasy picara's drawing upon her inner resources, strengthened by her autonomy, so that she acts as an individual agent in effecting and affecting her own destiny. For example, the picara is constantly trying to improve herself: Green's Terrilian wants to learn how to wield a sword although she knows that she will probably never use one. When she tries, the sword is far too heavy for her and her lover tries to use that as reason enough to dissuade her from learning. Later in the story, when she needs sword strength, it is not there. In compensation, however, her psychological powers grow so that she can defeat her enemies without physical strength. To be helpless is to be inferior; to have stamina is to be superior.

Inferiority, as it appears in fantasy, is not inadequacy or inability but it may be a lack of knowledge, the equivalent of the picara's lack of education. Madga is made to feel inferior when she cannot contribute physically to the upkeep of Thendara House except by tending the horses. Rheba, Maxwell's Firedancer, lacks knowledge of the whereabouts of her destroyed race. McIntyre's Snake lacks the needed knowledge of the offworld dreamsnakes' reproductive cycle, despite her scientific experiments to discover it. Only by chance, when she risks her own life to save that of her adopted daughter, does she find the secret that will enable her to breed the precious anesthetic snakes for her fellow healers. She also lacks sufficient knowledge to heal Jesse, the horsebreeder who dies of radiation poisoning from the contaminated post-nuclear crater; she is frustrated because she knows that earlier technology could cure the ills her people suffer. If isolation can be felt in the picara's overabundance of supernatural powers, her inferiority may also be felt in her lack of supernatural powers in a society where her powers are different. Aleytys is weaker in power than her enemy Kell but the driving need for survival has sharpened her wits beyond his.

Another level of inferiority exists in unequal opponents. Any inferiority lies in the amount of power, not in the power itself. For this reason, when a superior is pitted against an inferior, sympathy for the heroine is disjointed because she cannot win except through a *deus ex machina* or a ringer. For example, Morris' Estri is much weaker than her rival, whose species possesses supernatural powers that she has just begun to use. Her defeat of her enemy is obtained with her father's powers which are equal or superior to those of her enemy. Clayton's Serroi is only a pawn with powers in a game between greater gods, the "duel of sorcery" that gives the series its name. Green's Jalav is also the pawn of offworld, superior forces who are vicious emanations of her planets' "gods," Mida and Sigur. These gods are lesser or recalcitrant children who must be brought to order by an even more superior "god" who turns out to be Jalav's father. There is no way on earth (or on what serves as the home planet for the picara) that she can defeat such enemies.

Most fantasies end happily: good conquers evil; the wicked witch of the west is destroyed and the wizard is exposed as a snakeoil salesman, wandering rogue, or a picaro. If the black of her isolation has mixed with the pale yellow of her inferiority, the picara in a fantasy achieves a harmony unlike that of her earlier foremother. Her colors have muted and blended into the full figure of the picara, still sharply defined by the white of her autonomy. She has almost achieved completion—she is almost a full character, integrated and rounded, satisfied with herself, if not with her society. Yet, behind that tapestried figure flashes the spark of the picara that beckons for a new adventure, a new trick, a new lover, a new wealth, a new pattern of rainbow hues for her figure.

Chapter Ten
Conclusion

In making readers aware of the special qualities of tapestry weaving it is hoped, not only to help them to produce designs which are well suited to the medium, but also to give them a greater appreciation of the superb technical skill seen in the masterpieces of tapestry from the past. (Rhodes 9)

Imagine, if you will, that we are once more in the tapestry weaver's workshop. On the loom, the taut warp yarns are now nearly covered with figures and designs on the tapestried panorama. Sunlight floods across the stiff homespun of the underlying warp, the creamy crossing threads of the weft, the bright primary shades delineating outlines, the subtle shadows of the open slits, before resting for a moment on the white silk highlighting the picara's smile. Is she smiling or smirking, grinning, or gloating?

Why does she survive? Myth delineates the external symbols of internal journeys that all of us take. Yet just noting the hero's quest or the heroine's awakening alone do not sufficiently describe the picara. If she adopts the masculine quest motif, it is because the feminine awakening is beyond her capacity. Concerned only with her survival, the acceptance of motherhood never attracts her. Caught on the masculine plane, she never shifts to feminine intuition except to help her pull a confidence trick. The Jungian triadic structure comes close to outlining her figure but it fails because it limits her facets. Even her echoing the Great Goddess quaternity is too limited for her facile figure. Although she never combines the disparate elements of her personality into an integrated personality, it is in this hermaphroditic ambivalence that her appeal lies.

Picarisma, as we distinguished earlier, differs from *picarismo*. Where the trickster-picaro can laugh away the cruel reality of his world with a masculine shrug, the picara does not laugh. Ever. Survival is too serious. Survival is so serious that the picara must deny her feminine component to conduct her affairs in the most efficient way, unburdened by the baggage of emotional commitments.

She survives as we survive. The picara is that dark hidden atavistic core of self-centeredness that flashes out when our own survival is at stake. It is unreasoning, instinctive, untrammeled with conscience or morality, and it scares us. No amount of civilization can veneer it, no amount of religiosity can disguise it, no amount of literature can explain it. Her autonomy provides the best reason for her continued popularity. Independent from her background yet tightly woven into its fabric, the picara is distinguishable in all her art forms—tapestry, tale, novel, drama, courtesan portrait, bitch goddess, and woman warrior—because of her insistence on her autonomy. If we choose to explicate her design by breaking it down into separate colors, it is only to reunite those shades in the prismatic shifting of her character, highlighted by the white silk of her autonomy. Like an archetypal pattern, the picara's colors meld into a crystal figure of symbol which permits us to see the disparate hues of our own personalities.

Cut from the loom and hung against the castle or museum walls, tapestry is always meant to hang free, apart from the wall, so that the drafts of air move it gently as if it were a living picture. There, on her shifting tapestry, the picara's figure still stirs restlessly among other figures in the panorama. Occasionally she flirts with the picaro, with her staid businessmen, with her lovers, with her gulled victims. Seldom does she stay with her children or husbands; seldom does she stay with her background, country, or religion. She, like the tapestry, shifts to survive. She uses the slits in the tapestry to slide behind other figures to escape notice. She flutters in the leaves of books, breathes more easily in movies, and dances her intricate pattern across television screens.

In all her art forms, the picara represents more than the boyish trickery of the picaro or the wandering *angst* of the alienated anti-hero. She is the epitome of autonomy, of the social and economic individual, trapped in the tapestry of literature. Thus, her figure continues to flicker in the sunlight of the Mediterranean Great Goddess, in the candlelight of medieval tales, in the lamplight of historical novels, in the florescent light of science fiction, and in the torchlight of fantasy. The picara survives.

Works Cited

Abbey, Lynn. *Daughter of the Bright Moon*. New York: Grosset & Ace-Dunlop, 1979.

Adams, Nicholson B. and John E. Keller. *A Brief Survey of Spanish Literature*. Towata NJ: Littlefield, 1962.

Alter, Robert. *The Rogue's Progress: Studies in the Picaresque Novel*. Cambridge: Harvard UP, 1965.

Amazons! Jessica Amanda Salmonson, ed. New York: DAW, 1979.

Amazons II Jessica Amanda Salmonson, ed. New York: DAW, 1982.

Anchor Anthology of Short Fiction of the Seventeenth Century. Charles C. Mish, ed. Garden City NY: Doubleday, 1963.

Arbur, Rosemarie. *Marion Zimmer Bradley*. San Bernadino, CA: Starmont-Borgo, 1985.

Atwood, Margaret. *The Handmaid's Tale*. New York: Fawcett-Crest, 1985.

Auerbach, Erich. *Mimesis* W. Trask, trans. New York, 1957.

Auerbach, Nina. *Communities of Women: An Idea in Fiction*. Cambridge: Harvard UP, 1978.

Axhelm, Peter. *The Modern Confessional Novel*. New Haven Ct: Yale UP, 1967.

Barthel, Diane. *Putting on Appearances*. Philadelphia: Temple UP, 1988.

Barr, Marleen S. *Alien to Femininity: Speculative Fiction and Feminist Theory*. New York: Greenwood, 1987.

Baugh, Albert C. *A Literary History of England*. New York: Appleton, 1958.

Behn, Aphra. *Oronooko or the Royal Slave*. Lore Metzger, Introduction. New York: Norton, 1973.

Bell, Rudolph. *Holy Anorexia*. Chicago: U of Chicago P, 1985.

Benjamin, Harry (with R.E.L. Masters). *Prostitution and Morality* New York: Random, 1964.

Bernbaum, Ernest. *The Mary Carleton Narratives (1663-73)* Cambridge: Harvard UP, 1914.

Bibliography of Prostitution, A. Vern Bullough, ed. New York: Garland, 1977.

Bradley, Marion Zimmer. *City of Sorcery*. New York: DAW, 1985.

———— *Darkover Landfall*. New York, DAW, 1972.

———— *Hawkmistress!* New York, DAW, 1982.

———— [with Friends of Darkover]. *Free Amazons of Darkover*. New York: DAW, 1983.

———— *Lythande*. New York: DAW, 1986.

———— *Thendara House*. New York: DAW, 1983.

———— *The Shattered Chain*. New York: DAW, 1976.

———— *Sword and Sorceress III*. New York, DAW, 1986.

———— *Warrior Woman*. New York: DAW, 1985.

Brenan, Gerald. *The Literature of the Spanish People*. New York: Meridian, 1957.

Burford, E. J. *Queen of the Bawds or The True Story of Madame Britannica Hollandia and her House of Obsenitie, Hollands Leaguer*. London: Spearman, 1973.

Butler, Alban. *The Lives of the Saints*. Donald Attwater, ed. New York: Kenedy, 1956.

Cameron, William James. *New Light on Aphra Behn*. Auckland, NZ: 1961.

Campbell, Joseph. *The Hero with a Thousand Faces*. Princeton: Bolingen-Princeton UP, 1968.

———— *The Power and the Myth, with Bill Moyers*. Betty Sue Flowers, ed. New York: Doubleday, 1988.

Capote, Truman. "Breakfast at Tiffany's," in *Breakfast at Tiffany's: A Short Novel and Three Stories*. New York: Random, 1958.

Chandler, Frank W. *The Literature of Roguery*. 2 volumes New York: Random, 1958.

———— *Romances of Roguery*. New York: Franklin, 1899, 1961.

Chandler, Richard E. and Kessel Schwartz. *A New History of Spanish Literature*. Baton Rouge LA: Louisiana UP, 1961.

Chant, Joy. *When Voiha Wakes*. New York: Bantam, 1983.

Charnas, Suzy McKee. *Motherlines*. New York: Berkley, 1978.

———— *Walk to the End of the World*. New York: Berkley, 1974.

Clarke, Dorothy Slotelle. *Allegory, Decalogue, and Deadly Sins in La Celestina*. Los Angeles: U of California UP, 1968.

Clayton, Jo. *The Bait of Dreams*. New York: DAW, 1985.

Diadem Series

———— *Diadem from the Stars*. New York: DAW, 1977.

———— *Lamarchos*. New York: DAW, 1978.

———— *Irsud*. New York: DAW, 1979.

———— *Maeve*. New York: DAW, 1979.

———— *Starhunters*. New York: DAW, 1980.

———— *The Nowhere Hunt*. New York: DAW, 1981.

———— *The Snares of Ibex*. New York: DAW, 1984.

———— *Quester's Endgame*. New York: DAW, 1986.

———— *Shadow of the Warmaster*. New York: DAW, 1988.

Duel of Sorcery Trilogy

———— *Moongather*. New York: DAW, 1981.

———— *Moonscatter*. New York: DAW, 1983.

———— *Changer's Moon*. New York: DAW, 1987.

The Skeen Trilogy

———— *Skeen's Leap*. New York: DAW, 1986.

———— *Skeen's Return*. New York: DAW, 1986.

———— *Skeen's Search*. New York: DAW, 1987.

The Soul Drinker's Trilogy

———— *Drinker of Souls*. New York: DAW, 1986.

———— *Blue Magic*. New York: DAW, 1988

———— *A Gathering of Stones*. New York: DAW, 1989.

Contemporary Authors. Frances C. Locher, ed. vol. 81-4. Detroit: Gale, 1979.

———— Hal May, ed. vol. 87, 120. Detroit: Gale, 1987.

Daichman, Graciela S. *Wayward Nuns in Medieval Literature*. Syracuse: Syracuse UP, 1986.

Defoe, Daniel. *Applebee's Journal*. William Lee, ed., *Daniel Defoe: His Life and Recently Discovered Writings*. London, 1869.

———— *Conjugal Lewdness: Or Matrimonial Whoredom*, Maximillian Novak, ed., New York: Scholars Facsimile and Reprints, 1967.

———— *The History and Remarkable Life of Colonel Jack*. Samuel Holt, ed. New York: Random, 1965.

———— *The Life and Adventures of Mrs. Christian Davies, commonly called Mother Ross*. Sir Walter Scott, ed., Vol. 8. Oxford: Oxford UP, 1840-1.

_____ *Moll Flanders*. George A. Starr, ed. New York: Oxford UP, 1971.

_____ *The Review*. Arthur Secord, ed., New York: Scholars Facsimile and Reprints, 1938.

_____ *Roxana or the Fortunate Mistress*. Jane Jack, ed. New York: Oxford UP, 1964.

Delahaye, Hippolyte. *The Legends of the Saints*. Trans. Donald Attwater. New York: Fordham, 1962.

Donoghue, Denis. "The Values of Moll Flanders," *Sewanee Review*, LXXI (1963): 273-303.

Du Plessis, Rachel Blau. *Writing Beyond the Ending: Narrative Strategies of Twentieth-Century Women Writers*. Bloomington: Indiana UP, 1985.

Durant, Will and Ariel. *The Age of Louis XIV: The Story of Civilization*. Vol. VII. New York: Simon, 1963.

Durkheim, Emile. *The Division of Labor in Society*. London: Metheun, 1933.

Feldman, E. "Prostitution, The Alien Woman, and the Progressive Imagination, 1910-15." *American Quarterly* 19:192-206.

Fraser, Antonia. *The Warrior Queens*. New York: Knopf, 1989.

Gilman, Stephen. *The Art of La Celestina*. Madison: U of Wisconsin P, 1956 Westport CT: Greenwood, 1976.

Gold, Penny Schine. *The Lady & the Virgin: Image, Attitude, and Experience in Twelfth-Century France*. Chicago: Chicago UP, 1985.

Goldin, Stephen and Mary Mason. *The Rehumanization of Jade Darcy*. New York: NAL (Signet), 1988.

Green, Sharon. *Lady Blade, Lord Fighter*. New York: DAW, 1987.

_____ *Mists of the Ages*. New York: DAW, 1988.

_____ *The Rebel Prince*. New York: DAW, 1987.

Diana Santee Spaceways Series

_____ *Mind Guest*. New York: DAW, 1984.

_____ *Gateway to Xanadu*. New York: DAW, 1985.

Far Side of Forever Series

_____ *The Far Side of Forever*. New York: DAW, 1987.

_____ *Hellhound Magic*. New York: DAW, 1989.

Jalav Amazon Warrior Series

_____ *The Crystals of Mida*. New York: DAW, 1982.

_____ *An Oath to Mida*. New York: DAW, 1983.

_____ *Chosen of Mida*. New York: DAW, 1984.

_____ *The Will of the Gods*. New York: DAW, 1985.

_____ *To Battle the Gods*. New York: DAW, 1986.

The Terrilian Series

_____ *The Warrior Within*. New York: DAW, 1982.

_____ *The Warrior Enchained*. New York: DAW, 1983.

_____ *The Warrior Rearmed*. New York: DAW, 1984.

_____ *The Warrior Challenged*. New York: DAW, 1986.

_____ *The Warrior Victorious*. New York: DAW, 1988.

Greenberg, David F. *The Construction of Homosexuality*. Chicago: Chicago UP, 1988.

Greenwald, Harold and Aron Krich. *The Prostitute in Literature*. New York: Ballantine, 1960.

Grimmelshausen, Hans Jacob Christoffel, von. *Courage the Adventuress and The False Messiah*. Trans. Hans Speier. Princeton: Princeton UP, 1964.

_____ *The Runagate Courage*. Robert Hiller and John Osbourne, trans. Lincoln, NB: 1955.

_____. _Simplicius Simplicissimus_. Trans. George Schulz-Behrend. New York: Bobbs Merrill, 1965.

Hall, Nor. _The Moon and the Virgin: Reflections on the Archetypal Feminine_. New York: Harper, Colophon, 1980.

Hambly, Barbara. _The Ladies of Mandrigyn_. New York: Del Rey- Ballantine, 1983.

_____. _The Witches of Wenshar_. New York: Del Rey-Ballantine, 1987.

Harman, Thomas. "Caueat or Warening for Common Cursetors, Vvlgarely Called Vagabondes," Edward Viles and F.J. Furnivall eds., _EETS, ES_, No. 9. London, 1937.

Hatfield, Theodore M. "Some German Picaras of the Eighteenth Century," JEGP, XXXI (1932), 511-27.

Hawley, John Stratton. _Saints and Virtues_. Berkley: U of California P, 1987.

Head, Richard. _The English Rogue_. Michael Shinagel, introduction. Boston: New Frontiers, 1961.

Heilburn, Carolyn. _Reinventing Womanhood_. New York: Norton, 1979.

Heinlein, Robert. _Friday_. Boston: Holt, 1982.

Heroines of Popular Culture. Pat Browne, ed. Bowling Green, OH: Popular Press, 1987.

Hibbard, George R. _Three Elizabethan Pamphlets_. London, 1951.

Hill, Rowland, M. "Aphra Behn's Use of Setting." _MLQ_ VII (1946), 201-6.

Hiral, Ange-Marie. _The Revelations of Margaret of Cortona: The Franciscan Magdalene_. Trans. Raphael Brown. N.C.: Franciscan Institute, 1952.

History of Private Life, A. Roger Chartier, ed. Arthur Goldhammer, trans. Cambridge MA: Belnap P of Harvard UP, 1989.

Hodgell, P.C. _Godstalk_. New York: Atheneum, 1982.

Hunter, J. Paul. _The Reluctant Pilgrim: Defoe's Emblematic Method and Quest for Form in Robinson Crusoe_. Baltimore, 1966.

Hutman, Norma Louise. "Universality and Unity in the _Lazarillo de Tormes_." PMLA, LXXVI (1961), 469-73.

Huizinga, J. _The Waning of the Middle Ages_. New York, 1967.

Jensen, Margaret Ann. _Love's Sweet Return: The Harlequin Story_. Bowling Green, OH: Popular Press, 1984.

Jung, Carl G. _Man and His Symbols_. Garden City NY: Doubleday, 1964.

Karr, Phyllis Ann. _Frostflower and Thorn_. New York: Berkley, 1980.

_____. _Frostflower and Windbourne_. New York: Berkley, 1982.

King, Betty. _Women of the Future: The Female Main Character in Science Fiction_. Metuchen NJ: Scarecrow P, 1984.

Kirkman, James. _The Counterfeit Lady Unveil'd_. Spiro Peterson, ed. New York: 1961.

Klein, Viola. _The Feminine Character: The History of an Ideology_. 2nd edition. Urbana: U of Illinois P, 1971.

Lackey, Mercedes. _Arrow's Fall_. New York: DAW, 1988.

_____. _Arrow's Flight_. New York: DAW, 1987.

Lawner, Lynne. _Lives of the Courtesans: Portraits of the Renaissance_. New York: Rizzoli, 1987.

Lazarillo de Tormes. _Two Spanish Picaresque Novels_. Michael Alpert, ed. Baltimore MD: Penguin 1969.

Lazlett, Peter. _The World We Have Lost_. London: Metheun, 1961.

Lederer, Wolfgang. _The Fear of Women_. San Diego: Harbrace, 1970.

_____. _The Kiss of the Snow Queen: Hans Christian Andersen and Man's Redemtion by Women_. Los Angeles: U of California UP, 1986.

Lee, Tanith. _A Heroine of the World_. New York: DAW, 1989.

The Birthgrave Trilogy
——— *The Birthgrave* New York: DAW, 1975.
——— *Vazkor, Son of Vazkor.* New York: DAW, 1978.
——— *Quest for the White Witch.* New York: DAW, 1978.
The Novels of Vis
——— *The Storm Lord.* New York: DAW, 1982.
——— *Anackire.* New York: DAW, 1983.
——— *The White Serpent.* New York: DAW, 1984.
Lewis, R.W.B. *The Picaresque Saint.* New York: 1961.
Life of Long Meg of Westminster, The. Anchor Anthology of Short Fiction of the Seventeenth Century, Charles Mish, ed. Garden City NY: Doubleday, 1963.
Loos, Anita. *Gentlemen Prefer Blondes.* London: Brentano, 1926.
Lynn, Elizabeth A. *The Sardonyx Net.* New York: Berkley, 1981.
The Chronicles of Tornor
——— *Watchtower.* New York: Berkley, 1979.
——— *The Dancers of Arun.* New York: Berkley, 1979.
——— *The Northern Girl.* New York: DAW, 1980.
Macqueen-Pope, William. *Ladies First: The Story of Women's Conquest of the British Stage.* London: Allen, 1952.
Marston, John. *The Dutch Courtesan - Marston.* ed. M.L. Wine. Regents Renaissance Drama Series, Bison Books (67-68) Catalogue, Univ. of Nebraska P., 1967.
Markun, Leo. *Prostitution in the Medieval World.* Girard KN: Haldeman-Little Blue Books, n.d.
Mason, Shirlene. *Daniel Defoe and the Status of Women.* St. Alban's VT: Eden, 1978.
Maxwell, Ann. *Name of a Shadow.* New York: Avon Books, 1980.
——— *Timeshadow Rider.* New York: TOR, 1986.
Firedancer Series
——— *Firedancer.* New York: NAL (Signet), 1982.
——— *Dancer's Illusion.* New York: NAL (Signet), 1983.
——— *Dancer's Luck.* New York: NAL (Signet), 1984.
McCaffrey, Anne. *The Coelura.* New York: TOR, 1988.
——— *The Crystal Singer.* New York: Del Ray-Ballantine, 1986.
——— *The Renegades of Pern.* New York: Ballantine, 1989.
——— *The Ship Who Sang.* New York: Ballantine, 1976.
McDonnell, Ernest W. *The Beguines and Beghards in Medieval Culture.* New York: Octagon, 1969.
McIntyre, Vonda N. *Dreamsnake.* New York: Dell, 1978.
——— *The Exile Waiting.* Garden City NY: Doubleday, 1975.
McKillip, Patricia. *Fool's Run.* New York: Warners, 1987.
Middleton, Thomas. *The Roaring Girle, The Works of Thomas Middleton,* A. H. Bullen ed. 8 vols. New York, 1964.
Miller, Stuart. *The Picaresque Novel.* Cleveland: Case Western Reserve UP, 1967.
Millett, Kate. *The Prostitution Papers.* St. Albans: Paladin, 1973.
Mitchell, Margaret. *Gone With the Wind.* New York: Macmillian, 1937.
Mitchell, Timothy. *Violence and Piety in Spanish Folklore.* Philadelphia: University of Pennsylvania UP, 1988.
Moon, Elizabeth. *The Deed of Parsenarrion.* New York: Baen, 1988.
——— *Oath of Gold.* New York: Baen, 1989.
Monteser, Frederick. *The Picaresque Element in Western Literature.* Alabama: Alabama UP, 1975.

Morgan, Charlotte E. *The Rise of the Novel of Manners*. New York: 1963.

Morris, Janet. *Cruiser Dreams*. New York: Berkley, 1981.

—— *Dream Dancer*. New York: Berkley, 1980.

—— *Earth Dreams*. New York: Berkley, 1982.

High Couch of Silistra

—— *High Couch of Silistra*. New York: Bantam, 1977.

—— *The Golden Sword*. New York: Bantam, 1977.

—— *Wind from the Abyss*. New York: Bantam, 1978.

—— *The Carnelian Throne*. New York: Bantam, 1979.

Nicholl, Allardyce. *The History of the English Drama*. Vol. I, 3rd, 5th Editions. New York: Macmillian, 1940, 1955.

Norton, Andre and Susan Shwartz. *Imperial Lady: A Fantasy of Han China*. New York: TOR, 1989.

Novak, Maxmillian E. "Crime and Punishment in Defoe's *Roxana*," JEGP, LXV (July 1966): 445-65.

O'Donnell, Peter. *Dragon's Claw*. New York: TOR, 1978, 1987.

—— *Last Day in Limbo*. New York: TOR, 1976, 1988.

Parker, Alexander A. *Literature and the Delinquent: The Picaresque Novel in Spain and Europe 1599-1753*. Edinburgh: Edinburgh UP, 1967.

Patai, Raphael. *The Hebrew Goddess*. New York: Avon, 1967, 1978.

—— *Sex and Family in the Bible and the Middle East*. Garden City: Doubleday, 1959.

Pearson, Carol. *The Hero Within*. New York: Harper Row, 1986.

Pearson, Carol and Katherine Pope. *The Female Hero in American and British Literature*. New York: Bowker, 1981.

Progress of Romance, The: The Politics of Popular Fiction. Jean Radford, ed. New York: Methuen-Routledge & Kegan Paul, 1986.

Rhodes, Mary. *Small Woven Tapestries*. England: Branford, 1963.

Riggan, William. *Picaros, Madmen, Naifs, and Clowns: The Unreliable First-Person Narrator*. Norman, OK: U of Oklahoma, 1981.

Rojas, Fernando de. *The Spanish Bawd: La Celestina Being the Tragic-Comedy of Calisto and Melibea*. Trans. J.M. Cohen. Baltimore, MD: Penguin, 1964.

Rosinsky, Natalie M. *Feminist Futures: Contemporary Women's Speculative Fiction*. Ann Arbor, MI: UMI Research P, 1982,4.

Ruiz, Juan. *The Book of Good Love*. Trans. Elisha Kent Kane. Introduction John Esten Keller. Chapel Hill, U of North Caroline P, 1968.

Russ, Joanna. *The Adventure of Alyx*. New York: Simon-Pocket, 1983.

—— *The Female Man*. 1975. Reprint. New York: Gregg, 1977.

—— *We Who Are About To...* New York: Gregg, 1978.

Salmonson, Jessica Amanda. *The Swordswoman*. New York: TOR, 1982.

—— *Tomoe Gozen*. New York: Ace, 1984.

Sargent, Pamela. *The Shore of Women*. New York: Bantam, 1986.

—— *Watchstar*. New York: Pocket, 1980.

Schlauch, Margaret. *Antecedents of the English Novel: 1400-1600*. London: Metheun, 1963.

Schlobin, Roger. *The Literature of Fantasy: A Checklist*. New York: Garland, 1979.

—— *Urania's Daughter's: A Checklist of Women Science-Fiction Writers, 1692-1982*. San Bernadino: Starmont-Borgo, 1983.

Seymour-Smith, Martin. *Fallen Women*. Ontario: Nelson, 1969.

Shinagel, Michael. *Daniel Defoe and Middle Class Gentility*. Cambridge: Harvard UP, 1968.

Shinn, Thelma J. *Worlds within Women: Myth and Mythmaking in Fantastic Literature by Women.* New York: Greenwood, 1986.

Sieber, Harry. *The Picaresque.* London: Methuen, 1977.

Spencer, Jane. *The Rise of the Woman Novelist.* New York: Blackwell, 1986.

Spivack, Charlotte. *Merlin's Daughters: Contemporary Women Writers of Fantasy.* New York: Greenwood, 1987.

Stanton, Domna, ed. *The Female Autograph Theory and Practice of Autobiography from the Tenth to the Twentieth Century.* Chicago: U of Chicago P, 1984.

Starr, George A. *Defoe and Spiritual Autobiography.* Princeton: Princeton UP, 1965.

Stevick, Philip. *The Theory of the Novel.* New York: 1967.

Stirling, S.M. and Shirley Meier. *The Cage.* New York: Baen, 1989.

The Survey of Modern Fantasy Literature. Frank N. Magill, ed. Winston Salem: Salem, 1983.

Sutherland, James R. *Defoe: A Collection of Critical Essays.* Englewood Cliffs NJ: Prentice, 1938.

Tarr, Judith. *The Lady of Han-Gilen.* New York: TOR, 1987.

Tepper, Sheri S. *The Gate to Women's Country.* New York: Bantam, 1988.

——— *Northshore.* New York: TOR, 1987.

Thackeray, William M. *Vanity Fair.* John W. Dodds, introduction. New York: Holt, Rinehart and Winston, 1955.

Thompson, Bertha. *Sister of the Road.* New York: Macauley, 1937.

Thompson, C.J.S. *The Mysteries of Sex.* New York: Causeway, 1974.

Utter, Robert, and Gwendolyn Needham. *Pamela's Daughters.* New York: Russell, 1936.

Vinge, Joan D. *Catspaw.* New York: Warner, 1988.

——— *Psion.* New York: Delacorte, 1982.

——— *The Snow Queen.* New York: Dell, 1980.

——— *World's End.* New York: TOR, 1984.

Waage, Frederick O. "Meg and Moll: Two Renaissance London Heroines," *Journal of Popular Culture,* 20 (1986): 105-18.

Ward, Benedicta, S.L.G. *Harlots of the Desert: A Study of Repentance in Early Monastic Sources.* Kalamazoo, MI: Cistercian Publications, 1987.

Watt, Ian. *The Rise of the Novel.* Berkley: U of California P, 1964.

Weinstein, Donald and Rudolph Bell. *Saints and Society: The Two Worlds of Western Christendom, 1000-1750.* Chicago: U of Chicago P, 1982.

Whitbourn, Christine J. *Knaves and Swindlers: Essays on the Picaresque Novel in Europe.* New York: Oxford UP, 1974.

Winsor, Kathleen. *Forever Amber.* New American, 1944, 71. Signet.

——— *Star Money.* New York: NAL-Signet, 1950.

Yolen, Jane. *Sister Light, Sister Dark.* New York, TOR, 1988.

——— *White Jenna.* New York: TOR, 1989.

Index